FRANKLIN D. ROOSEVELT

Also by William E. Leuchtenburg

Flood Control Politics

The Perils of Prosperity, 1914–1932

Franklin D. Roosevelt and the New Deal, 1932–1940

New Deal and Global War

The Great Age of Change

Franklin D. Roosevelt
A PROFILE

EDITED BY

WILLIAM E. LEUCHTENBURG

AMERICAN PROFILES

General Editor: Aïda DiPace Donald

American Century Series
HILL AND WANG : NEW YORK

ACKNOWLEDGMENTS

I am indcbted to Esther Liberman and Dorothy Harden, who photocopied the selections in this volume, and to Christopher Micum Leuchtenburg, who wielded the stapler with his usual dexterity and good humor.

Contents

Introduction

Of the making of controversies about Franklin Delano Roosevelt there is no end. In his lifetime, he was literally worshiped by many Americans. One Congressman compared him to Jesus Christ and in a poll of New York schoolchildren God ran him a poor second. Yet he was just as strongly detested by others who, as one historian has noted, depicted him "as a liar, a thief, a madman, a syphilitic, and a communist." Since his death, scholars have kept the coals of disputation live. Some, like Basil Rauch, have contended that the "study of Roosevelt's words and of all his actions will confirm the instinct of the younger generation that another hero-President has lately been added to the company of George Washington, Thomas Jefferson, Andrew Jackson, Abraham Lincoln, Theodore Roosevelt, and Woodrow Wilson." Others, like Edgar Eugene Robinson, have asserted that Roosevelt's reign resulted "in a weakened Constitutional system, in imperiled national security, in diminished national morale, in deteriorated political morality, and in an overburdened economy."

Roosevelt's admirers argue that he was a creative leader not only of the United States but of the Western world at a time when democracy was in peril. They point out that he inspirited the nation in the dark weeks of March, 1933, and that by the end of the Hundred Days the country had regained much of its self-confidence. Roosevelt, they note, inspired faith in man's ability to master events instead of being victimized by them; he saw the world as an unfinished universe in which men must act to shape their destiny. At the same time, he offered fatherly reassurance of his own capacity to make the world more secure. He combined courage in the face of hardship with openness to ideas, he raised public issues that had long been submerged, and he showed skeptics that government could be efficient and still democratic. Elected for an unprecedented four terms, he led the country through the Great Depression, expanded the responsibility of the national government, took giant strides toward the achievement of social justice, guided the country through a victorious war against the Fascist powers, and laid the groundwork for America's entrance into the United Nations.

Roosevelt's critics, however, raise doubts as to whether he was truly a history-making man. They argue that nothing fundamental was altered in the Age of Roosevelt, that the United States at the end of the era remained pretty much what it had been in the beginning, a capitalist nation that rewarded the acquisitive instinct and tolerated a wide range of social injustice. Moreover, they assert that whatever changes did occur were the result less of Roosevelt than of impersonal forces that the President only dimly understood. His conservative campaign in 1932 has been cited to show that he did not intend to be a change maker, and the contradictory character of New Deal measures has been adduced as evidence that Roosevelt lacked a clear sense of direction.

Writers have differed too about whether Roosevelt was a conservative or a liberal. Although most perceive him as a reformer, some view him as an enlightened Tory who preserved capitalism and who never revealed more than "a-basket-for-the-poor-family-down-the-lane approach to social problems." Radicals have complained that he missed an opportunity to nationalize the banks, that he failed to discipline the nation in collectivism, and that he gave indifferent support to the planners like Rexford Tugwell. They see him, at best, as a broker who mediated among interests and who moved only as far as the pressures exerted on him required. They note that groups like the sharecroppers who could not articulate their demands got short shrift in the broker state, and that Roosevelt agreed to measures like insurance of bank deposits and the Wagner Act only because Congress compelled him to do so.

Yet others are convinced that F.D.R. was the paladin of social reform. "He takes his place," writes Henry Steele Commager, "in the great tradition of American liberalism, along with Jefferson, Jackson, Lincoln, Theodore Roosevelt and Wilson." Roosevelt, it has been pointed out, often showed his concern for unrepresented groups, as in his sponsorship of the Federal Arts Project, and frequently drove liberal legislation through a hostile Congress, as in his persistent fight for the death sentence on holding companies. Richard Rovere has written:

He led us, I think, magnificently. In the early years, to be sure, he was called upon merely to lead us back to where we had been—to keep the ship of state afloat and head it back to its moorings in the snug harbor of 1929. But that is almost always the way statesmen prove themselves. What more did Lincoln do? No more—and yet, in the doing, a great deal more. For the Union restored was not the status quo ante bellum but something very different. And while there was vastly less misery and danger in the late thirties than in the early thirties, the late thirties were very different from the late twenties. It has taken daring and imagination and high intelligence to hold this society together, and the exercise of these virtues proved in itself creative.

Some writers, indeed, have protested not that the New Deal was too conservative but that Roosevelt was a radical who overturned venerated American institutions and even fostered a Communist conspiracy. When in the 1950's Senator Joseph McCarthy asserted that the recognition of Soviet Russia in 1933 had ushered in "twenty years of treason," he was voicing a common suspicion. "Roosevelt's leadership," Edgar Eugene Robinson has written, "was the façade behind which a less understanding but profoundly convinced revolutionary leadership was provided in Congress, in administrative departments, in the press, on the radio, and in the colleges and schools." Yet many writers have observed that if Roosevelt had the squire's contempt for business, he also had the squire's sense of tradition and his conservative instinct to safeguard property rights. Like Lord Grey, who was also damned as a traitor to his class, F.D.R. sought to avert serious class conflict by timely concessions. As a consequence of New Deal measures, it has been argued, capitalism was resuscitated and the Socialist movement all but destroyed. "What cut the ground out pretty completely from under us," observed the Socialist leader, Norman Thomas, "was Roosevelt in a word. You don't need anything more."

Roosevelt has often been portrayed as the founder of the Welfare State in America. Sir Isaiah Berlin has even written that he was "the greatest leader of democracy, the greatest champion of social progress, in the twentieth century." For the first time, it has been said, the United States government recognized that men have inherent social rights and that the government must be responsible for guaranteeing at least a minimal livelihood. Yet F.D.R.'s critics have asserted that the Social Security Act was an appallingly limited piece of legislation which compared unfavorably with that adopted in European countries decades before. Moreover, they deny that the United States has achieved even today the rudiments of a Welfare State.

Political scientists and historians have quarreled about Roosevelt's performance as a party builder. F.D.R.'s champions contend that he put together a new coalition that ended a period of Republican supremacy that dated back to the Civil War and inaugurated a new era of Democratic preponderance. They point out that F.D.R. was the only victorious Democratic Presidential candidate in a century to win more than 50 per cent of the vote. They credit the "Roosevelt coalition" with a successful appeal to the masses in the great cities, and note in particular that in the 1930's the Negro broke his historic tie to the Republican party. Other writers dispute these claims. They state that the real builder of the metropolitan coalition was not Roosevelt but Al Smith. Analysts like James MacGregor Burns argue that the President missed an exceptional opportunity to reshape the party by failing to encourage progressive dissidents in states like Wisconsin. Furthermore, Roosevelt, it has been said, was too concerned with advancing his own political interests. As a consequence, at his death, the Democratic party was left divided and leaderless and the prey of entrenched Southern oligarchs and Northern machine bosses.

An even livelier controversy has centered on Roosevelt's economic policies. Critics have pointed out that recovery in the United States was tardier than in almost any other major country. They note that as late as 1939 ten million Americans were still jobless and they argue that only war pulled the nation out of the Depression. They contend that Roosevelt moved in the wrong direction by adopting restrictionist economics in the National Recovery Administration (N.R.A.) and the Agricultural Adjustment Administration (A.A.A.) and by embarking on the gold-buying fiasco. Conservatives claim that government meddling impaired business confidence and thus slowed recovery, while Keynesians lament the fact that Roosevelt proved unwilling to embrace massive deficit spending. On the other hand, F.D.R.'s partisans allege that he inherited from his predecessor an economy so badly impaired that it would inevitably take some years before recovery could be achieved. They insist that significant gains were made under F.D.R., and some believe that prosperity would have been restored even if war had not come. Roosevelt's willingness to break taboos about budget balancing has seemed more remarkable than his reluctance to subscribe to Keynes's unorthodoxy. Most important, it has been said, the New Deal provided a series of underpinnings for the economy that make another depression unlikely.

Almost all commentators have agreed that F.D.R.'s approach was untheoretical, but they have differed about whether this was a virtue or a defect. Roosevelt's critics have emphasized that he was untutored, especially about economics, and that his intellectual interests were superficial. They deplore his preference for puttering with ship models and stamp collections to reading and reflection. It was Roosevelt himself, they note, who said that he was "the least introspective man in the world." They recall his reply when his wife asked him whether their children should go to church: "I really never thought about it. It is just as well not to think about things like that too much." His shallowness and lack of learning, it has been asserted, meant that, as President, he was required to live beyond his intellectual means and that he was reduced in policy making to "catch-penny opportunism."

Those who have been impressed by Roosevelt's record, however, deny that he was ill-informed. Daniel R. Fusfeld has claimed that Roosevelt got a good grounding in economics at Harvard, and had demonstrated his competence in economic matters long before he entered the White House. Others have been astonished by F.D.R.'s grasp of detail in a wide spectrum of subjects. The publisher J. David Stern recalled an occasion when the President recited the average price of ten commodities in 1933 and ten years before and was correct on 90 per cent of them. In June, 1940, *Time* reported:

For three weeks he had discussed battlefield contours in military detail with U.S. experts; again and again they have whistled respectfully at his apparent knowledge of Flanders—hills, creeks, towns, bridges. The President's particular forte is islands; he is said to know every one in the world, its peoples, habits, population, geography, economic life. When a ship sank off Scotland several months ago, experts argued: Had the ship hit a rock or had it been torpedoed? The President pondered latitude and longitude, said: "It hit a rock. They ought to have seen that rock." Naval Aide Daniel J. Callaghan recalled the rock, disagreed. "At high tide, Mr. President, that rock is submerged." No such thing, said the President, even at high tide that rock is 20 feet out of the water.

Roosevelt's sympathizers claim that his "untheoretical" methods made possible a "pragmatic" approach that liberated government from the prison of orthodoxy. Uncommitted to dogma, Roosevelt was free to break traditions and to encourage experimentation. Disrespectful of the classic taboos, he showed a hospitality to new ideas that made the 1930's such a remarkable decade. Yet, they add, for all the improvisation and innovation, New Deal thought was more coherent than has often been recognized, for his administration, as Roosevelt said, had "a consistency and continuity of broad purpose."

Historians have also disagreed about whether Roosevelt should be hailed as a master of the art of compromise or faulted as a vacillator. Roosevelt, it has been said, alertly recognized the necessity of heeding the demands of a great many divergent interests and working out arrangements that would reconcile them. His critics, however, see F.D.R. as too often the fox rather than the lion, too unwilling to impose the national interest on parochial groups, too much a temporizer rather than a leader. Such disapprobation has been voiced both by radicals, who believe the President should have scourged businessmen, and conservatives, who castigate him as a demagogue who truckled to labor.

Judgments about whether Roosevelt was a dynamic leader or a timeserver have frequently hinged on a writer's assessment of the President's character. Some have seen him as a deeply moral man, as a Christian and a Democrat motivated by idealism and a sense of social responsibility. Others have viewed him as a Catiline willing to cater to any demand that would serve his lust for power. H. L. Mencken said of F.D.R.: "If he became convinced tomorrow that coming out for cannibalism would get him the votes he so sorely needs, he would begin fattening a missionary in the White House backyard come Wednesday." To some, Roosevelt's buoyant optimism has seemed admirable; others have deplored it as "Eagle Scout" superficiality and as the insouciance of a man unaware of his own limitations. Not a few of his admirers would concede that Roosevelt had been a rather superficial, supercilious man in his youth but claim that he underwent a "spiritual transformation" after he was crippled by poliomyelitis; he emerged, in Will Durant's words, "softened and cleansed and illumined with pain." Other writers, however, deny that his paralysis resulted in an emotional *crise*.

Both those who esteem Roosevelt and those who abhor him have found it difficult to penetrate his reserve. Roosevelt rarely revealed himself even to intimates. Not even to his minister would he speak of sorrows or disappointments. He seldom confided even in his own family. "You are a wonderful person but you are one of the most difficult men to work with that I have ever known," Harold Ickes told the President bluntly one day. "Because I get too hard at times?" Roosevelt parried. "No, you never get too hard but you won't talk frankly even with people who are loyal to you and of whose loyalty you are fully convinced. You keep your cards close up against your belly." After years of study, many historians have remained puzzled about what kind of man was hidden behind Roosevelt's mask of amiable gregariousness.

Questions about Roosevelt's character have also influenced the whole current of discussion about the President's foreign policy. Collective-security advocates have stigmatized F.D.R. as weak-willed while nationalists have execrated him as deceitful. Internationalists have charged that Roosevelt bowed to the isolationists in scuttling the London Economic Conference, agreeing to neutrality legislation, blocking aid to Loyalist Spain, and delaying too long in intervening in World War II. On the other hand, isolationists have arraigned Roosevelt as a big-navy man who seized on every opportunity to meddle in foreign affairs and who ultimately led the United States into a needless war to cover up his domestic failures. His supporters, however, respond that the President sought both to preserve peace and to mount resistance to fascist expansion and that war came only when these two goals proved irreconcilable. Once again, disputes over Roosevelt's character are significant. Isolationist critics claim that by deceptive statements such as his "again-and-again-and-again" speech in the 1940 campaign and his misrepresentation of the Battle of the Atlantic Roosevelt attempted to lead the country into war with Germany and that when this failed, he provoked the Japanese assault at Pearl Harbor even though it required sacrificing the men and ships at the base. In meeting these charges, Roosevelt's supporters are sometimes divided; some argue that the President's conduct was straightforward while others state that Roosevelt did good by stealth, that only by a degree of misrepresentation could he have led a nation deceived by the isolationists into a necessary war against the Axis. All of them agree, however, that the allegations about Pearl Harbor are bizarre.

World War II hatched a new flock of controversies about Roosevelt. Rexford Tugwell has written that in war he was "a very different kind of Roosevelt." Some writers have credited the

President with many of the achievements of the war years: the victory over the Axis, the unanticipated social gains, the creation of the United Nations. Others have contended that America's war aims were compromised by the means employed: the internment of Japanese-Americans and the deals with collaborationists in North Africa and Italy. Above all, historians have quarreled about the diplomacy of the war. They have disagreed about whether Roosevelt was a skillful statesman who succeeded, where Wilson had failed, in leading the United States into an international association of nations, or was a blunderer who threw away the sacrifices of the war at Yalta and other conference tables.

Finally, writers have differed about the legacy Roosevelt left. A new generation of radicals, distrustful of centralized power, looks back at the New Deal achievements with suspicion. A new generation of conservatives rehearses the old arguments against the New Deal and claims that the attempts to create a Welfare State has produced a Poorhouse State with a permanent class of reliefers. To these arguments, Roosevelt's admirers make two replies. One is that he reigned at a time of perpetual crisis, that if he could only see six months ahead, he almost always had a six-month answer ready. The other is that Roosevelt was, in John M. Blum's words, "the most daring democrat of his time." He made the American government more responsive to the needs of the people than had any other man who had ever held the office of President.

Less than two years after the President's death, Hamilton Basso wrote: "When the historian of the future gets around to evaluating the character and influence of Franklin Delano Roosevelt, he is going to have a man-sized job on his hands." The student who wishes to develop his own interpretation of Roosevelt faces no easy task. He will quite probably find that just at the point when he feels reasonably certain that he knows how to assess Roosevelt he will come upon a new insight that will jar his conviction of certitude. Yet there are rewards, too, in the attempt to decide F.D.R.'s place in history, for few men have so dominated their times as he did. To come to terms with the significance of the protagonist of the Age of Roosevelt is to move a long way toward comprehending the meaning of both domestic and foreign affairs in the twentieth century.

WILLIAM E. LEUCHTENBURG

Dobbs Ferry, N. Y.
February 10, 1967

Franklin D. Roosevelt, 1882–1945

Franklin Delano Roosevelt was born on January 20, 1882, in Springwood, Hyde Park Township, Dutchess County, New York. As an aunt later said: *"Il a été un beau cadre"* ("He was brought up in a beautiful frame."). Both the Roosevelts and the Delanos were prosperous merchant families who enjoyed the comfortable lives of Hudson River gentry. Young Franklin sailed, hunted with bow and arrow, was tutored in French, toured Europe; in short, he was raised in the manner of a young English gentleman. As befitted a gentleman, he entered Groton at fourteen with a mind, as one writer noted, "like a jackdaw's nest, full of shiny bits of unrelated knowledge." Four years later, in 1900, he enrolled at Harvard where he joined the Harvard Republican Club, edited the *Crimson,* and studied, not very diligently, with Frederick Jackson Turner, Josiah Royce, and A. Lawrence Lowell. In 1904, he entered Columbia Law School, which quickly bored him; he did not take a degree, but in 1907 was admitted to the bar. He married Eleanor Roosevelt, his fifth cousin, once removed, in 1905, and the marriage survived a number of vicissitudes, the chief of which was the overbearing presence of Franklin's mother.

Unexcited by work with a prestigious New York law firm and stirred by Theodore Roosevelt's rhetoric and deeds, Roosevelt decided to enter politics in 1910. After touring Dutchess County in a red Maxwell decorated with flags and bunting, he won election to the State Senate as a Democrat. In Albany, he gained a reputation as a patrician reformer, and in 1912 he opposed Tammany to support Woodrow Wilson for the Democratic Presidential nomination. Wilson rewarded him by appointing him Assistant Secretary of the Navy, a post that gave some rein to his advocacy of a "large" policy in foreign affairs. By 1920, he was well-enough known to be named as the Democratic Vice-Presidential candidate on a ticket with James M. Cox, but Cox and Roosevelt were buried in the Harding landslide.

In 1921, after swimming in the cold waters off Campobello in New Brunswick, Canada, Roosevelt was stricken with poliomyelitis, and it appeared that his career was ended; he was to remain a cripple for the rest of his days. But with the encouragement of his wife and of his devoted aide, Louis Howe, he kept up his political interests while pursuing a business career. He nominated Alfred E. Smith for the Presidency as the "Happy Warrior" in 1924, and in 1928, when Smith ran for the Presidency, Roosevelt won election for Governor of New York State by a narrow margin. When Roosevelt scored a thumping victory in 1930 in his bid for re-election, he immediately became the leading candidate for the Democratic Presidential nomination in 1932. His stand for public power, his interest in farm questions, and his unemployment program made him the favorite of the liberal wing of the party. He secured the Democratic nomination in 1932, and after a campaign in which he promised a "New Deal" for America, he defeated Herbert Hoover in an election in which he carried all but six states.

Roosevelt's first hundred days in office proved to be a remarkable time of innovation in which Congress approved sixteen significant measures, including laws creating the National Recovery Administration (N.R.A.), the Agricultural Adjustment Administration (A.A.A.), the Tennessee Valley Authority (T.V.A.), and the Civilian Conservation Corps (C.C.C.). The "Second Hundred Days" of 1935 saw such new departures as the Social Security Act and the Wagner Labor Relations Act. In 1936, running on the record of the New Deal, Roosevelt scored the greatest electoral victory in more than a century; in his race with Alfred M. Landon, he captured every state except Maine and Vermont. Yet just a few months after this overwhelming victory, Roosevelt met the first of a series of defeats. The abortive struggle to "pack" the Supreme Court, the recession of 1937–1938, and resentment at the sitdown strikes halted the forward surge of the New Deal. Still, Roosevelt remained strong enough to push through such new legislation as the wages and hours law of 1938 and to win re-election to unprecedented third and fourth terms by defeating Wendell Willkie in 1940 and Thomas E. Dewey in 1944.

By the time he campaigned against Willkie, Roosevelt was compelled to shift much of his attention from domestic to foreign concerns. Through most of his first two terms, he had pursued a cautious foreign policy. By 1940, however, he was advocating all-out aid to the Allies in their struggle against the Fascist powers in World War II. After the Japanese attack on Pearl Harbor in December, 1941, the United States entered the war against the Axis. For the next three and a half years, Roosevelt both led the nation in war and, at a series of conferences at Casablanca, Quebec, Cairo, Teheran, and Yalta, laid plans for the peace settlement. On April 12, 1945, shortly before the end of the war in Europe and the convening of the United Nations he had helped to create, Roosevelt died of a cerebral hemorrhage at Warm Springs, Georgia.

W.E.L.

FRANKLIN D. ROOSEVELT

CHARLES A. BEARD

✪

Roosevelt's Place in History

Historians are accustomed to say that contemporaries cannot precisely measure the stature of a distinguished figure of the times, correctly appraise his character, or determine his place in history. "Perspective," they contend, is necessary for this intellectual operation. In other words, we cannot be very sure of any judgment on Franklin D. Roosevelt, but by assiduous research in all the known papers we may write a definitive biography of Thomas Jefferson and assign him to his appropriate position in history.

The negative part of this argument is convincing enough. The assumption, however, that "perspective" will enable someone to perform the operation is just an assumption. Nobody knows what "perspective" in history actually means. It belongs to optics, not to any branch of humanistic studies. The position of no statesman in history is now determined, even though he has been dead a thousand years. New books are constantly being written on Caesar. To successive ages and classes he appears in different guises, and doubtless will so appear and reappear in the ages to come. The physical Caesar is dead. The historical personality still lives. Perhaps some day all the surviving original sources dealing with Caesar's life will be known. Even then no definitive biography will be written or can be written. He was a part of history and history is always being rewritten.

Reprinted from *Events*, Vol. III (February 1938), pp. 81–86, by permission of Current History, Inc.

1

One hundred years from now the private papers of President Roosevelt may all be open to scholars; that is, the surviving papers. Likewise the papers of many contemporaries will then be available. Things will be known that are not now known. But at that distant time a multitude of things now remembered, known, and felt will have disappeared forever.

Perhaps a biography of President Roosevelt written now would be truer than one written in 2038, or less true. Indeed what would a true biography look like? To ask the question, to pose the problem is to suggest the complexity of the idea.

Undoubtedly more will be known about his place in history by the year 2038, that is, his place up to that year. But how much of that position can be ascribed to his talents and character and actions? Nobody knows. Philip Guedella once remarked that a statesman's place in history largely depends upon his exit. If Lincoln had lived through the scandals of Reconstruction and the gilded age, he might not loom much higher than Blaine. His tragic ending contributed to his immortality.

Although the exit affects the verdict of history, the power of a statesman to divine history helps even more. Slavery was doomed. The verdict was ringing in 1861. Lincoln had insight enough to discover and facilitate it. Had the League of Nations proved an immediate success, Woodrow Wilson would occupy a different position in present history. In years to come it may be revived. If so, his place in popular judgment will be higher. To such whirls of fortune the fates of the greatest are subject.

What then can the historian—even one most competent in his craft and possessed of the widest knowledge—say about President Roosevelt now? He may recite innumerable facts not generally known or perhaps forgotten. On these he can be checked up. But when he says that Roosevelt is "great" or "little" or "wise" or "foolish," or pronounces such judgments in academic language, he is merely expressing his opinion, and the sources of his opinion lie partly or wholly outside the facts recited.

For these and other reasons, I am convinced that biography is not a science or an art inexorably bodying forth "the truth." It is more nearly a form of village gossip, sublimated, elevated, and transfigured. Like gossip, it is amusing, diverting, moving, tragic, comic, or grandiose, according to the social setting, talents, and animus of the biographer. And, as prevailing interests, conflicts, and ideas change, the images of distinguished historic characters, whether ancient or recent, will be altered, retouched, or perhaps broken for a time. Once the Bolsheviks in Russia condemned Peter the Great as a kind of enemy of mankind. Now those who speak in the name of Bolshevism have restored Peter to the position of a grand national figure. So it goes. Writing biography is a dangerous trade.

If this is true, nobody really knows Franklin D. Roosevelt or what he will do in the years to come or what his position will be in the long verdict of history. Yet what seem to be some of his characteristics may be discovered and set down. What he has said and done, he has said and done for all time, though the meaning may not be entirely evident, now or ever.

Franklin D. Roosevelt came from a well-to-do family, somewhat removed by possessions from the turmoil and struggle of industry and business. Although he spent much time on a landed estate and is often called a landed gentleman, his private income has not been wholly or mainly from the soil. There is something of the landed gentleman in his character—noblesse oblige, love of open spaces, and dislike of the money-grubbing plutocrat. Yet there is in his system none of Washington's cold austerity or Washington's aloofness from the vulgarisms of common intercourse. He combines some of the landed gentleman's stubbornness with the affability of the forum and jocosity of the cocktail party.

Being neither a landed gentleman in the strict sense nor a businessman nor a farmer nor a labor leader, President Roosevelt stands somewhat outside the active interests now in conflict. By experience and ideas he is separated from them. Well versed in the realistic writings of the Founding Fathers, he recognizes that many a righteous battle so-called is what he characterizes as another "classic conflict of ideas and interests." Yet he does not appear to have made any "system" of thought for himself. He is an eclectic, an improviser, or seems to be. His image of American economy is almost that of the New Freedom—small business, *laissez faire* in the main, competition, fair profits, and all the rest. Much of his legislation has been designed to make businessmen carry out the theory of business which they and the common run of economists profess on ceremonial occasions. According to that theory businessmen are all engaged in producing wealth—a beautiful fiction which Thorstein Veblen punctured about forty years ago, and Congressional hearings are puncturing every few weeks.

In supporting labor legislation President Roosevelt has not departed radically from precedents or from his theory of business enterprise. He accepts with organized labor the capitalist system of production and seeks to put labor in a better position to bargain for a share of the returns. He discards the raw class bias of American capitalists, as British capitalists have discarded it. In agriculture also he departs a little from the theory of the automatic market and the automatic distribution of wealth under the operation of the price mechanism. In that branch of economy the President accepts the agrarian theory that the mechanism exploits agriculture for the benefit of industry and that government intervention is necessary to "redress the balance."

All in all the President evidently proceeds on the assumption that with the lopping off of excrescences and the correction of particular faults the American system of economy can and will run on indefinitely, at least well enough to avoid a general breakdown. There are millions of unemployed. The plight of tenants, sharecroppers, and field hands is still distressing. Natural resources are being depleted. Billions of tons of topsoil are washing out to sea every year. The economic configurations and interests of foreign countries are closing against foreign trade of the old style. Autarchy remains unbroken in its development. Yet the American system of economy may function well enough to escape an alarming disaster, at least for many years.

What President Roosevelt would do in case this prophecy proves false, no one knows. Doubtless he does not know himself. Indeed speculation on that point is largely idle, for the forms of the crisis, if it comes, can be only dimly discerned now. Action would, of necessity, be related to the circumstances of the calamity.

In his refusal to cross bridges before he gets to them, President

Roosevelt obeys an old and realistic tradition in American politics. Lincoln never adopted the system of unconditional emancipation. He understood it, but did not commit himself to it. That slavery was highly objectionable to him all informed persons knew at the time, but he was elected President on an almost minimum program. His act of emancipation, when it came, was shaped by the exigencies of the hour, by circumstances not of his own choosing.

Whether President Roosevelt will be called upon to perform a major operation in American economy is now unknown. The circumstances of 1933 were propitious for such a stroke of state, but he avoided it. In case of another crisis, he might well pursue the same course, unless the very nature of events forced him to make a major decision. Doubtless this would fit the mood of the country, if things did not get out of hand generally. Should American economy continue to hobble along on a 60 or 70 per cent level of production, then, in respect of domestic affairs, his place in history is more likely to be akin to that of Jackson or Theodore Roosevelt than that of Washington, Jefferson, or Lincoln; that is, spectacular but scarcely important.

Hovering over the scene is the prospect of war. That President Roosevelt would struggle in the last ditch to keep the country out of foreign wars may well be doubted. He has, to be sure, expressed hostility to war. But realists in politics, while accepting the sincerity of his present intentions, take no stock in such declarations by rulers anywhere. Besides, President Roosevelt is more or less obsessed by the universal philanthropy of Woodrow Wilson. Like Wilson, he feels that America is morally bound to do good everywhere and imagines himself able to know the good in each and every case. Students of Wilson's letters and papers know that Wilson was eager to play a grand part on the world stage. That he might make himself the greatest man in all history by keeping the United States out of war never seemed to occur to him. At all events Wilson took the easiest way, for keeping the country out of the war might have brought on an economic collapse of almost revolutionary consequences.

Believing that he is under moral obligation to help decide the agelong quarrels of Europe and Asia, President Roosevelt has resisted every effort of Congress and the country to impose limits on his powers of intervention abroad. More than this. He has managed to destroy the letter and spirit of the first neutrality legislation and to acquire for himself almost dictatorial powers over American economy in relation to diplomacy and war—by the Neutrality Act of 1937. He would not have done this unless he believed that he was bound to help pass on the righteousness of foreign quarrels and intended to use all his powers, old and new, for such interventionist purposes. The policy of silence is foreign to the exuberance of his nature.

In case of a major war in Europe or Asia, there is ground for believing that he will speedily get the United States into the fray. That he could carry the country with lofty sentiments is highly probable. Americans are the prize sentimentalists of the known universe. But with what outcome? Here too even probabilities are elusive. That Americans will be euchred at the peace conference, whether they lose or win the war, is fairly certain. That President Roosevelt would ride high on war glamour for a time, goes without saying.

Then would come the reaction. Even President Wilson's official biographer, Ray Stannard Baker, finds himself literally compelled by the facts of revealed papers and the consequences of the high crusade to regard his hero as a tragic rather than a history-making figure. Indeed the World War did not bring forth a single figure now deemed heroic in stature and mold. The abyss of social revolution lies too near for hero making in the old style. Hence by involving the United States in war, President Roosevelt might well find himself on the way to a third-rate place in history with Wilson rather than to immortality with Washington and Jefferson. It might be otherwise, of course, so uncertain are conjectures, but such seem to be probabilities of high degree.

In one respect, however, President Roosevelt is unique among the Presidents of the United States. He has discussed in his messages and addresses more fundamental problems of American life and society than all the other Presidents combined. He has pointed out evils, distresses, and tensions that men in high places had hitherto blandly ignored. He has done this with vigor, consistency, and a rare power of expression that promise to place some of his addresses among the very greatest state papers of this country and all time. Even when his most severe Republican critics have finished their indictments, it remains a fact that President Roosevelt has penetrated deeper into the aspirations and tragedy of American life than any of their heroes, even Lincoln himself. Whatever else may happen, it seems safe to say that President Roosevelt has made a more profound impression upon the political, social, and economic thought of America than any or all of his predecessors. If so, then he will occupy a place of his own in the long judgment of history.

DAVID M. POTTER

✪

Sketches for the Roosevelt Portrait

A few months after the death of Franklin Roosevelt, Frances
Perkins stated her conviction that no "definitive biography and
true appraisal" of the late President would be written for "many
years." In this surmise, she probably voiced a widespread opinion,
for the judgments of history are notoriously long delayed. The
length of perspective which seems necessary is suggested by the
fact that Freeman's life of Washington, Malone's Jefferson, Ran-
dall's study of Lincoln, and Link's Wilson—all potentially definitive—are now in process of being written after time lapses of as
much as a century and a half, and in no case less than a quarter
century, since the deaths of their subjects. For a figure so controversial as Roosevelt, it may be that History in a free society
actually cannot produce a biography that will pass unchallenged as
definitive. Certainly if a definitive verdict is returned at all, everyone seems to agree that the jury of historians will be out for
several decades.

What few people as yet realize, four years after Roosevelt's
death, is that while there may be no verdict in our day, most of the
evidence has already gone to the jury. Although only the future
can show what conclusions the biographer will reach, the present
has already revealed most of the facts of which he will have to take

Reprinted from The Yale Review, N.S. XXXIX (September 1949), pp.
39–53, by permission of The Yale Review. Copyright © 1949 by Yale
University Press.

8

account. Material has come to light on Roosevelt far more rapidly than on other Presidents, and there is more testimony available today pertaining to him than to any other public man in our history. This material consists partly of an immense archive emanating directly from Roosevelt himself, and partly from a copious body of papers, memoirs, and other writings by an astonishing variety of persons associated with him in every conceivable capacity, at every degree of real or fancied intimacy, and at every stage of his life from infancy to the grave.

The battalions of Men Who Knew Roosevelt provide the most striking material now available on him, but the extent of his own papers is also arresting. These papers bulk large partly because, in his twelve years as President, Roosevelt of necessity sent more annual messages, held more cabinet meetings, conducted more election campaigns, and met more press conferences than any of his predecessors in their four- or eight-year spans. Another factor in the rate of accumulation of his papers was the proliferation of his activities as President. In his extended travels and with his access to radio, he made speeches more frequently, and in carrying out expanded functions he issued executive orders at a far heavier rate than anyone who had preceded him. As war President, he sent and received an immense number of communications, the volume of which is barely suggested by the fact that he addressed 800 cablegrams to Winston Churchill and received 950 from the Former Naval Person.

Yet neither the chronological length of Roosevelt's service nor the degree of his activity has contributed so much to swell the record as has the technological process of recording and preserving words that at any previous time would have been as perishable as the breath with which they were uttered. For many figures important in American history the record is astonishingly fragmentary, and when an editor speaks of the "complete works" of such a figure what he really means is all of that fraction of the works which happens to have survived. But for Roosevelt, the term complete is literal, almost in a sinister degree. Every back-platform impromptu address is recorded; every routine greeting to a civic or professional gathering is preserved; the words of every press conference were transcribed, and there were 711 such conferences during the first two terms alone. Historically, the fullness of the record approaches perfection, but as it does so, ironical consequences ensue. For the individual memorialized, it affords the embarrassment of perpetuating his most inane words and preserving in amber a great many flies which are hardly worth catching. For the editor, it presents the necessity of excluding known documents rather than discovering unknown ones. Thus when Judge Samuel I. Rosenman undertook to edit the *Public Papers and Addresses of Franklin D. Roosevelt* for the first eight years of the Presidency, he excluded many extemporaneous and informal addresses, most of the executive orders, Presidential proclamations, and official letters, 80 per cent of the press conferences, and virtually all of the White House statements, vetoes of private bills, and transmittals of departmental reports. With only the Congressional messages and important speeches fully represented, the work still ran to nine bulky volumes. Without laboring the point, it is safe to say that the utterances and activities of Franklin D. Roosevelt are more fully recorded than those of any other figure in American history.

All of this has been understood by historians for some time, but more recently another extensive category of records has come into play. This is the rapidly growing accumulation of published reminiscences and papers by those who were associated with the President.

These come today in a quick succession which contrasts strikingly with the delay that attended such publications in the past. Consider, for example, the case of Abraham Lincoln. It was seven years after his death in 1865 before the first volume by a personal associate, Ward H. Lamon, appeared; it was twenty-three years before the first volume by a member of his cabinet, Hugh McCulloch, was published; General Grant's "Memoirs" waited until 1880, Seward's personal papers until 1890, Nicolay and Hay's biography also until 1890, Gideon Welles's diary until 1911, Edward Bates's diary until 1933, and the opening of Lincoln's own papers until two years ago. No member of his family wrote memoirs of any sort. By 1924, when Woodrow Wilson died, the tempo of reminiscence had altered. Four cabinet members, William J. Bryan, David Houston, Franklin K. Lane, and William C. Redfield were represented by books which appeared before Wilson's death or within four years thereafter. The House papers, the Walter Hines Page papers, and the life of Wilson by his personal secretary, Joseph Tumulty, were also published within the same four-year limit. But the Pershing and McAdoo memoirs and the Newton D. Baker papers were withheld until seven years after, the Lansing memoirs for eleven years, and those of Josephus Daniels for twenty (though Daniels had published a brief biography of Wilson earlier). Wilson's daughter and his widow published books about him fourteen and fifteen years, respectively, after his death.

Four years after Roosevelt's death there are very few surviving major figures yet to be heard from, except perhaps, Henry Wallace on the civilian side, and General Marshall, General Arnold, and Admiral King from the armed forces. Within the family circle, his mother wrote *My Boy Franklin;* his wife has written two volumes of memoirs, only one of which has yet appeared in book form, though both have been published serially; his son Elliott has written *As He Saw It.* Aspects of his early political career are illumined by the memoirs of Josephus Daniels, under whom he served in the Navy Department, and of James M. Cox, for whom he was Vice-Presidential running mate in the election of 1920.

But it is the Presidency, of course, that has generated a profusion of memoirs. From Roosevelt's cabinet, we have no less than eleven books or serialized accounts written by or based on the papers of nine members of the official family. These vary widely, of course, in length, in value, and in the extent to which they hold a focus upon the President. At one extreme, Frances Perkins used her long acquaintance with Roosevelt and her acutely perceptive observations of him to write *The Roosevelt I Knew,* which concerns itself exclusively with the character and career of F.D.R. At the other, Cordell Hull made his voluminous memoirs primarily an account of State Department diplomacy, and he frequently left Roosevelt unmentioned for scores of pages at a time. Similarly, Henry L. Stimson's *On Active Service in Peace and War* is an autobiography, and it does for the War Department what Hull's account does for State. Neither of these deals primarily with Roosevelt, but both are major sources for the history of Roosevelt as President. Probably the most valuable single work on F.D.R., however, is Robert E. Sherwood's *Roosevelt and Hopkins*. Harry Hopkins' unusual intimacy with Roosevelt, the extraordinary fullness and perspicacity of his papers, and Mr. Sherwood's skill in organizing these papers and presenting a narrative to accompany them, combine to make a record which can hardly be matched by any future writer.

Compared with these four, other memoirs by cabinet members seem thin and gossipy. Inasmuch as Henry Morgenthau compiled while in office a nine-hundred-volume "diary," on which he has set a staff of historians to work, we may yet expect an important contribution, but thus far he has produced only a rather offhand series of articles in *Collier's*—which has been, incidentally, the principal vehicle for the serialization of the Roosevelt literature. Daniel C. Roper's autobiography devotes substantial space to Roosevelt as he seemed to an old Wilsonian, but it does not convince one that Mr. Roper either knew or understood Roosevelt very well. Harold Ickes published his *Autobiography of a Curmudgeon* in 1943, and has recently discussed his *Twelve Years with F.D.R.* serially in the *Saturday Evening Post*. Like Ickes, James A. Farley has also published twice, and with a somewhat more special reason, for his *Behind the Ballots* in 1938 expressed an approbation of Roosevelt which he no longer felt when he wrote *Jim Farley's Story* ten years later. Edward Stettinius, Jr. with his serialized *Roosevelt and the Russians* which appeared this year, gave his account of the Yalta Conference and of the last months of Roosevelt's Presidency. Taking the cabinet as a whole, no one except Wallace who served for as much as two terms has left his experiences unrecorded.

Outside the cabinet, people connected with Roosevelt in every conceivable way have added to the record. Churchill's *History of the Second World War* is in process of developing the story of a great international collaboration, and Eisenhower's *Crusade in Europe* gives brief but trenchant attention to the commander in chief. Old New Dealers like Raymond Moley, Hugh Johnson, and

Donald Richberg wrote about the first years of the administration, John N. Garner described in *Collier's* his consistent dissent from the New Deal, and Donald Nelson, Edward Stettinius, and James F. Byrnes provided accounts of the War Production Board, Lend-Lease, and the Yalta Conference. Roosevelt's foreign policy and his relations with members of the diplomatic service are treated not only by Hull, but also in Grew's *Ten Years in Japan,* Davies' *Mission to Moscow,* Dodd's *Ambassador Dodd's Diary,* Winant's *Letter from Grosvenor Square,* Hayes's *Wartime Mission in Spain,* and Sumner Welles's *Where Are We Heading?* None of the ambassadorial volumes devotes much space to Roosevelt, but all contain accounts of interviews and other salient details which the future historian will seize upon.

These memoirs from public life by no means exhaust the list. Almost every form of personal association with Roosevelt has been made the basis for a script. As White House physician, Ross McIntire has written a history of Roosevelt's health, and his account has provoked sharp controversy. In *Thank You, Mr. President,* Merriman Smith has described Roosevelt's relations with the press. The two principal Secret Service officers have told about protecting Roosevelt's safety, in their competitively titled volumes *Starling of the White House* and *Reilly of the White House* (Reilly was Starling's successor). The White House housekeeper, Henrietta Nesbitt, has revealed the details of the domestic routine in her *White House Diary.* But it remained for Louis Adamic to demonstrate how slight an association with Roosevelt could be capitalized when he took one meal with the President and Mr. Churchill, and made of the evening a book, *Dinner at the White House.* Had this been serialized, perhaps the soup, the fish, et cetera, might each have been the subject of an installment.

Whether motivated by the sense of historic obligation to posterity or by the enticements of commercial publishing, Roosevelt's associates have waived their rights of privacy with unparalleled promptness. It does not follow, of course, that their candor is always equal to their volubility, but the historian has invariably had to reckon with the disingenuous element in a narrative, and in the present case he at least has the narrative far sooner after the event than usual. Perspective may still be lacking, but he has already a plethora of materials upon which to work.

From these copious sources, certain features of the final portrait of Franklin Roosevelt begin to emerge fairly clear. It will be a long time before the portrait can assume finality in its details, for there are nine thousand cubic feet of Roosevelt's personal papers at the Hyde Park Library which must wait to be assimilated by scholars. Moreover, security officers will restrict or even prevent the use of parts of this material, as they have already restricted Mr. Sherwood in his freedom to quote directly some of the items in the Hopkins papers. But none of this is likely appreciably to alter the picture of Roosevelt as seen by his contemporaries. Of these contemporaries, there may not be an entirely even balance: for instance, we lack Stalin's narrative to supplement Churchill's, and, in general, Roosevelt's adversaries were in a poorer position to report on him than his supporters. But many of the friendly memoirs, such as that of Frances Perkins, are remarkably frank, and the production of memoirs has by no means been confined to the Palace Guard. For instance, Farley was not a Third Termer, Hull was not a New Dealer, and Stimson was not a Democrat. If the final portrait is to be made from preliminary sketches by various hands, the available sketches fortunately view Roosevelt from widely divergent angles.

What are the composite characteristics which these sketches seem to portray? Some of the qualities which appear markedly will astonish no one; others are perhaps less in accord with public impressions. Certainly it has long been well understood that Roosevelt was an extrovert rather than an introvert, that he was primarily a man of action, that he had an inexhaustible gusto for associations with people, that he thought in terms of the value of the goal rather than the dependability of the approach to it, that he was given to imaginative and even daring decisions, and that he possessed a good share of personal courage and buoyance which carried him through his illness and seemed to be strengthened by that ordeal. But less recognition has been given to his strong traditionalism in personal affairs and his fondness for quiet and undramatic surroundings in daily life. So much has been said of his political adroitness that we have ignored how notably he excelled in direct action and how poorly he used the tactics of indirection. So much has been said of his impulsiveness and of his humanitarian way of letting the heart rule the head that most people have lost sight of his great capacity for assimilating factual information and for applying it in his decisions on public questions. Such emphasis has been given to his tendency to dominate that his readiness to be guided by military and naval advisers, as well as his scrupulous nonintervention in military affairs below the level of over-all command, is frequently overlooked.

Some of these qualities may be, in part, inconsistent, but Roosevelt's personality was not a simple one in any case. Frances Perkins says he was "the most complicated human being I ever knew"; Morgenthau speaks of him as "extraordinarily difficult to describe"; and Sherwood considers that "his character was not only multiplex, it was contradictory to a bewildering degree." Moreover, Roosevelt was not a man who revealed himself freely. True, he often assumed the tone of intimacy, as in his fireside chats, in calling all the world by first name, or in his boisterous jokes and his banter with the press, but this intimacy was directed towards gaining confidence from others rather than imparting it to them. Even his personal letters, which are now available as far as 1928, in two volumes, betray little of his aspirations and his anxieties. They are as unrevealing as the letters of George Washington, and suggest that like Washington he was a "code man" who had fixed himself upon a model (perhaps of Groton, Harvard, and Hudson River society), and who found small place for personal introspection in such a role. For him a letter was an instrument of social communication, not of self-expression.

Here one may remark that many points which relate to the intimate side of Roosevelt's life are impenetrable, not because the material pertinent to them is concealed, but because it is opaque. For instance, when Mrs. Roosevelt published in the *Ladies' Home Journal* a series of missives called "Letters from Our Honeymoon," it might be supposed that she had gone pretty far in revealing the details of a romance. But in fact one can read many of Roosevelt's letters to her, and all of her account, in *This Is My*

Story, of the first nineteen years of her marriage to him without getting more than an inkling as to what either one of them meant to the other.

This should not be taken to imply that Roosevelt hid his most intense thoughts. It is more probable, simply, that all his energies were turned outward, and that his life was one of action rather than of reflection. Even in a leisure which was sedentary because it had to be, he collected stamps instead of, say, reading novels. When stimulated by concern for his place in history, he responded not by writing an *apologia* but by building a library.

Another aspect of this same quality was that Roosevelt thought in terms of situations rather than in terms of principles. There is very little evidence that he had much capacity for abstract or philosophical reasoning. Frances Perkins declares that his "mentality was not intellectual in the sense in which that word is ordinarily used. . . . He had to have feeling as well as thought. His emotions, his intuitive understanding, his imagination, his moral and traditional bias, his sense of right and wrong—all entered into his thinking, and unless these flowed freely through his mind as he considered a subject, he was unlikely to come to any clear conclusion or even to a clear understanding." He was devoid of ideology, as Frances Perkins also shows with her story of the dialogue between Roosevelt and a young reporter:

"Mr. President, are you a Communist?"
"No."
"Are you a capitalist?"
"No."
"Are you a Socialist?"
"No!" he said with a look of surprise as if he wondered what he was being cross-examined about.
The young man said, "Well, what is your philosophy, then?"
"Philosophy?" asked the President, puzzled. "Philosophy? I am a Christian and a Democrat. That's all."

When one considers the complex economics involved in some New Deal measures, it seems an important and damaging statement to say that Franklin Roosevelt, like Theodore Roosevelt, who also grappled with major economic questions, did not understand economics as such. Yet this is what most of the comment seems to mean, and Frances Perkins "was never able to make out that even during the days of his illness he had read substantially in the field of economics." This deficiency would go far to explain why Roosevelt was more successful in his war on the Axis than in his war on the Depression. The arts of strategy, tactics, and logistics are pre-eminently practical, and despite the constant accusation that he was addicted to "crazy theory," he was in fact never comfortable unless he could visualize a program in practical, concrete terms. It was when dealing with such conceptual matters as deficit finance and economic nationalism that he was least effective, but when he could compare arms shipments to Britain with garden hose, he seemed quite indomitable. The pragmatic nature of military and naval problems suited him exactly, and it must be significant that, while the success of the New Deal recovery program is questioned by many economists, the success of Roosevelt's war leadership is recognized by all who were in a position to appraise it. Stimson says that "the army never had a finer commander-in-chief," while Eisenhower declares: "With some of Mr. Roosevelt's political acts I could never possibly agree. But I knew him solely in his capacity as leader of a nation at war—and in that capacity he seemed to me to fulfill all that could possibly be expected of him."

The pragmatic mind characteristically learns by an assimilative rather than a strictly rational process, and this, too, was applicable in the case of Roosevelt. Perhaps no form of learning depends so completely upon assimilation as the knowledge of a given piece of terrain, and it is notable that both his wife, who knew all his other qualities, and General Eisenhower, who, professionally would take knowledge of terrain for granted, were especially impressed by Roosevelt's ability to grasp and remember all the features of a countryside. Both suggest that his mastery in this field amounted to genius. As a means of assimilative learning, Roosevelt relied upon talks with people rather than upon more formal sources of information. Frances Perkins says that he could " 'get' a problem intimately better when he had a vicarious experience through a vivid description of a typical case. Proceeding 'from the book' no matter how logical, never seemed solid to him."

Closely related to Roosevelt's pragmatic attitude was his talent

for direct and decisive action, coupled with a certain ineffective-
ness when the straightforward approach was precluded. He was at
his best when he could cut through complexities to a simple result.
When for instance, on March 4, 1933, he faced the accumulated
and complex economic chaos resulting from four years of Depression, his response was to ask for executive power "to wage a war
against the emergency, as great as the power that would be given
to me if we were in fact invaded by a foreign foe." Another of his
great moments came after the Japanese blow at Pearl Harbor,
when Secretary Hull wanted him to review for Congress the recent
history of Japanese-American relations, but when, instead, he
determined to send a terse and sharply focused war message,
which by its own brevity and decisiveness symbolized the end of a
frustrating period of doubts and unresolved discussions. He preferred clear-cut solutions, and we cannot safely suppose that it was
entirely the difference in the two international situations which
caused Woodrow Wilson and Franklin Roosevelt to seek the diverse goals of "peace without victory" and "unconditional surrender."

Decisions of great magnitude, such as the adoption of the plan
to invade Western Europe or the appointment to supreme command of Eisenhower, who had held the rank of temporary colonel
in 1941, evoked qualities of certitude and confidence in Roosevelt,
where they would have caused vacillation and loss of nerve in
many men. But when no clear-cut action was possible, or when
oblique tactics were adopted, he was surprisingly inept. This was
strikingly demonstrated in his attempt in 1937 to reconstitute the
Supreme Court without openly raising the issue of judicial supremacy; even Robert H. Jackson, who led the assault on the Old
Court and who defended Roosevelt with every syllable, admitted
that the plan "lacked that directness which was his genius." The
1940 convention, where he felt that he could not either renounce
or announce his candidacy, again showed Roosevelt at his worst.
The election campaign of that same year, when he perceived the
vital stake of the United States in the war then raging, but felt
himself compelled to declare "again and again and again" to
American parents that "Your boys are not going to be sent into

any foreign wars," was another time of eclipse for his stronger qualities. The "purge" of 1938, when he could not bring himself either to support the conservative Democrats or to ostracize them personally ("God bless you, Walter" were his words to Senator George), also saw him at the same kind of disadvantage. But perhaps there is no clearer example of this weakness than the fact that at Yalta, Roosevelt had logically either to refuse Russia's demand for three delegates to the U.N. or to put the best possible face on the fact that he had yielded; he did neither, and consequently the news leaked to the public in the most damaging way possible.

His deeply rooted preference for prompt action and for bold, imaginative, clear-cut decision made him, of course, unusually responsive to novel and unorthodox ideas. His critics insisted that he would embrace any crackpot notion that came along, but they ignore the fact that if his readiness to experiment was sometimes a weakness it was also, simultaneously, an element of strength. Many a "safer" man than Roosevelt might have avoided some of his mistakes and failed also to sponsor the Manhattan Project. No one has made this point so neatly and so unwittingly as John T. Flynn. In 1940, Flynn mentioned two items especially to illustrate Roosevelt's gullibility in accepting fantastic ideas: one was his enthusiasm, in the twenties, for a retail vending machine which later proved a failure; the other was his belief that this country could produce fifty thousand planes—which Flynn believed palpably impossible. Flynn's more recent *The Roosevelt Legend* retains the characterization of Roosevelt, but omits this pregnant illustration.

A corollary of the criticism that Roosevelt accepted fantastic ideas was the belief in some quarters that he acted impulsively and without any effort to inform himself—that he was a heedless improviser, a "gay reformer" playing recklessly with interests which he had not even attempted to understand. Raymond Moley, for instance, relates that when Roosevelt flew to Chicago in 1932 to accept the nomination, he went to the platform with two acceptance speeches which had been thrust upon him, and read in part from one, in part from the other. By a kind of perversity, Roosevelt himself encouraged this belief. As Sherwood remarks, he "for some reason . . . liked to picture himself as a rather frivolous fellow." He even implied that the announcement of the "unconditional surrender" policy was an unpremeditated utterance, but the Hopkins papers prove that it had been carefully prepared in advance. In many other matters, the record shows how diligent and attentive to details he could be. His important speeches were refined through several drafts; he studied them rigorously for every implication and controlled their length to a matter of as little as twenty-five words. By close questioning of the hundreds of people who came to his office, he accumulated and retained an immense store of information, which, it must be said, he used extremely well, especially in the conduct of the war. Eisenhower says, "I was struck by his phenomenal memory for detail." Henry Stimson testifies to his close personal attention to affairs, especially as concerned the armed forces. Cordell Hull offers the opinion that, "No President since Jefferson or the Adamses had a wider knowledge of peoples and conditions abroad."

On the personal side, there are two qualities that seem to stand out most of all. One was Roosevelt's high courage, the other his inordinate sociability.

The story of the spiritual stamina with which he fought against surrender to his illness is so well known that comment becomes superfluous. It is interesting, however, to note the moral influence of his attitude upon others. Sherwood writes of the President on his way to his office: "This progress to the day's work by a crippled man was a sight to stir the most torpid imagination; for here was a clear glimpse of the Roosevelt that the people believed him to be—the chin up—and the air of irrepressible confidence that whatever problems the day might bring he would find a way to handle them. The fact that this confidence was not always justified made it none the less authentic and reassuring. When I saw the President go by on these mornings, I felt that nobody who worked for him had a right to feel tired. That was not an unusual feeling; it went all through the wartime Administration in Washington, extending to all sorts of people, some of whom disagreed with him politically, and most of whom never laid eyes on him."

Sherwood observes two important qualities which lay at the base of Roosevelt's courage, but were much less apparent than his personal dauntlessness. One was his religious faith, the other his idealism. Both attributes were to some extent concealed by his apparent cynicism and his pretense of worldliness and freedom from illusion. He was, moreover, at times hard and even vindictive. But Sherwood believes that "his religious faith was the strongest force . . . that was in him," and that "his idealism was actually no less empyrean than Woodrow Wilson's." Frances Perkins believes that the faith which he developed during his illness was "a solid basis for his future inner security in time of stress," and that "what he cared about was improvement in people's lives."

His humanitarian concern for the betterment of people's lives was partly a product of his idealism, partly a result of his consuming interest in people as such. This sociability has been difficult to analyze for it was clear that his cordiality of manner was not always sincere, and the genuineness with which he addressed millions as "my friends" is often questioned. Apparently he sometimes used familiarity as a means of evading an issue or concealing an impasse, just as Lincoln used humorous anecdotes for the same purpose. But this does not mean that Roosevelt was lacking in a real warmth toward people, any more than it means that Lincoln was lacking in a real sense of humor. In fact he liked a surprising number and variety of people, only a small proportion of whom he ever met. He liked them so well that he sought strenuously to meet them on their own terms. As Michael Reilly of the Secret Service bluntly remarks, he was "never one of the boys," though he tried very hard to be, and indeed, "It was such a good try that it never quite came off." Perhaps the hardest try he ever made was when he addressed Stalin as "Uncle Joe." But the significant point is Roosevelt's eagerness to remove every barrier, rather than his failure completely to do so. "People," says Ross McIntire, "were as necessary to him as meat and drink." "He would rather talk to people," says Frances Perkins, "than to sit at his desk and be President," and she adds that when he spoke on the radio, his mind was focused on the people listening. "As he talked, his head would nod and his hands would move in simple, natural, comfortable gestures. His face would smile and light up as though he were actually sitting on the front porch or in the parlor with them."

This warmth of spirit was not unnatural in a man who, in his home life, was surprisingly sentimental and old-fashioned. His rooms were crowded with family pictures; his leisure was oriented toward the familiar scenes at Hyde Park; his Christmas was marked by the reading of Dickens and by the use on the tree of burning candles, which the F.B.I. could never induce him to replace with a safer form of illumination.

These qualities and others, both of his leadership and of his personal character, are among the things of which the definitive biography will have to take account. Just how it will construe them, one can only surmise, especially since history is a product of the times in which it is written. How it will explain his career in the light of these qualities, how it will analyze the significance of their impact upon public affairs remains to be seen. But if it accepts the testimony of his contemporaries, these are the characteristics which history will attribute to Franklin D. Roosevelt whether it is written a decade or a century hence.

✪

FDR: Pragmatist-Idealist

The time for historical re-evaluation is always now. The common-place assumption that each generation rewrites its past is rarely better illustrated than by the outpouring of studies, polemic and scholarly, on Franklin D. Roosevelt and the New Deal. There are so many widely—even wildly—diverse interpretations of what the New Deal really was that one is driven either to despair or to cynicism. Now that the New Deal has become ancient history (as it is at least to earnest undergraduates), a brief historiographic essay may not be out of order.[1]

Many critics of the New Deal have argued that the New Deal marked a radically new departure in political action and social thought. There is rather general agreement, for example, that the New Deal was something more than and different from the Progressivism in which it was nourished because it came to office in the midst of a terrible domestic crisis. Fourteen million unemployed and six-cent corn demanded programs that the reformers of an earlier and more prosperous age dared not countenance. But the

---

[1] In addition to Wayne S. Cole's essay on Roosevelt's foreign policy, "American Entry into World War II: A Historiographical Appraisal," *Mississippi Valley Historical Review*, XLIII (1957), 595–617, see Richard L. Watson, Jr., "Franklin D. Roosevelt in Historical Writing, 1950–1957," *South Atlantic Quarterly*, LVII (Winter 1958), 104–126.

Reprinted from *Pacific Northwest Quarterly,* Vol. LII (1961), pp. 50–55, by permission of the author.

hypothesis that American politics broke with the past in the 1930's goes quite beyond this obvious conclusion.

Samuel Lubell began his study *The Future of American Politics* with the assumption that "the distinctive feature of the political revolution which Franklin D. Roosevelt began and Truman inherited lies not in its resemblance to the political wars of Andrew Jackson or Thomas Jefferson, but in its abrupt break with the continuity of the past."[2]

Richard Hofstadter, in his analysis, *The Age of Reform,* elaborated upon this theme. Where Progressivism attacked bigness, sought to purify politics by destroying the "machine," was individualistic in its philosophy, and Protestant, nativistic, and middle class in orientation, the New Deal accepted bigness in the economy, worked cheerfully with the political bosses, looked to the organized group for its support and for its rationale, and incorporated lower-class, new immigrant groups into its coalition. But most significantly of all, Hofstadter suggested that whereas Progressivism had been moved by old-fashioned, absolutist, even utopian ideals, New Dealism referred to hardheaded, pragmatic principles. The Roosevelt leadership represented, he concluded, a "heartening rediscovery of the humane instincts of the country," and it got things done; but the "New Deal, and the thinking it engendered, represented the triumph of economic emergency and human needs over inherited notions and inhibitions."[3]

Writing in 1941 just as Dr. Win-the-War was taking over from Dr. New Deal, Edgar Kemler, a recent Harvard graduate and intern in the Interior Department, anticipated these hypotheses in an ironic essay he entitled *The Deflation of American Ideals: An Ethical Guide for New Dealers.* Sketching what became almost a caricature of Progressivism, Kemler dwelt on its spiritual impetus, its illusionary postulates, its moralistic objectives, its millennialism. The New Deal left behind its "Puritan" antecedents and

[2] Samuel Lubell, *The Future of American Politics* (New York, 1952), p. 3.
[3] Richard Hofstadter, *The Age of Reform: From Bryan to F.D.R.* (New York, 1955), pp. 314, 323. For an earlier discussion to the same points, see Eric Goldman, *Rendezvous with Destiny: A History of Modern American Reform* (New York, 1952), Chapters 14–16.

embarked on baldly realistic programs. Its concern was not with abstract ethical or religious principles, he argued, but with political and economic realities. As for bigness in the economy, it set about "to manage rather than destroy."

Wilson's ideals were "flimsy stuff" beside the toughness of the New Deal. The New Deal had done with "moral indignation" and turned to "social engineering." The New Deal was geared "to the wholesome animal needs of the community." Whereas Progressivism had been a "race horse," the New Deal was a "mule, whose value [lay] not in its beauty and morality but in its practical usefulness in a world of hard economics." The New Deal, in short, was nondoctrinaire, undogmatic, pragmatic.[4]

From a position well to the political right came an evaluation of the Roosevelt leadership not substantially dissimilar. Edgar E. Robinson, a spiritual as well as an actual neighbor of Herbert Hoover, concluded in his study, *The Roosevelt Leadership,* that the New Deal had "changed not only the direction but the fabric of American society and had done much to alter the American spirit of self-reliance and faith."[5]

Accompanying the insistence that the Roosevelt program marked a drastic shift in emphasis and direction of political thought and practice is the charge that the New Deal was devoid of a coherent body of belief. The observation that the administration never possessed a blueprint for the reconstruction of American society is not much more than a truism. Members of the administration have testified to this point that the New Deal had no central plan, no preconceived theoretical position, that Roosevelt himself "had a genuine indifference to *systems* of all sorts."[6]

Students of the Age of Roosevelt have elaborated upon this theme. James MacGregor Burns, for example, emphasized F.D.R.'s lack of a master plan for the remaking of America. "Everything conspired in 1932 to make Roosevelt a pragmatist, an

[4] Edgar Kemler, *The Deflation of American Ideals: An Ethical Guide for New Dealers* (Washington, D.C., 1941), *passim.*

[5] Edgar Eugene Robinson, *The Roosevelt Leadership, 1933–1945* (New York, 1955), p. 375.

[6] Rexford G. Tugwell, "The Progressive Orthodoxy of Franklin D. Roosevelt," *Ethics,* LXIV (October 1953), 19.

opportunist, an experimenter." He had no vision of a greater America apart from a series of tangible particulars, including dams and parks and rural electrification. The President failed to remake the Democratic party in the image of reform because, deficient in the power of positing long-range objectives, he was willing to patch together a haphazard system designed to offer partial and temporary solutions to full and persistent problems. Roosevelt played too often the fox, devious and crafty, too rarely the lion, direct and bold.[7]

Eric Goldman, in the same manner, described Roosevelt as "Restless and mercurial in his thinking, a connoisseur of theories but impatient with people who took theories seriously, he trusted no system except the system of endless experimentation." Admitting that "even the most casual doctrinaire has his ideological guideposts," Goldman noted Roosevelt's roots in patrician reform, in T.R.'s New Nationalism, Wilson's New Freedom, and Hoover's Associationalism. But liberalism, under the New Deal, became casual about means, he laments. It chose too often the expedient rather than the proper course. It became careless about political morality, too willing to make deals with corrupt men at home and abroad. Liberalism came, too readily, to acquiesce in "means that changed the end." Liberalism was debilitated by loose pragmatism, demoralized by moral relativism.[8]

More hostile in his criticism was Edgar E. Robinson, who saw the New Deal as the product of revolutionary forces and described its leadership as "tragic" because of deficiencies of "intellectual grasp and moral discrimination." Such unity as the New Deal exhibited arose not out of any deeply held philosophy, but out of the pressures of necessity. The source of failure was Roosevelt's inability "to justify the means or establish the ends he had in

[7] James MacGregor Burns, *Roosevelt: The Lion and the Fox* (New York, 1956), p. 156. Burns quite approves of the particular measures achieved by the New Deal, as do also Hofstadter, Goldman, and Kemler; they regret, apparently, the lost opportunity of reconstructing American society.

[8] Goldman, *Rendezvous with Destiny*, pp. 324–325, 450. Much to the same points, see Daniel Aaron, *Men of Good Hope* (New York, 1951), p. 293; and Paul T. Homan, "The Pattern of the New Deal," *Political Science Quarterly*, II (1936), 161–184.

view." In brief, there was as a consequence of the New Deal a loss of national integrity and standards because of the "wide acceptance of the view that 'the end justifies the means.' " The New Deal was a corrupting influence ultimately because of the kind of pragmatism it practiced, devious and crude (and terribly successful if one applies the pragmatic test to 1932, 1936, 1940, and 1944).[9]

A notable proponent of this view that the New Deal was "bereft of a coherent and plausible body of belief" was Richard Hofstadter, who in a sparkling essay on F.D.R., "The Patrician as Opportunist," rang the changes on that theme. In the Roosevelt program, said Hofstadter, there was no thread of consistent policy, no far-seeing plan, but rather a hodgepodge of contradictory experiments. F.D.R.'s intuitive grasp of the practical and his flexibility were, at the same time, assets permitting constructive accomplishments and liabilities which weakened liberalism by undermining its long-range objectives. Accustomed after twelve years to clever, dynamic, personal leadership, American liberalism was left, at his death, "rudderless and demoralized" and "all but helpless."[10]

Most forcefully, however, do we find this interpretation insinuated throughout the first three volumes of Arthur M. Schlesinger, Jr.'s, *The Age of Roosevelt.* An epic account of Roosevelt and the New Deal, grand in design and packed with detail, these volumes again and again express admiration for a President whose "determination was to keep options open within the general framework of a humanized democracy." The kind of pragmatism Schlesinger sees in the New Deal possessed an ultimate virtue, though it often led to confusion and drift and inconsistency, because it preferred "existence to essence" and favored flexibility and action over dogma and doctrine. "The great central source of

[9] Robinson, *Roosevelt Leadership,* pp. 14, 388, 408.
[10] Richard Hofstadter, *The American Political Tradition and the Men Who Made It* (New York, 1948), Chapter XII, vii, 311. The "demoralization" of contemporary liberalism was more apparent in 1948, after three years of domestic drift and cold war, than it was in 1955 when, in the *Age of Reform,* the significance of the New Deal was more positively stated.

its energy," he concludes, "was the instinctive contempt of practical, energetic, and compassionate people for dogmatic absolutes."

Thus it is that those he designates as "Platonists," whether of the right or the left (Herbert Hoover, John Dewey, or Earl Browder), win his scorn for "considering abstractions the ultimate reality." Those who paralleled most closely the chief's knack for improvisation become the heroes of the story. Harry Hopkins, Marriner Eccles, Molly Dewson, Justice Harlan Stone are moved by a practicality that embraced both ends and means. The New Deal may have lacked "ideological commitment" and "intellectual clarity," but it marched toward humane goals and relied on the means of pragmatic, democratic politics.[11]

These interpretations add up to a large but still partial truth. Franklin Roosevelt himself, not unaware of the charges of opportunism leveled at him during his lifetime, countered his critics with a candid confession of inconsistency, which he justified (somewhat less candidly perhaps) by the pressure of circumstances, "insufficient knowledge," and "the need of experimentation." But through all these inconsistencies, he said, "I trust that there also will be found a consistency and continuity of broad purpose."[12] The New Deal was pragmatic, of course. No one, least of all the New Dealers themselves, would care to deny the obvious cheer with which the Roosevelt administration went about its business of experimenting with new devices for recovery, relief, and reconstruction. The promise to try something, anything, to stimulate economic advance was an obvious answer to the general drift of policy and deadlock of political purpose which had characterized government for more than three years.

New Deal pragmatism was more than a simple pledge to experimental action, however. It rested on the assumption that man's social environment could be altered by a deliberate and knowing manipulation of political forces. To Roosevelt, govern-

[11] Arthur M. Schlesinger, Jr., *The Crisis of the Old Order* (Boston, 1957), *The Coming of the New Deal* (Boston, 1959), *The Politics of Upheaval* (Boston, 1960); the quotations are from the third volume, pp. 651, 647, 176, 263.
[12] Samuel I. Rosenman, ed., *The Public Papers and Addresses of Franklin D. Roosevelt* (New York, 1938), I, xiii.

ment could become "the instrument of our united purpose to solve for the individual the ever-rising problems of a complex civilization." Through the agencies of government, men could feel their way toward the institution of "practical controls over blind economic forces and blindly selfish men."[13]

Felix Frankfurter's views certainly represented part of the New Deal consensus, especially so because they could fall back so comfortably on unchallenged assumptions of right and wrong. His endorsement of Al Smith's candidacy in 1928 had been defended: "Happily, Smith has no set, doctrinaire 'principles,' but possesses a mind free for new experience and responsive to its directions." Governor Smith had achieved "great things for liberal causes"; his mind was "fertilized by the concrete event." It was not only Smith's realism, however, that commended him to all good liberals: it was also because he possessed "a deep understanding of political liberty," because he had "infused his government with human sympathy which transcends even tolerance," because he enjoyed a cast of mind "that feels the common qualities of men, that values the moral dignity and the love of life implanted in all, and is capable of neighborliness with all sorts and conditions of men however different their accents of speech."[14]

Frankfurter later found it easy to shift his affections to another Governor of the Empire State who would display the same happy knack of combining an empirical view of life with devoutly held commitments to all the moral principles of the democratic way: respect for man's dignity, the love of liberty, human sympathy, simple neighborliness. This was not a foot-loose pragmatism, but one anchored firmly to the moral absolutes of the long tradition of reform liberalism.

Rexford G. Tugwell, probably one of the most doctrinaire of the New Deal family, was himself torn between pragmatism and idealism. Roosevelt, Tugwell knew from experience, was capable of using, at different times and even all at the same time, the apparently self-contradictory means of planning, regulation, and fragmentation to meet the economic problems of the 1930's.

---

[13] *Ibid.* (New York, 1941), VI, 1.
[14] Felix Frankfurter, *Law and Politics* (New York, 1939), pp. 320–328.

Inconsistencies there were in abundance, but clearly established goals as well. What appeared on the surface to be casual or even flippant policy decisions were rather, Tugwell notes, painstakingly derived; it was just that Roosevelt chose deliberately to obscure his policy-making procedures.

F.D.R.'s pragmatism rested upon an unshifting foundation of ultimate principles—neighborliness, moral humanitarianism, religious faith, the conservation of natural and human resources, the need for social balance and for security if individual liberty and opportunity were to be preserved and extended. These commitments, Tugwell holds, were rarely made clear or complete primarily because the political life required "appeasement, accommodation, reconciliation, adjustment, compromise."[15]

Assuredly the New Deal was pragmatic. It was even guilty of "catch-penny opportunism" on frequent occasion. But if its theories did not add up to a logically consistent, coherent system of social philosophy, they were in the grand tradition of reform liberalism, and they did constitute a viable and vigorous, if admittedly hodgepodge, program for constructive action. This latter view can be found pursued in monographs written by Daniel Fusfeld, Bernard Bellush, and Thomas H. Greer, among others.

Daniel Fusfeld, in his monograph *The Economic Thought of Franklin D. Roosevelt and the Origins of the New Deal,* traced F.D.R.'s economic background. He persuasively argued that Roosevelt, if not a profound scholar, was remarkably well read and widely informed in the field of economics.

His views on basic economic matters were well articulated—particularly in such areas as labor, big business, welfare legislation, conservation and power, and regional planning—and were the basis of the policies he advocated as well as the advisers and administrators he chose.

Weak in the area of depression economics (a glaring enough deficiency), Roosevelt came to the Presidency with a philosophy

[15] Rexford G. Tugwell, *The Art of Politics* (New York, 1958), p. 245; see also Tugwell, *The Democratic Roosevelt* (New York, 1957).

of economics rather better thought-through and more coherent than his critics, contemporary or historical, have granted. While he was prepared "to shift his ground, and compromise in order to reach his goals," those goals were unambiguous in concept for the most part. Fusfeld indicates that F.D.R. more often learned by ear than by eye, that his responses were "derived primarily from the climate of opinion of his time," and that his system of thought was flexible enough to permit adjustment to new evidence and new theories; he also portrays, however, a president less capricious and less casual in these matters than is often assumed.[16]

Bernard Bellush's study, *Franklin D. Roosevelt as Governor of New York,* bolsters this general hypothesis that F.D.R. came to the Presidency, out of the gubernatorial experience primarily, clearly anticipating the major aspects of what would later evolve into the New Deal. The campaign of 1932 may have been one in which basic issues were as much confused and glossed over as clarified, but "Roosevelt had already formulated the bases for a program when he campaigned for the presidency in 1932."

Particularly in the areas of labor relations, conservation, agriculture, unemployment relief, public works, and social security, the fundamental principles upon which much of the New Deal would be built were firmly laid in this earlier period. Economic developments and political events would establish the context within which principles and programs would be implemented. F.D.R. would continue to respond, as he had, with "an open-minded, pragmatic approach," but this kind of pragmatic leadership was not devoid of the direction that experience and ideals could provide.[17]

Thomas H. Greer, in a similar vein, has summarized the social and political ideas of F.D.R. and concluded that the New Deal possessed "intelligible and consistent" objectives. Characterizing the President as a "practical philosopher" (rather than as "the

[16] Daniel Fusfeld, *The Economic Thought of Franklin D. Roosevelt and the Origins of the New Deal* (New York, 1956); the quotations are from pp. 4–5.
[17] Bernard Bellush, *Franklin D. Roosevelt as Governor of New York* (New York, 1955); the quotations are from pp. xii, 282.

patrician as opportunist"), Greer traced the sources of Roosevelt's thought—his education, his reading, "his absorbing interest in history," and "his capacity for learning by direct experience and through personal associations." F.D.R. was an innovator, to be sure, a practical reformer and a master politician, but programs were moved and informed by a philosophical system, not always consistent, but as coherent as statesmen can usually afford.[18]

Harry Hopkins, in a moment of exuberance, may have stated the common sense of the matter when he said to Robert Sherwood:

You and I are for Roosevelt because he's a great spiritual figure, because he's an idealist, like Wilson, and he's got the guts to drive through against any opposition to realize those ideals. . . . You can see the real Roosevelt when he comes out with something like the Four Freedoms. And don't get the idea those are any catch phrases. *He believes them!* He believes they can be practically attained.[19]

The rationale of the New Deal was in direct line of descent with the many strands of thought and belief which had made up the traditions of reform liberalism. It was eclectic. It was a theory fit for practicing politicians interested in and skilled at staying in power. To suggest that the New Deal consensus constituted a logically consistent, coherent, formal system of social thought would be to err grievously.

What Clinton Rossiter has written of the political theory of the Revolutionary generation might well apply, on a lower level of brilliance, one fears, to the consensus of the 1930's. The leaders of the American Revolution, he writes, were "makers of history with a flair for speculative generalization, not philosophers in single minded search of ultimate truth." The philosophy they pieced together was "earnest faith rather than ordered theory." Its genius was evident in its capacity to fashion real institutions for the

---

[18] Thomas H. Greer, *What Roosevelt Thought: The Social and Political Ideas of Franklin D. Roosevelt* (East Lansing, Mich., 1958); the quotations are from pp. ix, 140.

[19] Robert E. Sherwood, *Roosevelt and Hopkins* (New York, 1948), p. 266.

implementation of popular ideas.[20] Hyde Park was not Monticello, to be sure; yet the similarities cannot be denied.

The New Deal was firmly rooted in the past, and its contributions, for better or for worse, became part of the mainstream of American life. Above all else, the New Deal was a conservative force; it sought to preserve and to extend the faith and the institutions of liberal democracy. Identifying himself as a "true conservative" because he sought to defend a system of "private property and free enterprise by correcting such injustices and inequalities as arise from it," Roosevelt saw that only through the adjustment of institutions to a changing world could truly worthy ways be maintained.

Civilization was a living tree, he noted, which the liberal wished to keep alive and beautiful and functional by pruning it of its dead branches. The liberal he identified as one who worked "to control the processes of change, to the end that the break with the old pattern may not be too violent." Society was a living organism not easily distorted or deflected from its source. To resist growth was, however, to stunt and disfigure the natural processes of history. Statecraft was to be directed toward the preservation, extension, and redefinition of the community's essential values under conditions of increasing complexity.[21]

Out of pressing need the New Deal evolved a program; from the past it drew its inspiration. The inventiveness of the New Deal operated more in the arena of program than abstract policy. That it was not devoid of lively and viable theories, however, is abundantly clear. It succeeded, where it did succeed, not only because it was administered by clever politicians, not only because it proposed real, if always partial, answers to real and present problems; it succeeded also because its idiom drew from a tradition still revered in the American heart.

[20] Clinton L. Rossiter, *Seedtime of the Republic* (New York, 1953), p. 439; also see Rossiter, "The Political Philosophy of F. D. Roosevelt: A Challenge to Scholarship," *Review of Politics*, XI (1949), 87–95.

[21] F.D.R., *Public Papers* (New York, 1938), V, 389–390; F.D.R. quoted in Anne O'Hare McCormick, *The World at Home* (New York, 1956), p. 133.

★

Franklin D. Roosevelt: The Ordeal

Despite his appearance of vitality and excellent health, Roosevelt was, as he later granted, thoroughly fatigued. The unpleasantness* in Washington had forced him to cut short his vacation at Campobello; at the end of July he returned there. "I thought he looked tired when he left," his secretary, "Missy" LeHand, wrote Mrs. Roosevelt a few days later. But Campobello vacations to Roosevelt meant substituting long days of sports and physical exertion for his usual strenuous regimen in the city. His way of resting would have worn out most men.

Van-Lear Black took Roosevelt back to Campobello aboard his yacht, the *Sabalo*. When they ran into dirty weather, Roosevelt took over the navigation, since Black's captain did not know the Bay of Fundy waters. For hours he remained at the wheel, battling the fog, until he brought the yacht safely into Welchpool Harbor.

The next day was sunny, and they fished for cod from the *Sabalo's* tender. "I baited hooks, alternating between the fore and aft cockpits of the motor-tender, crossing beside the hot engine on a three-inch varnished plank," Roosevelt once recalled. "I slipped

Reprinted from *Franklin D. Roosevelt: The Ordeal*, pp. 97–105, 120–121, by Frank Freidel, by permission of Little, Brown and Co. Copyright © 1954, by Frank Freidel.

* A highly partisan subcommittee of the Senate Naval Affairs Committee had charged that Roosevelt, as Assistant Secretary of the Navy, had approved vice investigators' engaging in homosexual acts to trap sexual deviates [ed.].

—overboard. I'd never felt anything so cold as that water! I hardly went under, hardly wet my head, because I still had hold of the side of the tender, but the water was so cold it seemed paralyzing. This must have been the icy shock in comparison to the heat of the August sun and the tender's engine."

Although Roosevelt did not feel well, he continued his usual active routine. Wednesday, August 10, 1921, was no exception. In the afternoon, while the Roosevelts were sailing in their small yacht, the *Vireo,* they saw a forest fire on one of the islands and went ashore to help put it out. Roosevelt cut evergreen branches for himself and his children, and for several hours they flailed at the flames. "Late in the afternoon we brought it under control," he recalled. "Our eyes were bleary with smoke; we were begrimed, smarting with spark-burns, exhausted." The remedy, Roosevelt thought, would be a swim. So with his children he dog-trotted two miles along the hot, dusty roads across the island of Campobello, swam across a narrow fresh-water lagoon inside the beach, and dipped into the frigid waters of the Bay of Fundy. Then they ran back in their bathing suits.

"I didn't feel the usual reaction, the glow I'd expected," Roosevelt recalled. "When I reached the house the mail was in, with several newspapers I hadn't seen. I sat reading for a while, too tired even to dress. I'd never felt quite that way before."

During supper, Roosevelt quietly remarked that he thought he had a slight attack of lumbago, excused himself and went upstairs to bed. "The next morning when I swung out of bed my left leg lagged but I managed to move about and to shave. I tried to persuade myself that the trouble with my leg was muscular, that it would disappear as I used it. But presently it refused to work, and then the other."

When Anna Roosevelt carried a tray into her father's room, he greeted her with a cheerful smile, and even a wisecrack. There was nothing to be cheerful about, for his temperature was 102. Mrs. Roosevelt was worried, and the children alarmed. She sent for their old friend, Dr. E. H. Bennett in Lubec, who, despite Roosevelt's pain and paralysis, diagnosed the illness as no more than an ordinary cold. In order that the house might be quiet, Mrs.

Roosevelt sent the children and some guests off on a three-day camping trip. Even with the reassurance of Dr. Bennett, she was too concerned about her husband to go with them.

The next morning, Friday, August 12, Roosevelt could not stand up, and by evening had even lost the power to move his legs. They were numb, but very sensitive to the touch. He ached all over, was at least partly paralyzed from the chest down, and his thumb muscles had become so weak that he could not write.

By Saturday, Mrs. Roosevelt and Dr. Bennett decided they must call in a consultant. Louis Howe, who was visiting at Campobello, helped them canvass the resorts. They located a famous elderly specialist, Dr. W. W. Keen of Philadelphia, who was staying at Bar Harbor. He diagnosed the paralysis as due to a blood clot in the lower spinal cord, prescribed heavy massage, predicted that Roosevelt would recover, though perhaps not for a long time—and sent a bill for six hundred dollars. Mrs. Roosevelt sent to New York for a masseuse; meanwhile she and Howe massaged her husband as best they could. The heavy kneading of his feet and lower legs was exceedingly painful to him, since they were hypersensitive. Still worse, it was exactly the wrong treatment, and further damaged the muscles.

For several days, he continued to have serious fever and to show no improvement. It was difficult to get a nurse, so Mrs. Roosevelt herself took care of him and slept on a couch in his room.

A week after the first chill, his temperature returned to normal, and despite the acute depression that normally accompanied this illness, Roosevelt's spirits bobbed upward. "I think he's getting back his grip and a better mental attitude though he has of course times of great discouragement," Mrs. Roosevelt wrote. "We thought yesterday he moved his toes on one foot a little better which is encouraging." She added, referring to the specialist's prediction that it might take a long time for her husband to recover, "I dread the time when I have to tell Franklin and it wrings my heart for it is all so much worse to a man than a woman."

Whatever the dark feelings Roosevelt must have had, he kept them to himself at the time. Years later he confided to Frances

Perkins that for the first few days he had been in utter despair, feeling that God had abandoned him. Then his buoyancy and strong religious faith reasserted themselves; he felt that he must have been shattered and spared for a purpose beyond his knowledge. As he had been brought up to do, he displayed none of the black side of his feelings to his family; incredibly soon he was making light of his affliction. Only a week after he was taken ill, he wrote, "Thanks to a severe chill which I lay to vagaries of the Bay of Fundy climate, which has more tide and more kinds of weather than any other place in the globe, I am spending a considerably longer vacation than I intended under the stern eye of a doctor who refuses to allow me to more than look at my mail and sign a few letters each day."

Roosevelt's uncle, Frederic A. Delano, meanwhile was consulting several specialists, who from Delano's description felt certain that the disease was infantile paralysis. They recommended that the massages and manipulations stop, since the patient must have time to rest and rebuild slowly. On August 25, Dr. Robert W. Lovett, a Boston specialist on poliomyelitis, arrived and confirmed this. He stopped the massaging and suggested hot baths. Fortunately for Roosevelt's morale, Dr. Lovett considered it a mild attack, and thought Roosevelt might recover completely.

On the first of September, Sara Delano Roosevelt, who had been in Europe, arrived at Campobello, and immediately entered into the gay spirit of the sickroom. She wrote her brother:

> I got here yesterday at 1:30 and at once . . . came up to a brave, smiling, and beautiful son, who said: "Well, I'm glad you are back Mummy and I got up this party for you!" He had shaved himself and seems very bright and *keen*. Below his waist he cannot move at all. His legs (that I have always been proud of) have to be moved often as they ache when long in one position. He and Eleanor decided at once to be cheerful and the atmosphere of the house is all happiness, so I have fallen in and follow their glorious example. . . . Dr. Bennett just came and said "This boy is going to get all right." They went into his room and I hear them all laughing. Eleanor in the lead.

The first stage of the illness was over, and Roosevelt was ready to begin working to regain the use of his legs. Even more impor-

tant to him than this was the question of whether he would be able
to return to his career. Sara Roosevelt firmly believed that for him
to do so would kill him, and strongly voiced her opinion that he
should not. Her son was an invalid; an invalid he would continue
to be. Therefore he should give up all thought of future participation in business and politics. He had had a brilliant career already,
even though he was only thirty-nine, and was well entitled to
retire. He should return to Hyde Park, which he loved, to the life
of a country gentleman, and a collector of books and stamps. In
effect, he would have been returning to her full domination, and
would have been assuming the way of life of his elderly ailing
father, her beloved James, whom she had nursed twenty years
before.

Roosevelt would have none of this. The struggle against his
mother's wish for him to retire went on for months, but fortunately
he did not have to fight it alone. Eleanor Roosevelt thinks that if it
had been a necessity for him to retire he could have done it and
not been unhappy. However, it was not necessary; she, Howe, and
Dr. George Draper, who was taking over the treatment, felt that
for Roosevelt to retire would be "a terrible waste," and fortified
him with spirits as indomitable as his own. Even before Roosevelt
was sure he had infantile paralysis, he was impatient to return to
his career. Within two weeks after the attack, Mrs. Roosevelt was
planning to move him to New York City for treatments because,
"if, as he hopes, he can carry on his various business activities it
can only be done there." On August 22, he authorized President
Henry Noble MacCracken of Vassar College to name him on a
committee for an endowment drive, and on September 12, he
accepted membership on the Executive Committee of the Democratic Party in New York State. Thus, there was literally no period
when he was out of public life. He came to a determination to go
on and make a further career for himself, Mrs. Roosevelt has said,
at a time when he was lying in bed and working for hours to try to
wiggle a big toe.

At the same time, Howe, who had spent years building a reputation for square dealing with newspapermen, fed vague explan-

ations to a press association correspondent who came over from Eastport almost every day. He managed to keep the news that Roosevelt was seriously ill out of the newspapers until August 27, when he could couple with it the information that "he is now improving." Thus, from the outset Howe helped create the illusion —so important if Roosevelt were to continue active in politics— that there was nothing vitally wrong.

Howe's greatest difficulty came on September 13 when a private railroad car arrived at Eastport to take Roosevelt to New York. The crowd of well-wishers and reporters would have been shocked to see Roosevelt helpless on a stretcher. Besides, the invalid was a shy man who would have been keenly embarrassed over displaying his weakness in public. Consequently, Howe started a rumor that Roosevelt would land at a dock at the far end of town, then signaled the motorboat to bring him in at the near end. His stretcher was loaded onto a luggage cart and bumped up a long, sharp incline to the train. It was a physical as well as a mental ordeal, for every jolt caused him excruciating pain; yet when he spied eight-year-old Franklin, Jr. he managed to smile, wave, and convey the impression that nothing very much was wrong. His stretcher was passed through the window of the railroad car, and he was comfortably settled before the crowd spied him. When the *New York World* correspondent saw him in the car, "Mr. Roosevelt was enjoying his cigarette and said he had a good appetite. Although unable to sit up, he says he is feeling more comfortable."

Thus Roosevelt returned to New York City without letting the public learn that he was suffering from anything more than a passing illness. After he had arrived at the Presbyterian Hospital, Howe gave the story to the newspapers that Roosevelt was suffering from poliomyelitis and had lost the use of his legs below the knees. But he quoted Dr. Draper, who had been Roosevelt's school chum: "He will not be crippled. No one need have any fear of permanent injury from this attack." After *The New York Times* ran this news on its front page on September 16, Roosevelt wrote Adolph S. Ochs, the publisher:

While the doctors were unanimous in telling me that the attack was very mild and that I was not going to suffer any permanent effects from it, I had, of course, the usual dark suspicion that they were just saying nice things to make me feel good, but now that I have seen the same statement officially made in the New York *Times* I feel immensely relieved because I know of course it must be so.

I am feeling in the very best of spirits and have already been allowed to take up part of my somewhat varied interests.

If anything, Howe had succeeded too well in creating the impression that Roosevelt had suffered only a slight handicap from which he was quickly recuperating. Herbert Pell sent a note asking him to attend a meeting of the Democratic Executive Committee on October 11. Howe scrawled on the margin, "Mr. Pell had better wake up & hear the birdies!" Even Roosevelt had to admit to another political associate that the newspaper accounts were "a trifle optimistic."

Undoubtedly Howe was aiming his emphatic forecasts of quick and complete recovery at Roosevelt as well as at the public, for the sad fact was that Roosevelt was still a very sick and badly crippled man. Dr. Draper, who was a skillful specialist, now found his former optimism (based on Dr. Lovett's diagnosis) quite unjustified. Roosevelt continued to suffer from agonizing sensitivity. It hurt him even if someone touched the sheet on his bed. Over a period of weeks he would now and then run a temperature as high as 102. He made little or no improvement. At the same time that Roosevelt was determined that he was going to leave the hospital on crutches in two or three weeks, Dr. Draper was confiding to Dr. Lovett that he feared the back muscles were so seriously damaged that his patient might not even be able to sit erect. He felt that the maintenance of Roosevelt's morale was paramount, and in cooperation with Mrs. Roosevelt and Howe he worked diligently to sustain it. Dr. Draper wrote, "He has such courage, such ambition, and yet at the same time such an extraordinarily sensitive emotional mechanism, that it will take all the skill which we can muster to lead him successfully to a recognition of what he really faces without crushing him."

Yet slowly Roosevelt did make progress, and because he did, it is questionable whether he ever faced up completely to his condition. He still had sufficient power in his arms to pull himself up by a strap over his bed and thus turn himself over. Dr. Draper did not examine his arms, in order not to disturb his belief that they were unaffected; indeed, Roosevelt took considerable pride in their strength.[1] When Daniels visited him in the hospital, he beckoned his former chief close to the bedside, then suddenly launched a blow that sent him reeling. "You thought you were coming to see an invalid," Roosevelt laughed, "But I can knock you out in any bout."

He did recover the entire strength in the muscles of his arms, and as he developed them, they became very powerful. His back muscles too recovered, and despite Dr. Draper's forebodings, there came a day when he was able to sit up. On October 28, 1921, he went home to his 65th Street house, able to pull himself up by a strap and, with some assistance, to swing himself into a wheel chair. His state of mind was excellent, and his hope for the future boundless. "I . . . am getting along well and expect to be walking on crutches in a very few weeks," he wrote on December 8. "The doctors say that there is no question but that by the Spring I will be walking without any limp."

But the months of pain and strain were by no means over. In January, 1922, the muscles behind his knees began to tighten and pull his legs up under him. Dr. Draper had to put both legs into plaster casts. During two weeks of agony, wedges, driven a bit deeper each day, stretched the tendons back.

In February, Roosevelt was able to put on braces of steel, weighing seven pounds each, and stretching from his hips to his shoes. With the aid of these, he slowly learned to stand up once more and to walk with crutches. He was not really walking, but maneuvering himself with his hips; he was never again able to walk or even stand without support. He had no balance and no power in

[1] Ernest K. Lindley wrote that after over ten years, the close friends and business associates who visited F.D.R. in the hospital still reminisced about it "eagerly and with tones of wonder." "In essence they are all the same. Roosevelt gaily brushed aside every hint of condolence and sent them away more cheerful than they could make a pretense of being when they arrived. None of them has ever heard him utter a complaint or a regret or even acknowledge that he had had so much as a bit of hard luck."

his legs. However, at the time, he still either did not know, or did not choose to believe, that he was hopelessly crippled. With determination and enthusiasm, he began gentle exercises that he hoped in time would rebuild the strength of his leg muscles.

It was a most tense, unpleasant winter in the house on 65th Street. Everyone had outwardly to maintain a semblance of cheerfulness when there was nothing to be cheerful about. Roosevelt would get down on the living room floor with the younger children, but since they failed to realize his weakness, there was the danger that they would roughhouse with him too hard. The house was so overcrowded that Mrs. Roosevelt had to sleep on a cot in one of the boys' rooms. Through it all, Sara Delano Roosevelt, with her usual dogged vigor, worked unceasingly toward her goal to get Roosevelt to accept his invalidism as permanent and return to Hyde Park to retirement. She poked and prodded at every weak point in the family relationship—she was sure she knew better than the doctors and that her son must be kept quiet; the house was too noisy. She even worked to convince fifteen-year-old Anna that it was unjust for the girl to have a small fourth-floor room, while Louis Howe had a large third-floor room with bath. To do so was not difficult, since Howe, whose humor and interests were entirely adult, was not liked by the Roosevelt children. Also, Anna was at a difficult age and quite unhappy already. Sometimes at the dinner table she was so annoying to her father that he spoke severely to her and she left in tears. Consequently her grandmother was able to persuade her that her mother was not interested in her. Finally, Anna went to her mother and demanded a switch in rooms. Eleanor Roosevelt, preoccupied with her husband's illness, did not realize Anna's agitated state of mind, and rebuked her sternly.

Every bit of Mrs. Roosevelt's thought and energy was going into the fight on behalf of her husband. As had always been her habit, she maintained a phenomenal degree of outward composure. It never occurred to her to take Anna into her confidence and "consult with her about our difficulties or tell her just what her father was going through in getting his nerves back into condition." In retrospect she wrote, "I have always had a very bad tendency to shut up like a clam, particularly when things are going badly; and that attitude was accentuated, I think, as regards my children."

Even Eleanor Roosevelt's magnificent reserve could withstand only so much attrition. One afternoon in the spring, while she was reading to her two youngest sons, she began to sob uncontrollably, and cried for hours. When Elliott came home from school and found her crying in the living room, he fled; Howe tried to find out what was wrong and failed. Finally, she went into an empty room, locked the door, and slowly pulled herself together. It was the only time that she lost emotional control of herself, but it seemed to have a salutary effect upon Anna, who began to draw closer to her mother, and soon was confiding in her. As for Mrs. Roosevelt, "From that time on I seemed to have got rid of nerves and uncontrollable tears, for never again have either of them bothered me."

There has been much speculation about the effect of the illness and suffering upon Franklin D. Roosevelt. He did demonstrate immediately a truly incredible fortitude—but he had possessed it in large measure since childhood. His own reserve, the buoyant mask with which he hid his inner feelings, was so uncracked at the time and in following years that it is hard to gauge his emotions.

"Now, I don't want any sob-stuff in the relation of my experience," he warned a newspaperman in 1928. "Of course, it was a great shock to be stricken down at a time when, except for natural exhaustion after a hard campaign, I felt myself to be in the pink of condition. And it was rather humiliating to contract a disease of which 75 per cent of the victims are children. But I am thankful that my children were spared."

.   .   .   .

Gradually he adjusted himself to his limitations so well that he could work more effectively than ever before. Ernest K. Lindley, writing in 1931, declared:

He soon began to find that his inability to run around had compensating advantages which, in time, became a really powerful asset. He had always been a restless worker, frequently jumping up and down and dashing here and there through sheer excess of physical energy. He had always been vigorous in his exercise. He had seldom shown fatigue simply because he had been endowed with unusual vitality. Now that he was compelled to sit in one spot, all of his energy was of necessity concentrated upon the work before him. A bit removed from the hurly-burly, he was relieved of many petty irritations and the nervous wear and tear which is one of the most exhausting things about city life. He had an excellent excuse not to do what he did not wish to do; and at the same time, he could not resort to the normal human impulse to run away from a difficult problem. Every one came to see him; he spent neither time nor energy moving from this conference to that.

Many of the men who came in regular contact with him avow that they envied his even temper and clear head at the close of days which had worn them out. He impressed his close friends as having emerged from his illness less impetuous, more serene and judicially minded, though without loss of decisiveness.[2]

Eleanor Roosevelt observed that the main effect of the polio upon her husband was to accentuate his already great power of self-control. The fact that he had to decide on a course of treatment, and then wait a year or two to see its effect, forced him to the attitude that "once you make a decision you must not worry about it." This greatly influenced his future life. Many public men, after they have made a decision over which they have no further control, worry for fear it is not the right one. Roosevelt learned to put out of his mind the things he could do nothing more about.[3] "He could pull a curtain down and go to sleep," Mrs. Roosevelt has said. During the Presidency, and especially during the war, this was "a salvation to him." Polio gave him that capacity.

[2] From Ernest K. Lindley, *Franklin D. Roosevelt: A Career in Progressive Democracy,* copyright 1931, used by special permission of the publishers, The Bobbs-Merrill Company, Inc.

[3] Mrs. Roosevelt remembers that at the time of a banking crisis when F.D.R. was Governor that he sent for Lieutenant Governor Herbert Lehman, himself a banker, to give him advice. Lehman made the necessary decisions, and F.D.R. accepted them, but Lehman then paced the floor. F.D.R. could not pace because he could not walk. He sat in his chair and remarked that if Lehman, once he had made up his mind, would stop worrying, he would be much more useful the next day.

ARTHUR M. SCHLESINGER, JR.

✪

Behind the Mask

But the public image was one thing. The question remained: what was he really like underneath? Nothing more preoccupied and frustrated those around him than the search for an answer. If on the eve of the Presidency Franklin Roosevelt had seemed a baffling mixture of Eagle Scout optimism and hard-bitten resolve, two years in the White House only gave every facet of the contradictory character a higher polish and deeper and more inscrutable gleam.

II

Physically he changed little. His health was excellent, save for his continued susceptibility to the common cold and his chronic sinus trouble (for which he received almost daily treatment from the White House physician, Dr. Ross McIntire). He had pretty much abandoned his old effort to restore motion in his leg muscles and operated most of the time from his wheel chair—except for speeches, when he wore leg braces, or special occasions like the Sunday evening devotional service after Thanksgiving at Warm Springs in 1935 (described here by General Evans Carlson):

Reprinted from "Behind the Mask" in Arthur M. Schlesinger, Jr., *The Coming of the New Deal* (Boston, 1957), pp. 574–588, by permission of the publisher, Houghton Mifflin Company.

We had placed a chair at the roadside for the President's use, but when he drove up he waved the chair aside. Descending from the car he drew himself up and with magnificent dignity and superb will he walked down the ramp, through the door and forward to his seat amid the patients. Never will I forget that walk, which was performed in utter silence. No explanation was ever given for what must have been a supreme effort. But I sensed, and I felt that others present must have sensed, that it was made for the purpose of giving hope and inspiration to the assembled patients.

His energy rarely flagged. Sometimes a sustained bout of work darkened the circles under his eyes and accentuated the occasional trembling of his hands ("My boys' hands shake like that," Roosevelt would say. "It is a family trait"); but a few days under the sun at Warm Springs or sailing on blue water always restored his abundant vitality. Anne O'Hare McCormick reported in 1937, "Of all the leaders of his time, he is perhaps the least variable." Where the rulers of Europe seemed to her to have shriveled and aged under the glare of power, Roosevelt was more himself than ever— his hair perhaps a trifle thinner, his face and figure thicker, but the gestures, the warmth, the composure, the tempo the same. "Mr. Roosevelt is a unique figure in the modern world: the one statesman this writer has seen who seems able to relax."

Yet was not his air of relaxation itself a way of disarming and confusing those who sought to penetrate behind the mask? The surface, as Tugwell said, was all charm, or puckish humor, or absorption in fascinating detail, or delight in maneuver; only one thing seemed certain—that the significant area of operations was taking place a good way below. This area, Roosevelt plainly conceived, was no one's business save his own. "It was part of his conception of his role," remarked Tugwell, "that he should never show exhaustion, boredom, or irritation." He would rather have posterity believe that decision was simple for him, that he selected goals with careless ease and pursued them with serenity, than to admit to misgiving or foreboding. "The serious student," said Tugwell, "is forced to conclude that this man deliberately concealed the processes of his mind." It was partly this; it was partly too, as Herman Kahn has suggested, the Ivy League convention of casualness, now exhibited for the first time in the Presidency.

On one level, this became pure theatrics, sometimes of an obvious kind. Peggy Bacon commented on the bright, direct look, the frank, clear gaze of craft, "clever as hell but so innocent . . . a grand old actor." He turned on his dazzling smile, said one unimpressed White House functionary, "as if somebody had pressed a button and sent a brilliant beam from a lighthouse out across the sea"; to this man, who had served every President since McKinley, Roosevelt's private and public selves seemed more alike than those of any other President because his performance never stopped—because "he never failed to present himself as the leading actor on whatever stage was available at the moment." Those who saw him at close range tried forever to peer into what Robert Sherwood vividly described as "his heavily forested interior." Most of them concluded with Sherwood: "I could never really understand what was going on in there."

His first defense was the cordial, winning but essentially impersonal courtesy which both tantalized and defeated intruders. Dr. Hjalmar Schacht described him as "for all his frankness, possessed of a peculiar reticence." Mary Colum, visiting the White House on a literary occasion, noted "the amazing smile that was a combination of so many kinds of smile, and none of them evoked by any of the people he was addressing," the intelligent, unimpassioned face that seemed incapable of betraying anything but conventional graciousness—yet the hint of "untried intensity" within. "It is difficult to imagine stone or steel under that smooth, bright flow," Anne O'Hare McCormick once said; but she knew it was there. "Make no mistake," said Dr. C. G. Jung after seeing Roosevelt in 1936, "he is a force—a man of superior but impenetrable mind, but perfectly ruthless, a highly versatile mind which you cannot foresee."

III

These were chance visitors. Those who saw him enough to get behind the wall of conventional courtesy encountered next his sense of unassailable internal dignity. One or two interpreted this as snobbishness; but Roosevelt was not a snob. If it is true that people's backgrounds registered on his mind—that he had, for example, an odd weakness for European titles, however seedy—it is also true that lack of background made no difference. "Roosevelt, in his personal relationships," said Stanley High, "is wholeheartedly a democrat" of that "genuine and uninhibited sort" of patrician who had nothing to lose by friendliness or to gain by patronizing. "Snooty people are as much on his black list as prima donnas." His letters to Harvard deans show an evident anxiety to save his sons from "the lack of individuality and the narrowness" which he considered to mark "the club and Boston life of the average private school freshman." His three closest friends were a middle-class newspaperman, a Jew, and the son of a harness maker. "There was a quiet reserve about him," said a White House maid, "but Mr. Roosevelt never made me 'feel like a servant' or 'feel like a Negro.' " Jim Farley, the main source of the snobbishness story, tried to support it by ascribing to Eleanor Roosevelt a quotation ("Franklin finds it hard to relax with people who aren't his social equals") which she subsequently denied and which, in any case, was demonstrably untrue—as Ed Flynn said, "just silly. The Roosevelts were all gregarious to the point of foolishness." Before personal disappointment had embittered him, Farley himself rendered quite different testimony. "There isn't a snobbish bone in his body," he wrote in 1938. If some men born to high social position conveyed feelings of superiority, "I can honestly say I have never observed anything of the kind in Roosevelt. . . . His friends and personal companions are not chosen from any particular group of class."

It was not snobbishness at issue: it was Roosevelt's intense protection of his own interior privacy. "He never was 'one of the boys,' " wrote Mike Reilly of the Secret Service, "although he frequently made a good try. It was such a good try that it never quite came off." No one could be permitted to glimpse the wheels at work. "He never did let down the bars beyond a certain point," said Henry Morgenthau. "I would be the last to claim," said Donald Richberg, "that I ever became well acquainted with that inner man." Harold Ickes reached the conclusion that, however open and smiling the surface, "the core underneath was self-contained, and perhaps even inclined to reserve to the point of coldness." "Roosevelt," said Stanley High, "has a great many intimates, few close friends and no cronies." "Nobody that I know," said Hugh Johnson, "has ever really gotten within the aristocratic reserve of his inherently proud, even haughty, and, I will venture to say, lonely spirit."

Even his wife, to whom he was profoundly devoted, did not share his interior hopes or tribulations. She has written that he did not even tell her when he decided to run for the Presidency; this she learned from Louis Howe. "Franklin," she has said, "did not talk a great deal about the work that he was doing, either at meals or in private family conversation." Tugwell's summary of their relationship seems compassionate and exact: "Eleanor shared everything with Franklin that she was allowed to share and opened her faithful heart completely to his desires and needs. But Franklin himself did not possess the key to his own unconscious reticences, and there was very imperfect reciprocation." They were "linked by indissoluble bonds but not lost in each other as husband and wife might sometimes be."

IV

Some people who do not reveal themselves at work reveal themselves at play. But whose relaxation could have been less revealing than Franklin Roosevelt's?

The White House, of course, imposed new circumspections on a life already drastically limited by steel braces and a wheel chair. It was almost impossible to escape the atmosphere of official responsibility, even in the family rooms upstairs. And, though the Roosevelt regime brought a gay informality the Presidential mansion had not seen since Roosevelts last lived there, the White House still had defects from the viewpoint of thoroughly relaxed living. Most notable of all, perhaps, was the food. Mrs. Nesbitt, whom Mrs. Roosevelt had brought from Hyde Park as housekeeper, described herself as "small-town and a homebody" and believed in "plain foods, plainly prepared." This was fine for Mrs. Roosevelt, who could not care less what she ate; but the President, who enjoyed good cooking, spent his years in the White House in a state of ill-suppressed dissatisfaction. The most powerful man in the country, he could not command a good dinner. His guests were even more indignant. Tugwell described White House food and drink as "pretty awful." "On only one other occasion," wrote Ickes bitterly after a White House dinner, "have I ever tasted worse champagne."

In the White House, Roosevelt sought diversion above all in people and talk. He demanded to be informed and entertained; and he liked people who could pleasantly take his mind from what Francis Biddle once called "the horrible ennui of that wholly impersonal life." Old friends who knew nothing of official affairs here served a purpose—thus Vincent Astor or Henry Hooker. Among associates in government, he could relax only with those who shared his capacity to turn their backs on the daily routine. This is why Jim Farley failed to achieve intimacy—not because he was not in the *Social Register* but because he could talk of nothing except politics. In contrast, as Moley has noted, Ed Flynn was in the personal circle because he "always seemed bored with politics, had read widely and could amuse Roosevelt with items far from statecraft."

As a relief from the White House, Missy LeHand began in 1936 to arrange occasional parties at Harold Ickes's secluded house out beyond Chevy Chase Lake. Ickes, a gourmet, served excellent dinners; and Missy would select an entertaining group—Corcoran, perhaps, with his accordion; or Watson, Early, Hopkins, Morgenthau, McIntyre, later Bill Douglas and Bob Jackson, for an evening of poker. These evenings consisted mainly of idle, easy, kidding chat. They relaxed the President, but disclosed nothing and fitted admirably into his system of defense. "It is delightful to see how the President can enter in at a party," Ickes once wrote. "He had as good a time as anyone there, laughing and talking and joking. . . . Yet, in spite of all his fun-making, no one ever presumes to treat him with familiarity."

If the President's hobbies were more revealing, what they revealed was a set of contradictory traits. In some favorite diversions—the playing of cards, the mixing of drinks, the making of jokes—his habits were conspicuously broad and disorderly. At the

poker table (though he played for tiny stakes, "just for conversation," as the Vice-President, a serious poker player, said patroniz-
ingly) he adored reckless variations like seven-card stud with
deuces and one-eyed jacks wild or improbable improvisations like
"spit in the ocean." His style at rummy, according to Molly
Dewson, was similarly "bold, dashing, high-spirited." When he
mixed drinks, he always overdid the vermouth in the martinis and
the bitters in the old-fashioneds. His humor was slapdash, lacking
wit and consisting mostly of corny remarks which no doubt
sounded funnier at the time than they do in cold print. From a
press conference:

Q. Mr. President, does the ban on the highways include the parking
shoulders?
Roosevelt. Parking *shoulders?*
Q. Yes, widening out on the edge, supposedly to let the civilians
park as the military goes by.
Roosevelt. You don't mean necking places? (*Prolonged laughter.*)

Once when George Dern read the cabinet a long report on beet
sugar, Morgenthau could stand it no more and scribbled a note to
the President: "May I sing some soft music?" The note promptly
came back: "Yes, *chamber* music, or a *pot*pourri." When coins
were pouring into the White House for the campaign against polio,
Roosevelt sent a characteristic message to the mail clerk: "I hope
you are having a good dime." His match books for a time bore the
legend "Stolen from Franklin D. Roosevelt."

His attitude toward baseball sums up this cluster of traits: "I
am the kind of fan who wants to get plenty of action for his
money." Pitchers' duels, he supposed were all right, but "I get the
biggest kick out of the biggest score—a game in which the batters
pole the ball to the far corners of the field, the outfielders
scramble, and the men run the bases. In short, my idea of the best
game is one that guarantees the fans a combined score of not less
than fifteen runs, divided about eight to seven."

Yet despite all this, nothing absorbed him more than his stamp
collection; and stamp collecting obviously called on an entirely
opposite set of psychological characteristics. He spent many happy

evenings in his upstairs study, an album open before him, magnifying glass, tweezers, and hinges by his side; he found infinite pleasure in leafing through philatelic catalogues and ordering new items. In the 1920's Roosevelt had begun to specialize in stamps from North, Central, and South America and Hong Kong. By the thirties he had about twenty-five thousand stamps in some forty albums. Following the example of Hoover, who had also been a collector, Roosevelt asked the White House mail clerk to rescue unusual stamps from the incoming mail. The philatelic passion would seem to attest to a particular personality type with classic characteristics of meticulousness, tidiness, parsimoniousness, and obstinacy. Obviously such a hobby suited Hoover perfectly; but how to reconcile it with the disorderly, generous, and flexible Roosevelt? Yet it gave him more relaxation than almost anything else he could do in the White House and it clearly corresponded to some need in his bewildering personality.

V

Still, for truly effective relaxation, he had to get away. Travel much improved the opportunities for rest and for privacy. In 1933 he spent 92 days away from Washington; in 1934, 149; in 1935, 145. He liked moving around by automobile or slow train, refreshing himself by watching the countryside unroll before him. His favorite objectives were the places he knew best and which soothed him most—Hyde Park and Warm Springs. There he could give the slip to official cares, even to official supervision. Despite the assassination attempt at Miami in 1933, Roosevelt continued to chafe at the vigilant protection of the Secret Service. Where Hoover kept his White House under incessant patrol by four operatives on the ground floor and two on every floor above, Roosevelt ordered them all to stay in the Usher's office. Away from Washington he was even more insouciant. "I certainly do not want a high wire fence around the Warm Springs cottage!" Roosevelt told Chief Moran in early 1933. "The simplest protection would be, as before, a flood light covering each side of the house and front." "Nothing pleases my husband more, in Hyde Park or Warm

Springs," Eleanor Roosevelt said, "than to lose the Secret Service car which always follows him." When Colonel Starling, the head of the White House unit, wanted to cancel a trip in 1934 because of reports of an assassination plot, Roosevelt called the idea "absurd." "Every public appearance of a chief executive entails an element of risk; but . . . if anyone wants to kill me, there is no possible way to prevent him. About all that can be done is to guard against a second shot." The only thing that worried him was fire. Shortly after moving to the White House, he worked out a system for escape, involving even a canvas chute on which he could slide to safety. Starling later wrote, "His absolute lack of fear made it difficult at times for him to understand the safeguards with which we surrounded him. He liked to feel completely free, and he saw no reason why he should not be."

He could never feel completely free; but he found momentary refreshment observing the rose garden at Hyde Park, or driving his specially fitted car along the twisting woodland roads beside the Hudson, or looking at the view from the ridge where he would soon build his beloved Hilltop Cottage, or watching the blue herons at dusk at the Val-Kill pond, or picnicking on the Knob at Warm Springs, with its illimitable view of quiet green country receding dimly into the distance, or pausing a moment among lovely southern pines at twilight. Then the implacable round started again, and he returned to the memoranda, the cables, the phone calls from Washington, and the important guests.

The best escape of all was the sea: Roosevelt once told Ickes that sailing was the only way he could really rest. Except for swimming, it was the one exercise which remained to him after polio; combined with fishing, it gave him deep excitement and almost inviolable privacy. On his own boat, the *Amberjack,* he wore his oldest sweater and his dirtiest flannels and never shaved. Cruises on Vincent Astor's *Nourmahal* with nonpolitical friends (Ed Flynn, watching them embark, once observed sardonically, "The Hasty Pudding Club puts out to sea") were a cheerful antidote to the Presidency. And there were more formidable expeditions, like the one which Hopkins and Ickes never forgot on the *Houston* in the autumn of 1935 to Cocos Island, a densely

flowered islet of vivid green rising two thousand feet out of the
brilliant blue Pacific off the shores of Costa Rica. Lowered to the
chair in the stern of his special fishing launch, fighting sailfish and
pompano in the choppy Pacific, using all the power of his massive
arms and shoulders to reel in the fish, Roosevelt cast off weariness
and irritability under the healing beneficence of sun and spray and
salt.

VI

At work or at play, the defenses remained intact. He appeared
almost deliberately to surround himself by incurious people—the
Earlys, McIntyres, Watsons—as if to preserve his inner sanc-
tuaries. "It sometimes seems," Tugwell has perceptively noted,
"that those who were closest to him for the longest time were kept
there because they did not probe or try to understand but rather
because they gave an unquestioning service."

Some pressed too hard, of course. They were too curious or
insensitive or cared too much. It was when Roosevelt was thus
pressed that he resorted—almost, it would seem, as if he considered himself entitled to do so—to deviousness and to deceit.
Those who did not press rarely complained of being cheated. "I
knew Roosevelt for twenty years," said Molly Dewson, "and never
once did he give me double talk. In human intercourse, if a person
shies off from a subject, it is common sense not to press him and
force him into an evasive answer." Frances Perkins, who ordinarily restrained herself, said, "It is my final testimony that he
never let me down." Those who plunged ahead invited their own
punishment. "It was evident," wrote Richberg, "that he often
regarded the use of a deceptive statement as justified, particularly
in discussions with someone who was trying to get him to commit
himself to a position he did not wish to take."

There is no question that he took a certain relish in misleading
those who seemed to him to deserve it. What may have begun as a
necessity became on occasion a pleasure. "He was apt to see the
importance of immediate ends," said Tugwell acutely, "more
readily than the consequences of doubtful means"—and this
myopia became a pervading weakness of his Presidency. For

Roosevelt, the result tended to grow more essential than the method; and he never adequately recognized that casualness over methods might jeopardize or corrupt results. "Never let your left hand know what your right is doing," he once told Morgenthau. "Which hand am I, Mr. President?" Morgenthau asked. Roosevelt said, "My right hand, but I keep my left under the table." ("This is the most frank expression of the real F.D.R. that I ever listened to," Morgenthau noted, "and that is the real way he works—but thank God I understand him.") Once, rehearsing a speech, Roosevelt read a passage in what he called the T.R. manner. Tom Corcoran spoke up (as Richberg recalled it): "Oh, but Mr. President, the difference between you and T.R. is that you never fake." Roosevelt replied, "Oh, but Tommy, at times I do, I do!"

He did, of course; it became the last resort of his system of defense. Those who impaled themselves on it felt bitter resentment in consequence. Some never forgave him. Others, who adored him, were deeply upset and angry. "It is pretty tough when things like this can be said about the President of the United States," wrote Harold Ickes after a Democratic Congressman remarked to him that Roosevelt might have a hard time disproving Huey Long's charge that he was a liar, "and when members of his own official family and of his own party in Congress feel that his word cannot be relied upon. It hurts me to set down such a fact, but it is the fact, as I have had occasion to know more than once."

Roosevelt enjoyed mystification too much. But perhaps a measure of mystification is inherent in the Presidency. "There isn't enough time," Tom Corcoran once said, "to explain everything to everyone, to cajole everyone, to persuade everyone, to make everyone see why it has to be done one way rather than another. If a President tried to do this, he would have no time left for anything else. So he must deceive, misrepresent, leave false impressions, even, sometimes, lie—and trust to charm, loyalty and the result to make up for it. . . . A great man cannot be a good man."

VII

There are two sorts of greatness—the foursquare, all-of-a-piece, unitary, monolithic kind, possessed by Washington, Jackson,

Winston Churchill; and the glittering, elusive, pluralistic, impalpable kind, possessed by Jefferson, Henry Clay, Lloyd George, where levels of personality peel off with the delusive transparence of the skins of an onion, always frustrating the search for a hard core of personality underneath. The greatest statesman may perhaps, like Lincoln, combine both kinds: in the phrase of Archilochus, he is both hedgehog and fox. Franklin Roosevelt clearly belongs in the second category. He had, not a personality, but a ring of personalities, each one dissolving on approach, always revealing still another beneath.

Yet one cannot exhaust the Roosevelt mystery by saying that he was complicated. For, though the central core of personality remained impossible to pin down, one felt, nevertheless, beneath the dazzling variety on the surface, behind the succession of masks, a basic simplicity of mind and heart. His complexity was infinite, but it all pertained to tactics. On questions of essential purpose, he retained an innocence which was all the more baffling because of its luminous naïveté. "He sometimes tries to appear tough and cynical and flippant," Hopkins once told Sherwood, "but that's an act he likes to put on. . . . You and I are for Roosevelt because he's a great spiritual figure, because he's an idealist." This was true. It was his tactical deviousness which got him into trouble; it was the fundamental, tantalizing, intermittent but ultimately indestructible idealism which saved him.

He was complicated everywhere except in his heart of hearts. There he perceived things with elementary, almost childlike, faith. "What is your philosophy?" asked the young man. "Philosophy?" Roosevelt replied. "Philosophy? I am a Christian and a Democrat —that's all." And for him, his church and his party implied a series of lucid commitments—respect for persons, respect for nature, respect for freedom. He held to these commitments with a confidence he never questioned and a serenity which never faltered.

This inner well of serenity was the unending source of spiritual refreshment. Anne O'Hare McCormick called him "apparently the least worried man in the country." Gerard Swope once said to him that he marveled at the calm with which he carried the Presidential load. "I'll tell you, Gerard," Roosevelt replied, "at night when I lay my head on my pillow, and it is often pretty late, and I think of the things that have come before me during the day and the decisions that I have made, I say to myself—well, I have done the best I could, and turn over and go to sleep." "More than any other person I have ever met," said Dr. McIntire, ". . . he had equanimity, poise and a serenity of temper that kept him on the most even of keels." As Eleanor Roosevelt summarized his attitude: "You made up your mind to do a thing and you did it to the best of your ability. If it went sour, why then you started in all over again and did something else, but you never spent time repining." And she added significantly: "I have never known a man who gave one a greater sense of security. . . . I never heard him say there was a problem that he thought it was impossible for human beings to solve." "Roosevelt was a man," said Tugwell, "with fewer doubts than anyone I had ever known."

What was the source of this serenity? He himself offered no clues; he was, he used to say, "the least introspective man in the world." In part, of course, it was character, temperament, experience, triumph over catastrophe. "F.D.R. was very tough," said Francis Biddle. "He had got on top of life. Nothing could touch him." But it was something more than this. "He had," said Tugwell, "a source of detached exaltation which could not be touched by the outcome." "He felt guided in great crises," said Eleanor Roosevelt, "by a strength and wisdom higher than his own." Hugh Johnson put it more forcibly, perhaps too forcibly: "That he has some sort of messianic complex, none who is near him will deny."

Roosevelt unquestionably had a deep sense of religious assurance, though its character remains a puzzle. His faith was unanalyzed, nontheological, a matter of tradition and propriety, something which he felt but did not care to formulate. "I think it is just as well not to think about things like that too much!" he admonished his wife. He was by no means a regular churchgoer; "by the time I have gotten into that pew and settled down with everybody looking at me, I don't feel like saying my prayers at all." The divisiveness of dogmatic theologies bothered him: "In our religious worship we should work together instead of flying off on different tangents and different angles." Though a Senior Warden of St. James's Church at Hyde Park, he personally preferred Presbyterian, Methodist, or Baptist sermons to Episcopalian, and on Christmas tended to go to one of the big Methodist or Baptist churches in Washington ("What's the matter? I like to sing hymns with the Methodys"). For a time, he had even omitted his Episcopalian affiliation from his biography in *Who's Who,* not restoring it until 1924. Yet, as Robert Sherwood said, "his religious faith was the strongest and most mysterious force that was in him." He once wrote, "I doubt if there is in the world a single problem, whether social, political, or economic, which would not find ready solution if men and nations would rule their lives according to the plain teaching of the Sermon on the Mount." If nothing ever upset him, if his confidence seemed illimitable, it was because he deeply believed, with full reverence and humility, that he was doing his best in the eyes of God, that God was blessing his purposes, that he was at one with the benign forces of the universe.

VIII

In the end, a President of the United States must stand or fall by his instinct for the future as well as by his understanding of the past and his mastery of the present. Implanted within him, there must be an image, not necessarily—or even desirably—explicit or conscious, but profoundly rich, plastic, and capacious, of the kind of America he wants, of the vision of the American promise he is dedicated to realize, of the direction in which he believes the world is moving. Without such a sense, his Presidency will be static and uncreative. As Franklin Roosevelt's successor once put it, "The President's got to set the sights." This vision of the future becomes the source of his values; it justifies his strivings; it renews his hopes; it provides his life with its magnetic orientation.

It was this astonishing instinct for the future which above all distinguished Roosevelt, his extraordinary sensitivity to the emergent tendencies of his age and to the rising aspirations of ordinary people—a sensitivity housed at the same time within a personality and intelligence sufficiently conventional to provide in itself a bridge holding together past and future. Indeed, his very position on the breaking point between an old world and a new one gave him a special freedom and spontaneity which only a man can possess who is nourished by older values. When Roosevelt accepted the inevitability of change, he did so, not by necessity, but by conscious choice. He had made a deliberate decision, both temperamental and intellectual, in favor of adventure and experiment. "My impression of both him and of Mrs. Roosevelt," wrote H. G. Wells, "is that they are unlimited people, entirely modern in the openness of their minds and the logic of their actions." Nothing could daunt him, very little surprised him, he was receptive to everything, and not in a passive sense either, he received, not to accumulate, but to act; the future which he perceived was (this he deeply believed) to be in part his own creation. Wells summed him up: "The most effective transmitting instrument possible for the coming of the new world order. He is eminently 'reasonable' and fundamentally implacable. He demonstrates that comprehensive new ideas can be taken up, tried out and made operative in general affairs without rigidity or dogma. He is continuously revolutionary in the new way without ever provoking a stark revolutionary crisis."

The essence of Roosevelt, the quality which fulfilled the best in him and explained the potency of his appeal, was his intrepid and passionate affirmation. He always cast his vote for life, for action, for forward motion, for the future. His response to the magnificent emptiness of the Grand Canyon was typical: "It looks dead. I like my green trees at Hyde Park better. They are alive and growing." He responded to what was vital, not to what was lifeless; to what was coming, not to what was passing away. He lived by his exultation in distant horizons and uncharted seas. It was this which won him confidence and loyalty in a frightened age when the air was filled with the sound of certitudes cracking on every side—this and the conviction of plain people that he had given them head and heart and would not cease fighting in their cause.

✪

The Experimental Roosevelt

I

The New Deal was an incident in American history which arose out of the Great Depression; it was, indeed, part of a convulsive struggle to overcome the Depression. Most of its characteristics, however, developed out of traditional progressivism and most of its devices were accepted items in a general armory. Progressives were provided with an opportunity by the crisis; but they were not by any means compelled to invent improvised measures for its solution. The doctrinal differences between Republicans and Democrats, in those days (or, if it is preferred, between Hoover and Roosevelt) were not new differences. They were indeed very old. Of course the line-up had not always been as it was in 1932. Sometimes the progressives had been Republican —as in the days of La Follette and Theodore Roosevelt—but progressives had never seemed very much or very long at home with Republicanism; and their happiest Presidential leadership had been found, before Franklin D. Roosevelt, in Woodrow Wilson, who was the heir to Bryan.

It has to be said that progressives consorted very uncomfortably with Southern reactionaries among the Democrats; and it was

Reprinted from *The Political Quarterly*, Vol. XXI (July–September 1950), pp. 239–270 by permission of The Political Quarterly Publishing Company Ltd.

always a problem for Wilson, as it was to be later for President Roosevelt, to bring into legislative being a progressive program against the opposition of the Southerners. But it would almost be true to say that the New Deal of the thirties consisted of postponed items from Wilson's program, which had been abandoned in favor of preparation for war in 1916.

There is an actual continuity here too which is sometimes forgot. For President Roosevelt had been a very active and loyal member of the Wilson administration; and he had been an admirer as well as a distant (fifth) cousin of Theodore Roosevelt. He could quite legitimately think of himself as the inheritor of a tradition. That this was a relationship he felt deeply all his close associates were aware. It is not perhaps surprising, in view of all the circumstances, if he tended to respect the tradition rather literally, somewhat as generals are said to begin all new wars by using the tactics of the last one. The central tenet of American progressivism had always been the perfecting of *laissez faire* rather than the development of socialism (though sheer necessity had dictated the public ownership of municipal utilities). The post office was publicly owned in America, but the telegraphs and telephones, the railways, and the facilities for producing power were not. To meet the abuses of overcharging and poor servicing, the break-up of big corporations and regulation of the rest was relied on. And the regulatory commission was one of the favorite progressive devices. It had its national embodiment in the Federal Trade Commission; but it was best developed in states like Wisconsin and Minnesota, where progressives had been politically powerful. It was part of the progressive idea, in fact that the central government need not be powerful or active, a prejudice which had been handed down from frontier and agrarian days when all government was considered to be oppressive and the more remote and larger governments the most dangerous of all.[1]

---

[1] It will be remembered that the Democratic platform of 1896—the one on which Bryan first ran—had an emphatic declaration to this effect in its preamble: "During all these years the Democratic Party has resisted the tendency of selfish interests to the centralization of governmental power, and steadfastly maintained the integrity of the dual scheme of government established by the founders of this Republic of republics. Under its guidance

To the Governor of New York, who had once been a member of the Wilson administration and was, by family, allied with progressivism, most of the nation's ills quite naturally seemed to have come from not having carried out the progressive program. Big businesses had abused their trusts; they ought to have been broken up, and, where that had not been feasible, they ought to have been severely regulated. If they had the Depression might have been avoided.

The ills of 1932 were very nearly fatal ones. The Depression which had begun in 1929 had failed to "run a course," as, in theory, it ought to have done. It had seemed to deepen as the years had passed. But, also, since the government was Republican, and since the Republicans had purged themselves of all progressivism and were now conservative—indeed reactionary—such abuses as could have caused the Depression still existed. Nothing had been done to cure them. The alternative program was obvious. And if the Governor of New York should become President of the United States, as it seemed more and more likely that he might, it would be quite natural that he should turn out to be thoroughly, but orthodoxly, a progressive one. He would favor business regulation because it would seem to him that conspiracies to restrain trade had strangled it and because they had held prices too high and diminished consumption; he would be against "the money power" because the financiers had got a monopoly of credit which they withheld from small business and because they were behind the flagrant gambling in stocks. Aside from this, he would be against the development of strong central government, would indeed be in favor of minimum federal powers, would want expenses and taxes reduced, and most governmental functions to be decentralized— carried on by the states and municipalities.

This was in fact the kind of program President Roosevelt would

---

and teachings the great principle of local self-government has found its best expression in the maintenance of the rights of the States and in its assertion of the necessity of confining the general government to the exercise of powers granted by the Constitution of the United States." T. Roosevelt's New Nationalism took another line; but it did not impress itself deeply on the progressive tradition; that was still one of decentralization.

have liked to carry out. It was the furniture of his mind down into 1932; and his mind was never entirely purged of these preferences. If what was done in the New Deal is examined, much of it will be seen to be consistent with this inclination. There were, as time passed, many departures from the pattern. Some, indeed, of the measures adopted almost at once, in the haste of crisis, were quite out of harmony with it, and obviously owed their origin to an entirely different tradition. But the President did not adopt the alternative ideology, perhaps never quite understood it; he was, in fact, inconsistent. He consented to such measures as A.A.A. and N.R.A.—as well as to some later ones—with some misgivings, but in a desperate, experimental mood because orthodox measures were so clearly inadequate, and because the substantial agreement of the interests involved, which was one of his political methods, had been secured. To some others, such as the building up of a federal (central) relief organization, he gave only the most grudging consent and got rid of it at the earliest possible instant. And when a permanent social security system came to be worked out, he settled an internal argument in his official family by coming down on the side of state rather than federal administration. This was a momentous and revealing choice; it showed what side he would like to be on if he could.

It would not be inaccurate to describe what went on in the inner circles of the early New Deal as a struggle between old-fashioned progressivism and a new conception of the nation as an organism having a *gestalt* to be respected and developed. The technological developments since the First World War had prepared the way for this newer philosophy, but it was very far from having any wide acceptance. There were, as well, other conflicts, particularly of a political sort, which were more easily seen. And sometimes the contemporary inconsistencies were so confusing that it was uncertain which side of the basic ideological struggle the President himself had chosen. But to the insiders of that day it was clear enough that the President could be persuaded away from the old progressive line only in the direst circumstances and then only temporarily or if he could make for himself a satisfactory rationalization.

This doctrinal faithfulness to a view of things which was then symbolized by Justice Brandeis' name—because Justice Brandeis was a literal believer in littleness, and because Messrs. Frankfurter, Corcoran, Cohen, and the other second New Dealers were his disciples—led the President into numerous cul-de-sacs. There was the abortive early economy drive, given up only with the greatest reluctance; there was the rehabilitation, without reform, of the banking system within the Federal Reserve framework; there was later the enormous undertaking of reforming the securities exchanges which had such meagre economic results; there was the evasion of definition in setting up the TVA so that it had to be substantially surrendered later to local interests; and there was the hand-to-mouth handling of relief so that satisfactory administration could never be achieved. These and a dozen other items of the New Deal program owe their peculiar, often tortured, contradictory, or abortive character to the struggle which went on in those early days without any clear resolution, with one side at times dominating policy in some specific respect and the opposite side at other times winning out, but with each usually securing some concession which prevented it from having the force of clear conception. But in all that happened the basically dominant philosophy was progressive, and as time passed and the crisis lightened, progressives of the older, more orthodox persuasion became the more trusted lieutenants. These were the second New Dealers. By the end of 1934 the first New Dealers had mostly departed from the White House and with them the philosophy of an organic economy.

There is reason to believe that the President came to suspect the efficacy of recourse to the antitrust-plus-regulation devices. Partly this was the discipline of the office, and partly it was the approach of war. The war, even when it was only a distant probability, loomed large on the horizons of America; it was, even in that prospect, a vast and monstrous phenomenon. And it was enlarged in the President's mind a long time before the enlargement became a general apprehension. But when the probability of conflict did come to be entertained, it quickly became absurd to regard Brandeis-scale supply organizations as adequate to the rising needs. The insatiable appetite of the armies for every commodity being made, and many not yet heard of, could only be satisfied by mines, factories, organizations bigger than even big business had ever imagined, and certainly far beyond the most horror-struck conception of the antitrust believers. Considerations such as had always bothered the progressives were laid aside. Big business and "the money power" were enlisted as partners, if not wholly trusted ones, in the national effort. But, of course, *laissez faire* in America was of two kinds: that which existed only in the economists' texts (which was the orthodoxy of progressivism), and that which big business shined up and put out in the street before its establishments in the hope that people would identify it with what they had in their minds, and believe that what went on inside the shop was what they hoped was going on. A business which was able in any degree to manage its prices was by so much violating orthodoxy, and by so much deceiving its public. But most American products were, in those days, sold at managed prices, and a free market did not exist. The long deception had worn very thin. The real question was: who was to do the managing? And more and more, public discussion turned on this issue, rather than on the question whether management should be tolerated at all.

This was the question of central importance economically which would have to be come back to after the war, as President Roosevelt must finally have known. But not until then. Then its solution would be seen to require the institutional setting of well-planned relationships. But from the first looming of war on the horizon the question of incentive to produce vastly was so exclusively pressing that planned relationships were regarded with ill-concealed impatience by everyone concerned. The result of this would soon be a welter of waste and inefficiency, partially resolved by an allocations system (which would be as often disregarded as honored), but no permanent system within which the energies and resources of the nation might fall into cooperative relationship.[2]

[2] Still, the War Production Board, together with the overhead organizations in the Office of Emergency Management—the Office of Economic Stabilization and the Office of Mobilization and Reconversion—would be sufficient recognition that national life could not proceed on the theory that big businesses could be broken up and that the resulting little ones would

It is not of much use to personalize the struggle of ideologies, the first phase of which began when the professors were invited to Albany in the early spring of 1932. Most of it went on in the mind of the man who was about to become President. Although each view had its protagonists, who urged, when they could, the shaping of policy in the direction they believed it ought to take, and although they sometimes seemed to have a victory here or there, what actually happened was that the tough Dutch mind which had the final responsibility eventually came to grips with each issue and resolved it in accordance with a set of preferences no other mind was allowed to comprehend. The secrecy of the Roosevelt inner operations chamber was extraordinary. The greatest pains were taken to guard it from penetration; and artful devices of a most extraordinary sort were invented for the confusion of the curious. It is this which accounts for the diverse—not to say contradictory —accounts, by various associates, of the Presidential attitudes, convictions and commitments. Not even Mrs. Roosevelt, who made a lifelong study of the matter, can suggest anything very helpful about the mind whose decisions made more difference to our generation than any other. It is doubtful whether she, for instance, any more than many others, with what they must have thought adequate knowledge, thought of him, even in Albany days, as Presidential stuff. This doubtfulness about his capacity as a putative statesman is certainly a notable characteristic of many accounts of his approach to the office. Even the politicians, Farley and Howe, had no idea of the Tartar they were catching. A surface agreeableness, a charm, combined in the Albany and even in later

---

make goods and fix prices fair to the consumer. If President Roosevelt had himself furnished the continuity from war to peace it seems unlikely that he would have scrapped the institutions for conjuncture which had begun to take effective shape. He might have had to compromise under Congressional pressure and give up some of them. But it is logical to think that he would have resisted. If he had, and had been able to reshape these devices to peacetime uses throughout the fourth term which he only began, he might have recognized that he had mistakenly resolved the ideological battle of the Brain Trust against their successors in 1933. For that had been the issue then; and what the Brain Trust had wanted for peace was not only useful for war. It would have to be come to in America sooner or later.

years (although people gradually became accustomed to it) with a complete domination of his grave physical disability, led almost everyone, his intimates included, to underestimate the extent of his determination to have his own way. They were even unaware, in practically every instance, that he had a way.[3] And as for the method he used in reaching the inclinations which were unveiled from time to time, somewhat as lightning flashes from an innocent-appearing summer cloud, there were no clues which were of the slightest use to his would-be helpers.

II

The New Deal was a Roosevelt New Deal, not that of a Brain Trust, of a Machiavellian Kitchen Cabinet, of a Frankfurter, or of any one else or any other group. It would not be true to say that as Governor, as candidate, or as President he did not borrow a good deal or even, on occasion, allow his "advisers" (a word which made most of those intended to be included in this class smile somewhat wryly) some latitude. Numerous speeches in campaign days and early in the first term, contain phrases, sentences, even whole paragraphs of mine. I am sure that Mr. Adolph Berle could recognize as many; and, of course, Mr. Raymond Moley could identify even more. But it is important, I think, to say that such passages as I could claim are not mine at all in the context in which they appear. The phrase, sentence, or paragraph has been

[3] There were exceptions I would make to this. Missy LeHand, his lovely and sensitive secretary, was always aware and watched with amused tolerance the dashing of many hopes on the rock of his determination. Both Judge Rosenman and Mr. Raymond Moley were sensitive enough, and had experience enough, to know how tough a center the Roosevelt outer agreeableness really had. Harry Hopkins found out later. But all three of these associates were peculiar in this—that they sought to be only projections of the Roosevelt mind, if they could find out what its directive was. They had no desire to shape it. I doubt if any of them ever helped him to make it up, or even sought to. Mr. Moley's departure was occasioned by his unreadiness to change as the President changed, or perhaps an insensitiveness, caused by Washington's confusions, concerning the real situation. Roosevelt's message to the London Conference was a cruel blow to one who thought he was being the perfect reflection of his principal's intention, and he never really recovered from it. Nor did Roosevelt. He can hardly have looked at Mr. Moley after that without some feeling of shame.

tortured or persuaded, as the case may be, into a larger whole with a meaning not mine at all.

It was more or less the same way with legislation. There are at least a dozen people who are quite certain that they are the principal authors of the Agricultural Adjustment Act, the National Recovery Act, and all the other measures of importance which became law in the famous "hundred days" after inauguration. Sometimes the case is good. For the Agricultural Adjustment Act did include authorization for the favorite programs of several different groups. Some of these had histories in the sense of having been previously proposed, embodied in unsuccessful legislation, made part of political platforms or pushed by the Grange, the Farm Bureau Federation, or the Farmers' Union. The same was true of the National Recovery Act. Several different ideas for regularizing industry, making its competitions less chaotic, providing an over-all guide to its activities, were included; there were also thrown in the wage and hour provisions and the prohibition of child labor, which had only the relevance of conciliating pressure groups. And there was added the whole separate title under which public works and relief were authorized as "pump-primers." Worse hotchpotches than either of these twin Acts can hardly be imagined.

Nevertheless, all this was not carelessness on the President's part, any more than were the loose-jointed, cliché-filled, over-comprehensive speeches of the campaign. The President often felt that if many panaceas were authorized in a measure, the sponsors of each would at least not object; and it would be accepted by Congress with a minimum of argument or delay. And, once passed, with such generous authorizations, one or another or maybe several of the embodied schemes could be tried. So far as the President was concerned, the method was of no importance, however much it meant to its doctrinaire authors. He was interested only in results—and grand results at that. He often had to pacify disgruntled zealots or those who had interests involved in one method rather than another. But this, he counted, I feel sure, a lesser evil than staging a knock-down fight in the Congress—especially when he himself had no conviction.

As some of us gradually came to understand, he had in mind a wide welfare concept, infused with a stiff tincture of morality, in most respects like that of the progressives who had preceded him. But he had a more practical eye for results and a greater indifference about methods than any of them had had—with the single exception of his distant cousin Theodore (about whom there is legitimate question whether he can rightly be called a progressive at all). Most of the others—Bryan, La Follette, Wilson, for instance—had been evangelical (Bryan), contentious and cocksure (La Follette), or arbitrary (Wilson). President Roosevelt was none of these. Yet as I write this I realize I am being far from exact. For I am certain that he had intentions which were quite definite and not at all so loosely held that they could be called wide. They were simple, too, in his mind, I believe. In fact one of the clues to his character was that, however devious and seemingly confused his own methods or those he allowed to be used by his subordinates, the ends he sought were easily and quite securely carried in his mind, clear as precepts are to a child. He wanted all Americans to grow up healthy and vigorous and to be practically educated; he wanted workers to have jobs for which they were fairly paid and he wanted them to give a decent day's work for the pay; he wanted businessmen to work within a set of rules which seemed to him easily defined and, if adhered to, capable of righting most commercial wrongs; he wanted everyone free to vote, to worship, to behave as he wished within an accepted national scheme; he wanted officeholders to behave as though office were a public trust. It is easy to be speciously profound about President Roosevelt, and no doubt many historians will be; but it is my belief that everything he ever did or allowed to be done was, in the circumstances and in his view of them, calculated to bring about one of these simple and admirable ends.

He often did not know how. It was a complicated economic system which had gone all to pieces since the fall of 1929, and there were important pieces of it about which he had never had occasion to think. This was especially true of the money and banking system; and, of course, this seemed to be at the center of the storm, and its abuses, perhaps, the cause of it. When a business system breaks down, the paralysis is registered not first but most vociferously in the banks. And the banker behind his desk refusing to make loans which would start things going, unable to meet his own obligations because he has been too generous (as it suddenly appears) in the past, seems like the devil in the headquarters of this particular hell. His colleague, the investment banker, shares this guilt. He has saddled all his correspondent banks, and through them the nation's savers, with securities which everyone concerned should have known very well were thoroughly speculative, but which the underwriter is thought, somehow, to have guaranteed. It seems, at first, to the amateur—and the President was, in spite of having been a downtown lawyer for a bit, and having been briefly an officer of a Wall Street financial house, a complete amateur— that bankers ought to be punished who have behaved in these ways, and perhaps replaced by others who will behave differently. This assumed that they had been bad—had abused a trust, gambled with other people's money or led investors to take un-warranted risks. It also assumed that punishment and replacement were indicated. With him, as with other amateurs, the realization that the problems were too serious for such remedies to have any effect brought on an immediately succeeding impulse to treat the symptoms directly. If bankers would not now make loans enough, government must make—or guarantee—temporary ones for the emergency. If currency was short, more must be printed. If debts could not be paid because prices had fallen and what was to be paid back was more in value than what had been borrowed, the units of value could be cheapened and prices raised. Debts could thus be cleared away and confidence restored.

Governor Roosevelt, in the spring of 1932, when he had no further responsibility than that of writing speeches which would give people confidence in his Presidential candidacy, listened to everyone who might have anything revealing to say about the smash-up whose debris was piling up all around him. He consulted the orthodox. The men from Wall Street came, and their apologies were unconvincing; Carter Glass's assistants in preparing the Federal Reserve Act were sent for, among them Professor H. Parker Willis himself, who had thought that what had happened was impossible. His remedies, like those of the bankers, were indistinguishable from what was going on—deflation until slow recovery set in. Professor James Harvey Rogers was lucid about causes and even sympathetic to monetary manipulation as a remedy, although he knew that this alone was not enough. And then there were the unorthodox, from Irving Fisher to George Warren. The Fisher commodity dollar, the Governor could not understand; but in George Warren he met a man to whom everything seemed satisfyingly simple. Vary the amount of gold in the dollar, he said, and the price level can be run up or down, stabilization can be achieved, and business will be resumed. Warren's assurance appealed to the Roosevelt simplicity and gave the future President a confidence he had not felt about any other scheme.

He said remarkably little about all this, reflecting the confusion of his counsels and the realization that the orthodox would be horrified at the thought of actually trying the Warren remedy. Meanwhile, Hoover's Reconstruction Finance Corporation made emergency loans, the Farm Board desperately attempted to stabilize the prices which were most depressed, those of farm products. Still trouble piled on trouble. Loans to businesses and banks seemed to sink into the sterile economy like water into desert sand; the Farm Board bought wheat and cotton by the millions of carloads and prices did not respond. It was evident that these remedies were not enough. Finally, with the election over, and with inauguration approaching, the economic system began to dissolve at the center. Disorganization was complete. On Inauguration Day, every bank in the land was closed, and no one knew whether any of them would ever open again.

The new President had heard by now a plethora of talk from every kind of person who thought he knew anything at all about finance, but at inauguration time it was clear to him only that he would have to experiment. He did not know what to do and no one had completely commanded his confidence in any remedy. He did not dare try the Warren plan at once. That would induce more panic. He must have had a session with himself in one of the few waking moments he could steal in those days. And what he decided to do has always seemed to me entirely characteristic and revealing. He must first cut the nation off from outside influences,

for he had heard of sinister speculations in London, Paris, and
Amsterdam; he must make the banks safe from then on for
depositors' funds; he must enlarge loan funds; he must cheapen the
dollar; then people must get back to work, meanwhile being sure at
least of relief; and all the time he must go on encouraging the
confidence that all was really well. And, of course, this was what
he did. And presently he tried the Warren remedy, making Mr.
Henry Morgenthau Secretary of the Treasury to see it through. It
was, of course, absurd, and after a while was given up. It had done
no damage and no good.

When it was all over, the nation could not tell what had caused
the revival any more than it had been able to analyze the causes of
the Depression. Nothing much was changed; but the system was
running again. An opportunity for reform had been missed; but not
one which Roosevelt had heard about from any of the numerous
financial experts. Not one of them had any conception of a genuine
national banking system. And if he ever thought of trying to
establish one he must have given it up quickly when he considered
whether anyone could be got to run it. For there was no one, no
one at all. Was he satisfied? I think so, because his larger intention
had been carried out. The hungry were fed; the jobless were at
work; fear no longer haunted men who ought to be free from its
compulsions; children went to school decently fed and clothed.
And the men who had been greedy, irresponsible, and careless had
had a terrible lesson. Also a watch would be put on them now, and
if they became greedy again the government would interfere. This
was all simple. It amounted to security, freedom, and decency.
And President Roosevelt was one of those who knew well enough
that these were not values which may be established once for all.
They were administered virtues, requiring leadership, which he
was prepared to go on giving, and a trust which he knew the
people would thenceforth yield him as their protector.

III

This illustration—the way in which the financial debacle was
muddled through—shows, as others might, I think, what President

Roosevelt was determined to bring about and what he was only interested in as an experimental matter. There were occasions when, as I have said, those who had been, as they thought, very clever in creating some governmental device to meet a need, had got entangled in its extension of their personalities. They must defend it, they felt, against any and all detractors and competitors. These were, aside from the businessmen who were perishing in extreme anguish from loss of confidence (which they bitterly blamed the President for not restoring), the worst sufferers of those days. Some of them ought to be used as a case book for students of governmental psychoses. They were not always what somewhat later came to be known as "empire builders" either; they might not be possessed of that peculiar expansive compulsion which afflicted Mr. Ickes so continuously, was the secret vice of Harry Hopkins (while he made grand gestures to prove that it was not true), which helped to bring Mr. Leon Henderson's Office of Price Control into discredit, and was carried to the most absurd extremities by the businessmen who became wartime bureaucrats. Quite often, in fact, they were pure idealists, so pure that any shading or compromise was for them quite impossible, and any political trading affecting their enterprises, which went on in the White House, seemed the basest of betrayals.

Mr. Hull lived in prolonged agony from Rooseveltian carelessness about the sacred principles of free trade; Mr. George Peek died a lingering official death rather than consent to farmers being helped in any way except that to which he had given his heart; Miss Frances Perkins seldom had a serene moment because of the President's incorrigible tendency to think in terms of national rather than local administrative units; and General Johnson had a period, at the height of the excitement over the goings-on under the aegis of the blue eagle, when he ran to the White House several times a week for reassurance. The New Deal was a hectic time for these marshals of recovery. Some of them lived long enough to see the nation recover without their aid. That may well have been the bitterest experience of all.

The President had a therapy he used in such cases; for experience soon taught him that his carelessness about means would frequently bring this human flotsam to his doorstep. He called its homeopathic phase "holding hands"; and when this proved insufficient he resorted to "upping." And he devoted an unconscionable amount of time and thought to these affairs, although the victims could never be got to believe that he cared in the least, and often went away and talked dreadfully about him afterwards. These tirades came from deep down in injured personalities and were often recklessly uttered. Those who were tougher, less committed, who shared, perhaps, the Presidential disdain for means, or who were simply personally loyal (as Louis Howe, Mr. Rosenman, Stephen Early, Marvin McIntyre, Lowell Mellett, General Watson, and Frank Walker always were and as Harry Hopkins came to be in his and the President's last years) or who were working politicians (as Mr. James A. Farley was until the Southerners tempted him with suggestions of preferment), were thus able, from a central position in and about the White House, to observe an extraordinary procession of sensitive and dedicated natures coming up out of obscurity, being revealed momentarily in the Presidential sun, and declining again into furious obscurity.

These individuals seldom turned up again. For President Roosevelt had done all he could to repair the damage, and his failure always rested on his conscience, making the sight of one of the defections most unpleasant. He never "fired" anyone. There was, out of all the possibilities, only one case of contumacy. That, of course, was Mr. Arthur E. Morgan, first Chairman of the Tennessee Valley Authority. The rest perished with their works, or such of their works as were no longer in favor. But they went because matters were allowed to become intolerable for them. The squeeze was permitted to go on until the tortured victim cried out in pain—which means that he made a speech or a statement attacking his competitor or detractor—and presently after that even he could perceive the untenability of his position. He would have become the momentary hero of the opposition press; he would be "taken up" by the old Washington settlers, whose hatred of New Dealism was positively phobic; or the Liberty League, the Republicans, or Wall Street would, figuratively speaking, be seen in his company. The unsuitability, then, of further associations with the White House would be obvious.

That there was a squeeze going on—as when first Mr. Jerome Frank, for one reason, and later, Mr. George Peek for another, were forced out of Secretary Wallace's entourage—the President was never unconscious. Those who knew his weakness for not grasping really nasty nettles knew from small signs that he was peeking through his fingers. And when the blow-up came, they knew that it was not, as it seemed to be, a painfully unexpected occurrence. Sometimes they even suspected that there was a little Presidential malice involved. Harry Hopkins said to me, after we had watched one of these proceedings run its course, "You know, he *is* a little puckish." And that was not far from right, perhaps, although the observation failed to reach the source: an essential carelessness about means. There were cases which hurt him and which he tried desperately to remedy by "upping." This, of course, consisted in finding for the victim another, even more honorable, employment. And sometimes he kept people by him who had been terribly injured, but whose loyalties were greater than their hurts. Mr. Jerome Frank was one of these. He later became the distinguished Chairman of the Securities Exchange Commission and then an even more distinguished federal judge—both by Rooseveltian appointment.

I have said that this does not mean that there was any lack of Presidential interest in the devices of government calculated to reach an end. On the contrary, there was an omnivorous interest. But being committed to any of them would have been alien to a nature which was so thoroughly experimental about means, and at the same time so doggedly determined to attain ends. Even those closest to him were sometimes confused about what went on. We often mistook means for ends, shuddered at the wrong crises and were amazed that expected Presidential reaction failed to take place. I once offered to bet Harry Hopkins fifty dollars that the President would find a way to complete the Passamaquoddy power project which the private power interests and the politicians between them had treacherously killed. I thought the completion of this scheme (as well as the Florida Ship Canal) ranked as an end. I was quite wrong. But so was Harry. He refused to wager.

If, to future historians, the New Deal seems an unusually confused and heterogeneous approach to a socio-political problem (recovery from economic depression), it may be helpful if they recall that recovery was only part of the intention. President Roosevelt conceived that when the ship of state emerged from the flying mists of the economic hurricane, she might be transformed into the dream ship of Bryan, La Follette, Theodore Roosevelt, Wilson, and Brandeis. The means approved by orthodox progressivism, however, never seemed adequate when the crisis was really frightening, and recourse was had to means which could only have had their origin in minds dominated by the concept of national integration.

These historians will find, I think, when they move on from the years of the New Deal into the period of preparation for war and then of war itself, a very different kind of Roosevelt. In this endeavor he was not tormented by the ideals of *laissez-faire* progressivism, and even the orthodox at his elbow ceased to reproach him for departure. It was plain to everyone that the marshaling of the nation's whole strength in one mighty, singly conceived thrust was necessary if the Nazi-fascist threat was to be overcome. And the steady assurance with which the President advanced into the leadership of global strategy showed him at his best, just as his fumbling with the early New Deal showed him at his worst. He had ever to overcome popular reluctance before he could proceed from step to step. But, as we look back, we can see that his course was not only absolutely clear, but, for its end, correctly conceived. And his sense of timing, always good, was in this instance even better. He waited as long as he had to, but not so long as would be disastrous, before making each move. Frequently, especially in the early stages, he got his way by the smallest of margins—as when the Selective Service Act was approved in the House in 1940 by a majority of one. But always, once he had won, and events had moved as he had said they must, his people were compelled to acknowledge his rightness. He saw what must be done and he furnished the leadership for shaping the means.

The mistakes made in the advance toward war seem now to have been almost miraculously few. Because he saw so clearly the ultimate intention, and because he was perfectly free to adopt the means which seemed most suitable, he functioned at his best. It had never been so during the New Deal. There his intentions, although firmly held, were far less concretely visualized. Victory, or even a permanent international organization of nations, are much more easily objectified than are freedom, security, and social justice. And if the ends become specific more easily in the one case than in the other, so do the means. For the field of decision is occupied by the assured—those who are certain that they know the best ways; and their assertions can be impressive to the amateur even if they have no better support than derivation from inner preferences and have no demonstrable foundation.

The progressive means for attaining the ends President Roosevelt was from the first determined to attain in domestic policy, had, some of them, been tried as national devices and had failed. Antitrust legislation had been on the books for forty years and had again and again been strengthened after successive failures to achieve results. There had been a Federal Trade Commission since Wilson's time and, measured by its terms of reference, its achievements had been miniscule. So strong, however, is the hold on men's minds of orthodoxy, especially when it has been crystallized in political controversy and defended as a cause, that practical failure had had no effect. And even in the debacle of 1933 what was said by progressives was that what was needed was more of the same. And they were always on hand to urge these not only as recovery measures, but as the reforms needed to prevent future recurrences of such a sort. President Roosevelt felt that they were right. All he knew from the past told him so. Everyone he had most revered had believed that it was so. Yet his practical sense often led him to consent to quite different solutions.

These dilemmas were not happy ones for him, as may be imagined. And he knew that they would not be happy ones for progressive legislators. When he had to persuade Congressmen to vote for measures which, however necessary they seemed, neither he nor they quite liked, in this traditional sense, his discomfort betrayed itself. It was so, for instance, in the message which accompanied the submission of the Agricultural Adjustment Act, whose very name betrays the assumption of a federal duty to "adjust"—that is, to bring into better relationship the economic forces bearing on agriculture. The progressive program for farmers had always centered on attacking the "middlemen," breaking up their conspiracies, regulating their activities and forcing them to be fair. No New Dealer loved meatpackers, millers, and other processors; but it was obvious that the ten-year depression of agriculture had causes which ran deeper than middlemen's sins. So it was decided in wide and acrimonious conference to attempt the raising of prices by reducing national supplies. The President accepted the decision, but he said in his message to the Congress recommending the measures: "I warn you that this is a new and untrod path." And went on to say that if adjustment proved impractical he would be the first to acknowledge it. He may have been the more doubtful for knowing that there were several ways of reaching the adjustment we all talked of and not being sure which was likely to be most effective or, for that matter, which we would finally decide to use. He did not add that he would be glad if we had to give all of them up, but he might have. I have no doubt that he would have been glad at the time. But I think he changed. And I think I know why. It was, I believe, the actual experience of the Presidential office which made him, as time went on, less and less a believer in the vast and careless autonomy of *laissez faire* and more and more conscious of presiding at the center of a nobly living organism, the federal state. I know, on one occasion, when we met at Hyde Park to discuss the approach to some problem, perhaps a dozen of us, he began a little facetiously by saying: "Well, fellow socialists . . ." And I thought it not so facetious, really, as a sudden welling into voice of an unconscious which had been at work apprehending the nature of the Presidential task.

IV

The discipline imposed by the Presidency transforms those who are elevated to its central office. There can hardly be any position in the contemporary world which possesses quite this same power to penetrate personality and to shape and mold it to the national use. For the chief executive of the American government's vast functions is not only, in addition, the political chief of a victorious party, but also the chief of state of a great and expanding power. With the torrents of converging energy sweeping in upon him from the continent's enormously productive mines, farms, factories, and systems of distribution, he has daily to reconcile a hundred urgent interests and turn their energies, if he can, toward what he conceives to be the national good. He is required to give direction to the most powerful and most willful productive machine ever known. He is even required to keep it going when it shows signs of faltering and to smooth the way for its usefulness to the world. He would be a strange man, indeed, who, with these demands stretching his capabilities, would be able to remain the same human creature he had been before.

Also the President will have presided over a portentous political victory, as any democratic decision must be in a Western state, and be the acknowledged disposer of many thousands of fates. He may not have been the political boss of his party—in fact, few political bosses ever reach important elective offices of any kind— but after his election in a nationwide referendum, his prestige will be so enormous as to be almost beyond comprehension. He will have had more millions of votes cast for him by free choice than any man ever had before. And if, to many of those millions of voters, he may not have been much known before the campaign began, when it is over, and they have voted for him, he will be their chosen man. Each of them may have—and many will have —a proprietary interest in his fortunes. They will wish him well because he represents their judgment. Such an elected hero, supported as he is by that massed backing, not a passive, lethargic election-day kind of approval, but an interfering, vocal and very active kind of possessiveness (as can be told by studying the White House mail and telegrams), can no longer be the kind of person he was before this deification happened to him.

But added to the enormous powers of chief executive and of political leader there is the third: those of a chief of state. There must necessarily surround him, in this capacity, however simple and even shy a man he may be, the complete circumstance appropriate to the nation's prestige. The ceremonial of so exalted an office is necessarily highly formalized—it must be if embarrassing discriminations are to be prevented. And the President can never depart from the formality expected of him as the living symbol of his country's dignity and position. His life must be a kind of public show, lightened a little here and there by touches of his own inevitable humanity, by his pathetic attempts to break out of his confinement and circumvent formality—never very successful and growing less and less so as he becomes more and more the embodiment of his responsibilities. The American people are inconsistent and demanding in these matters. They require commonness and at the same time an almost unattainable virtue; sympathy and humanity, but also an untouchable justness.

The result of this discipline is that Presidents cease to be human creatures at all, almost, however human they must have been to have had the political appeal required for election. Then too they must have within their minds a firmly fixed conception of the nation's future which is the measure of every decision they may make. This is not something they may reveal, except in bits and patches; that would be to expose it to destruction by those whose interests it did not suit. Besides, like any working plan, it has to be changed as conditions change or as processes of judgment require it to be changed. It is therefore kept in the background. But if it does not exist it will make the life of the executive and politician almost impossible. He will again and again fall into inconsistencies; the judgments he must make many times a day will presently be seen to have no intelligible orientation. And ultimately he will lose the confidence of those who expect to be led against their own wills.

For democracies do demand that kind of leadership; and in the American democracy only the President—the people's own man, *all* the people's own man—can supply it. He must persuade them, almost bully them, often, into doing things which they are most reluctant to do. They have interests, prejudices, irresponsible preferences; they listen to gossip, are advised by a press they do not really trust, and by leaders they know to be incorrigibly local. They expect their President to be free from any interest or prejudice, to think singly of the national good, and to persuade them to its support. He must force the Congress, against its will, to do what has to be done, and he must often do it by raising the people—who want nothing so little as to be raised—against it.

This is what the American Presidency is and what it requires of its incumbents. This is why it is so important to understand the nature of the Rooseveltian procedure and to distinguish its permanent elements from those which he regarded as instruments for gaining the far more important ends.

V

The Presidency has not always been so demanding as it was in 1933. To find comparable expectations centering there it would be necessary to go back to Lincoln's time, when the fatal compromises written into the American Constitution faced resolution in an appeal to force which, it seemed, might well shatter the Union. It was the task of Lincoln to prevent a threatened dissolution, coming through the ordeal of conflict to the establishment of a brotherhood which until then had been merely a truce between hostile cousins. Until the Great Depression, like the approaching Civil War with respect to union, revealed that capitalism was not a system at all, and finally, after its failure to cure its multiple fractures, demanded a new leadership, the Presidency had never embodied, to quite the same extent, the hopes and fears of the whole nation. Not even the ordeal of Wilson, who, drawing back from war and hating it, finally embraced it as the fire in which a lasting peace might be forged, had been so inexorable. Governor Roosevelt must, in contemplative moments, have shuddered at the task he faced. The legend has grown up that he approached it with lightheartedness and even a careless grace. That fiction needs only an understanding look at the circumstances and at the man to be refuted. It is true, however, that he had a clearer conception of the requirements imposed by the office than any man who had assumed it in more than a century, and a more certain reliance on a strength not his own than any except perhaps Washington.

One of the realities about the Presidency is that those who come to it have then to be educated and that this can be a very expensive business. It sometimes seems almost providential that this period has never been fatal for the nation, so clumsy and so irresponsible have some of the new Presidents been. If they have come from the legislature they have to learn that there is inherent in the Constitution an opposition between the Congress and the President which a year of off-guard appeasement may enable the Congress to take such advantage of that leadership can never be re-established. If they come from governorships, they are apt to be inclined toward the view that states still have rights; and before they recover from that they may have damaged the federal power so severely as to require a decade or more of repair. So it goes, usually; but with Governor Roosevelt this, at least, was different. He knew the instrument with which he had to work and he intended to use it for all it was worth. He was aware of the dangers of Congressional hostility; he knew that cabinet members are not always trusted executive subordinates, but are often rivals for power; he had had practical experience of the states' weaknesses, and was the less apt, because of that, to concede them responsibilities they could no longer shoulder with any success; he knew that he had to be President of the whole nation and not only of those who had voted for him.

I could go on at some length with the advantages of this sort possessed by President Roosevelt which had not been possessed by any President before him. In spite of all this good fortune for the nation, however, it is well to recall that, like Lincoln, he was not omniscient or even always wise, that he had to find his way through confusing fact, conflicting counsel and inefficient or disloyal administration of his policies; and that, although his moral view was simple and clear, the exigencies he faced were such that the expedients for solution had to be found in costly trials and errors, not all of which would even prove relevant to the problems they sought to solve.

Everyone now knows how Lincoln fumbled with his problem, only gradually and painfully finding his way to the winning of the Civil War and, what was more important, the re-establishment of the Union: how one general after another failed him; how he had to struggle against the Congress and members of his cabinet, first for the power to wage real war, and then for the liberty to shape its strategy toward the softening rather than sharpening of its issues; and how fortunate it now seems that he was able finally at the bloodiest battlefield of all to talk of "binding up a nation's wounds." They are not far enough yet from President Roosevelt for just judgment; or perhaps they have forgot the earlier and less happy Roosevelt for the later and more certain war leader. In the first conflict with Depression, the fumbling pattern of 1860–1863 was reproduced. He found no generals who were both dependable and always wise. More and more his moral plan had to be contemplated in secret because less and less of it could be realized. He attained a kind of victory, as Lincoln did, but it was far from a clean-cut or final one; and it might have gone to pieces if the vast digression of war had not swallowed up and hid all its half-failures and distressing compromises. Still, with a serenity which nothing material could touch, he could always rebegin. For to him expedients were never really heartbreaking.

He took me with him one time to the little parish church at Hyde Park for a Sunday morning service. I cannot now recall how I happened to be alone with him that day; but I recall well enough why I was at Hyde Park. The National Recovery Administration had fallen into awful trouble. After a spectacular flight, the blue eagle's plumage was torn and ragged. General Johnson had become a pathological problem, a temperamental, ranting, dangerous head of an agency so perverted and rogue-minded that its extinguishment seemed the only possible way to cut the terrible loss it represented. The President had made mistakes in the case. He had given the general *carte blanche,* had allowed him liberties so extravagant that no excuse seemed possible, and had even, in effect, disbanded the National Recovery Board, his administrative control, because the general disliked explaining to anyone what he was up to. The President obviously had no one to blame but himself. And for the better part of a year the general had had much friendlier access to him than I, for instance, had had; and this was as true of all the others, except, perhaps, Mr. Samuel Rosenman, who knew better than some of us how to keep quiet when advice was not wanted.

We had been talking all the day before, just he and I, with some others coming and going, about the debacle of the N.R.A. and about what could be done. He was frank about the mistake, but, of course, he could not be frank in public; that was politics. There had to be a relatively unembarrassing way out. I was trying my best to think of something; but I was not having much luck. One part of the problem was to dispose of the general, whose cantankerousness and volubility made most of the usual possibilities unsuitable; the other much more important part was determining what ought to be done about N.R.A. By this time it was not only offensive to those who, like myself, profoundly distrusted big business, however much they felt it represented a necessary technological advance, and felt that any partnership with it had to be heavily weighted on the government side, but also those progressives who were against bigness in any case and were horrified by the very suggestion of partnership. The N.R.A. could have been administered so that a great collectivism might gradually have come of it, so that all the enormous American energies might have been disciplined and channeled into one national effort to establish a secure basis for well-being. That had been what I had had in mind in making my contribution to the law setting it up.[4] But the law had also included, as was the New Deal fashion, the ideas of the big businessmen themselves, who saw in the situation the possibility of a great super-trust, manipulating supplies, controlling prices and establishing narrower and narrower rules for what competition remained. They had no idea of admitting government to the partnership except as a minor convenience and cover. General Johnson was Mr. Bernard Baruch's handy man—had been for years—and he had run away with the whole administration. The President had consented to this: he had indeed shut all the rest of us off when we had tried to object; and he had sheltered General Johnson from any of the critical appraisal (except from a group of vociferous consumers who were allowed to register objections to codes through a deputy administrator) which might

[4] As I have said in *The Industrial Discipline and the Governmental Arts* (Columbia University Press, 1933).

have modified the progress of N.R.A. toward complete fascism and allowed the necessary machinery to be set up for establishing the government as the senior partner.

He now had to get out of a bad situation as best he could. Talking to me was, in this instance, I suppose, a kind of purge by confession. By repeating to me the objections I had been urging as best I could for a year or more and pointing out where the general had got to in his absurd subservience to the businessmen who had collected about him as deputies, code administrators, and so on, he let me know, and through me all those others who thought as I did, that he had been quite wrongheaded and even naughtily persistent in his wrongheadedness. He did not say he had been as pleased as the general to see all the "fat cats," as he called them, flocking to Washington and taking part in the recovery effort. He did not mention, though in a bitter moment I did not hesitate to point it out, that he had sent word to Secretary Roper, after a meeting of the Recovery Board (of which the Secretary of Commerce was Chairman), during which some criticism had been put forward, not to have any more such meetings. This had meant that there were thenceforth to be no intermediaries between the general and the President. It could be said after that, I told him, with more truth than when it had been said earlier about Mr. Raymond Moley, that if an appointment was wanted with the general it could only be had by asking the President to arrange it.

The fact was, and he knew it, that no one could be blamed but himself; and by having me at Hyde Park for a weekend and asking me for ideas about getting out of the trouble he was in, he was making amends. I knew well enough that others were working at the problem too; Mr. Donald Richberg, who expected and wanted to succeed, Miss Perkins who wanted N.R.A. abandoned except for its child-labor prohibitions, and many others, some through me, for power seekers are quick to sense the avenues to favor, and they knew from my renewed familiarity at the White House, and especially my week-ending at Hyde Park and my journeyings to Warm Springs, that I would very likely have something to do with shaping the resolution of the crisis.

I awoke on Sunday morning and lay a long time looking out on the fields and trees of that sweet countryside. My heart was as full as any heart can hold of affection for any other man. There was no doubt that he was too given to an artful contrivance I did not like, or even that he was confused about some means that had suddenly turned into ends—as he now saw N.R.A. had done—but there was also no doubt about his being essentially a whole, perhaps an intended, President. He was, I knew then, not a made President, but a born one. He came to the manipulation of powerful forces and vast interests as naturally as I did to the study of their incidence. He accepted into himself the collective personality of the American people in the same way, I thought, looking out at the meadows, that that old oak over there accepted into itself the whole arrangement of Nature just here and now, and lorded it over the field and its creatures with an unmistakable, unconscious, perfectly modest majesty. No monarch, I thought, unless it may have been Elizabeth or her magnificent Tudor father, or maybe Alexander or Augustus Caesar, can have given quite that sense of serene presiding, of gathering up into himself, of really represent-ing, a whole people. He had a right to his leeways, he had a right to use everyone in his own way, he had every right to manage and manipulate the palpables and impalpables. He would only do it for his country's good; he was part of an ordering of affairs which had a guidance. He had touch with something deeper than reason, all right. That secure innocence, within which he could be quite naughty but never really bad, came of resting on a bosom broader than most of us ever find.

As I started to say, I was going with him that morning to the Sunday service. The church at Hyde Park is hardly more than a small, old, stone-walled, ivy-covered chapel. But it exactly suited the President. We had been talking in his bedroom until time to go—I dressed, but he in his old sweater, with the morning papers scattered about, and one cigarette after another being fitted into the long holder he used. He was being very good, telling me what he meant to do in this way and that to bring the federal govern-ment into the people's service—not that he used such words. What he said was "Rex, we ought to do more for the poorer farmers," or "more to extend the forests," or "build more dams for power," or "put a floor under wages," or "make the planning board more effective." The whole broad and deep setting of such remarks as these needed, by now, no discussion between us. There were a lot of things not yet done on which both his new people, Corcoran, Cohen, and the others, and the old helpers, like Mr. Berle and me, could agree well enough. There were a lot of them to which the other crowd would never agree. They were after him, I knew, to scrap N.R.A., having the excuse of its outrageous mishandling; but I wanted it kept. It could still be the industrial counterpart, I thought, of the Agricultural Adjustment Administration, which, whatever its human defects, was rapidly knitting up American agriculture into a system. I would have liked to see industry become a system too, although not one managed by Mr. Baruch's friends or any other private interest.

He knew how all this stood well enough. And he was wondering, I thought, whether the nation was ready to become so self-conscious as I suggested it might, an organism, functioning to plan, eliminating many of the wastes of competition, gaining the advantages of thought and purpose which must come from nationally conceived programs of production. There was plenty of contrary evidence. The very thought of such a discipline turned the stomachs of his political runners and made Congressmen shudder. Theirs was a life of fantasy which they called realism, of caprice which they called freedom. It was fundamentally what had caused the breakdown which the President's bold words had done something to frighten into the background. But they liked the nostrums to which he had resorted hardly better than the disease. The clamor for a balanced budget rose to heaven from those businessmen who lived by its unbalance. They hated relief for the unemployed even though it supported an economy which they could then exploit. There was no sense in them. It really did not seem as though a great system, with direction and purpose, could be established with such people still in places of power. And it would take inspired leadership. The President, to do it, must be clear in his mind and much more certain about his instruments than he had been.

I knew well enough that it was doubtful whether he would do it.

He could not yet quite see the contours of such a system. And there were those others, preaching the virtues of littleness and freedom, always nagging at him, men some of whom he revered, like Brandeis, some of whom he was taking for his working team, like Messrs. Frankfurter, Corcoran, and Cohen. Yet I could see that the Presidency had done its work on him. He saw the nation, as none of the others did, whole; he saw part working with part, all functioning together: the men in the cities, the men on the farms, the men at sea, all working for each other as they worked for their families. And he was the centering point. He could not make the nation over. He could not make it other than it was. He could only make it more superbly what it was. Moreover, he had tried an experiment. The N.R.A. was my kind of thing. He pointed out that I had approved his choice of the general to administer it, which I had. I returned that I had thought it would have no chance at all unless Baruch was in on it—hadn't he himself reminded me that Mr. Baruch "owned sixty Congressmen"? And it was quite possible that the general had run away even from Mr. Baruch, for that gentleman was at least discreet. I pleaded, in other words, that because the experiment had gone badly it did not prove what the progressives were saying. It was simply not a good experiment. I begged for renewal—with a board for balance and sanity. This was one place in government where a board was indicated. Before he had begun to get ready for church he had been working on that, trying people over in his mind, wrestling a little with his dislike of boards. I gave him a name or two, and he liked them. He said we must talk of it more, but now it was time to go. Would I go with him?

We had lifted him into the back seat of the big open car—one of the few times I had been allowed to help. And he had patted the seat beside himself. I had got in and we had rolled down the drive to the Albany road, with the Secret Service car following cheerfully in the morning sunshine, and the Presidential cape blowing a little in the wind. We came up to the door of the church; and after his usual trouble with the braces we went in. And he worshiped, simply and humbly, singing the hymns, reading the responses, listening attentively to what seemed to me a meaningless sermon by a young rector. It was meaningless to me because I hadn't the hang of the Episcopal ritual and did not know what the doctrinal issues meant on which the rector dwelt. Also I was bothered a little by getting up and sitting down—which amused him because he had a special dispensation in that respect. Nevertheless, as the quiet moments came when the young rector preached and I looked sideways at him, I felt that I had lost. I was asking too much. It was not only N.R.A., it was the whole organic conception of the living nation, equipped with institutions for foresight, conjuncture and balance. It was not yet time for it. He would go on performing what he could of this function by main cleverness and personal manipulation. He would still be the quarterback of a team without any other direction. He had no possessive feeling for any lesser objectives than those with which he was in direct touch here in his church—the brotherhood of man in the fathership of God. With anything not indicated directly to a Christian gentleman he would temporize, experiment, tentatively put forward if it seemed to go in the right direction. But he would not give it or its administrators any kind of loyalty, bind himself to its history or their fortunes. He would not go far to persuade people of its desirability or risk much of his political capital to establish or maintain it.

I knew that N.R.A. was done for; and I hardly expected to see another attempt of the sort in my lifetime. I might have been full of lament. But somehow what I had perceived had communicated its perspective to me and I had borrowed a little of the President's equanimity. It can be imagined that this was for me a political event of the first importance. I had not only learned to understand more than I had before about a President but also much more about the Presidency.

VI

One time, shortly after inauguration, President Roosevelt, for my own good, told me a parable which I have on occasion repeated. I call it the parable of the truck driver, not because of any intended disparagement of that profession, more because I admire the toughness required to carry it on—as no doubt the President did

too. It was intended, besides comforting me, to illustrate the necessarily tentative nature of essays in administration. I came into the
President's office one day late in the spring of 1933 looking, I
guess, pretty tired and perhaps a little wan, as though things were
getting to be decidedly too much for me, as, in fact, they were. I
had been at it now since the very early spring of 1932, much of
that time immersed in outsize problems quite beyond any experience I had ever had before; and for several months had been
carrying almost the whole administrative burden of the old Department of Agriculture—while we tried to find ways of reforming
it—the Secretary necessarily spending most of his time on preparations for the Agricultural Adjustment Administration. I was also
serving on half a dozen interdepartmental boards in the Secretary's
stead, the most important of which were the National Recovery
Board and the Public Works Board; and I was still doing a certain
number of jobs for the President—acting as his familiar in the now
diminishing Brain Trust relationship. Probably, also, I was beginning to feel the unrestrained hammering of the press, which had
begun almost as soon as the panic of the bank holiday had
subsided. At any rate, I was in such a state of exhaustion or
discouragement as to be noticeable.

The President looked that day, as he did all through the first
term, more leisurely in his seersuckers, and, with his good brown
color, healthier than any physically immobilized man had any right
to look. The sun streamed through the doors open to the lawn and
a breeze crept around the walls, where by now all his ship pictures
were hung. His enormous shoulder and chest development fairly
loomed over his almost empty desk—empty, that is, except for
gadgets—hiding the shrunken legs below. The impression, too,
strong to miss, was one of enormous power and confidence. He
leaned back and blew out a long cone of cigarette smoke. "You'll
have to learn," he said, "that public life takes a lot of sweat; but it
doesn't need to worry you. You won't always be right, but you
mustn't suffer from being wrong. That's what kills people like us."
"But," I said, "I have to make the most awful decisions for a guy
like me. And I always have to make them too soon. It gets me
down."

"Well," he said, "if you have decisions, what do you think about me? And I sleep nights. I'll tell you what you can think of. If you were a truck driver, just put down in your chair, 50 per cent of your decisions would be right on average, they'd have to be. But you aren't a truck driver. You've had some preparation. Your percentage is bound to be higher. So long as you keep it over 50 per cent I won't get rid of you and send for a truck driver." He laughed one of those laughs which could be heard all over the White House in those days and which made harassed people out in the waiting room, newspaper correspondents lounging in the lobby, secretaries with problems they could not fathom, even the servants at the housekeeping look at each other and smile in sympathy. Those laughs echoed in the pervading gloom of that year from California to Pennsylvania and made everyone in the whole nation feel better, all except the sour reactionaries, who were already busy whispering that it was a sign of approaching mania—"the lousy bastards," as Harry Hopkins used to say!

Outside, the reporters surrounded me. They knew I wouldn't repeat anything the President had told me but, as Fred Storm said, they could always hope, couldn't they? "What had he been laughing about?" they wanted to know; and I was too enraged at the press by now and too conscious of its malice to dare tell them, as perhaps I should have done, the useful parable I had heard. But then, it may be that the nation, hanging on its saviour's words in those days, might not have liked to hear that its servants in Washington, who pretended, as far as seemed congruous, to be infallible, were only expected by the President to be as right as the law of averages required—a little righter than a truck driver, hauled in and put at a desk, would be. Besides, by that time, it had occurred to me that one of my wrong decisions might be more important than all my right ones. There was, after all, something amiss with the parable, even if it did illustrate the tolerance of a President who did not value any decision too highly. They were mostly about things which after all only appeared to matter at the moment. He genuinely did not worry lest they be taken wrongly. He had a source of detached exaltation which could not be touched by the outcome.

This was more a feeling of the certainty of goodness than of being guided. He had it to do himself and he had no expectation of being absolved in confessional. So he kept the faith as he went along. He thought others ought to do it too, although he got enormous enjoyment out of their sins and laughed as much as any man at their inabilities to behave. That this applied to nations as well as men, those of us who served him had occasion to learn. The issue of the war debts, it will be remembered, was all mixed up with the phenomena of the Depression. If the farmers in Iowa were embittered about their debts to their mortgage-holders (whom they roughly called "the money power"), the French and the British were equally embittered about the debts they owed the United States.

For several centuries in similar circumstances European nations had foreclosed on various parts of the world; but their sole response to repeated duns in these years was a press campaign in which America was pictured as Uncle Shylock. Hoover had been brought in 1932 to a moratorium, and before Inauguration a preliminary conference in Geneva was to be held to lay down the principles for a full-scale conference later. The Europeans intended to use this occasion to get their debts forgiven, and Messrs. E. E. Day and J. W. Williams, Mr. Hoover's emissaries, were quite prepared to cede the point so that some international monetary stability could be reached. But President-elect Roosevelt in Albany had different ideas. He was, in fact, outraged. We were, he said, being put in a hopelessly false position. Anyone would think that *we* owed *them* an apology. This was not the naïveté of Coolidge, who, when the debts were mentioned, said, "Well, they hired the money, didn't they?" But he could understand that both Coolidge and Hoover had been treated with intolerable arrogance. He meant to have things go differently. And if historians are puzzled still, as I understand they are, as to why the President that summer blew up the London Economic Conference when the Europeans thought they had things nicely fixed up with Mr. Hull, and even Mr. Moley, they might consider the President's habit of differentiating means and ends, and his carelessness about the one and his adamant respect for the other.

The issue of Russian recognition furnishes another illustration.

It was to be expected that the new and moral liberal regime would give up the stiff and prejudiced attitude set by Secretary of State Hughes in Harding's time and maintained through twelve Republican years. To Republicans Communism as an economic philosophy was sinful, and they had never wavered in their determination that the United States should take no official notice of it. Even before his inauguration President Roosevelt had given some intimation that his attitude would be a different one. I noted from time to time his various remarks when the subject arose and I could see that this was a matter on which he had very clear guidance. I naturally wondered, as in other instances, what it was and how he had arrived at it. After a good deal of waiting and watching, I arrived at what I thought was the answer; and from then on I was even more interested to see whether I had been right. The confirmation all through was so ample as to be overwhelming. In this one instance I had succeeded in working out a useful formula. I had learned from the hard experience of the campaign how little committed the President was to any economic system or device, even to one which might affect a whole nation. So he had toyed with the idea of a new national banking system, with governmentally dominated self-government for industry, and with national planning. He had been willing to have all three, as I had hoped, but he had approached each of them as gingerly as a cat might approach an oversized rodent it had cornered. He found them interesting to speculate about; they appealed to his highly developed manipulative faculties; he even worked out political preparations and administrative procedures. But his interest was that of a workman who might choose the kind of steel to go into a machine or the kind of fertilizer to put on a field. The steel or the fertilizer might have technical qualities of a fascinating sort, but if what was wanted was a certain result it was only sensible to let the wanted result dominate the choice of material or tool. Also the President of the United States measured or determined results in different terms from anyone else. They had first to be good for the nation and then had to be accepted by it; only after these criteria had been satisfied could the more strictly functional judgment be allowed to have its way.

So far as I was concerned, when once I had caught on to this formula, I was completely satisfied, whether the decision went for or against the system or device I felt was necessary. What more could anyone ask than that the best politician, the freest and least prejudiced mind, and the most dedicated President possible to imagine should consider his ideas. I thought at the time and, being stubborn, have continued to think since, that a determined leader could have put into operation all three of the devices I have mentioned (as well as others I have not); but I never felt in the least disgruntled about it and I never went on trying to arrange a situation in which he would find himself committed to something his judgment had gone against—an occupation which is one of the particular vices of cabinet members and others in positions of governmental importance. This was a loyalty which I know— because he once told me—that he valued.

I knew that Russian recognition had been tried over in his mind and determined on as expedient. The economic prejudices of his predecessors weighed not at all with him in spite of his progressive predilections; but there was another which did and which might have affected his decision except that he found it not to be official. That, of course, was the Communist attitude toward religion, which he went into thoroughly with me as he must have with others before he made a decision. And I have thought since, although it did not occur to me at the time, that his decision was partly determined by the belief that recognition would be helpful to religious Russians in the various ways any imagination can conceive.

It was that old experienced hand Litvinoff who was sent by the Politburo to negotiate when the President's decision became known. What happened in the incident I am about to relate, the President told me himself immediately afterward (he told others too, for they in turn told me so). When the signatures were affixed and Litvinoff was about to leave, the President said to him:

"There is one other thing; you must tell Stalin that the antireligious policy is wrong. God will punish you Russians if you go on persecuting the church."

I ought not to put this remark in quotation marks, because I cannot be certain of its literal accuracy. But I am certain that it is almost exactly what he said. Litvinoff was taken aback. It was altogether unexpected. And when he thought it over he realized the significance of the way in which it had been put. The President had not said that Russian antireligious policy would alienate opinion and create diplomatic difficulties. He had said it would precipitate divine punishment.

Litvinoff related this incident to others in a puzzled way. He spoke of it because he thought it had no diplomatic significance and so could be talked about: but also he was astounded and curious. He wound up by asking:

"Does he really believe in God?"

That, at least, I could have answered. I knew, for certain, that this was an end, not a means.

✪

Franklin D. Roosevelt:
The Patrician as Opportunist

> THE *country needs and, unless I mistake its temper, the country*
> *demands bold, persistent experimentation. It is common sense to*
> *take a method and try it. If it fails, admit it frankly and try an-*
> *other. But above all, try something.*
> —FRANKLIN D. ROOSEVELT

Once during the early years of the Wilson administration Eleanor
Roosevelt and her husband, then Assistant Secretary of the Navy,
were lunching with Henry Adams. Roosevelt was speaking earnestly about some governmental matter that concerned him, when
his aged host turned on him fiercely: "Young man, I have lived in
this house many years and seen the occupants of that White House
across the square come and go, and nothing that you minor
officials or the occupants of that house can do will affect the
history of the world for long."

It was not often that Adams' superlative ironies were uninten-
tional. Although the influence of great men is usually exaggerated,
Roosevelt must be granted at least a marginal influence upon the
course of history. No personality has ever expressed the American

popular temper so articulately or with such exclusiveness. In the Progressive era national reform leadership was divided among Theodore Roosevelt, Wilson, Bryan, and La Follette. In the age of the New Deal it was monopolized by one man, whose passing left American liberalism demoralized and all but helpless.

At the heart of the New Deal there was not a philosophy but a temperament. The essence of this temperament was Roosevelt's confidence that even when he was operating in unfamiliar territory he could do no wrong, commit no serious mistakes. From the standpoint of an economic technician this assurance seemed almost mad at times, for example when he tossed back his head, laughed, and said to a group of silver Senators: "I experimented with gold and that was a flop. Why shouldn't I experiment a little with silver?" And yet there was a kind of intuitive wisdom under the harum-scarum surface of his methods. When he came to power, the people had seen stagnation go dangerously far. They wanted experiment, activity, trial and error, anything that would convey a sense of movement and novelty. At the very beginning of his candidacy Roosevelt, without heed for tradition or formality, flew to the 1932 nominating convention and addressed it in person instead of waiting for weeks in the customary pose of ceremonious ignorance. A trivial act in itself, the device gave the public an impression of vigor and originality that was never permitted to die. Although, as we shall see, Roosevelt had been reared on a social and economic philosophy rather similar to Hoover's, he succeeded at once in communicating the fact that his temperament was antithetical. When Hoover bumbled that it was necessary only to restore confidence, the nation laughed bitterly. When Roosevelt said: "The only thing we have to fear is fear itself," essentially the same threadbare half-true idea, the nation was thrilled. Hoover had lacked motion; Roosevelt lacked direction. But his capacity for growth, or at least for change, was enormous. Flexibility was both his strength and his weakness. Where Hoover had been remote and abstract, a doctrinaire who thought in fixed principles and moved cautiously in the rarefied atmosphere of the managerial classes, Roosevelt was warm, personal, concrete, and impulsive. Hoover was often reserved with valued associates. Roosevelt could say "my old friend" in eleven languages. He had little regard for abstract principle but a sharp intuitive knowledge of popular feeling. Because he was content in large measure to follow public opinion, he was able to give it that necessary additional impulse of leadership which can translate desires into policies. Hoover had never been able to convey to the masses a clear picture of what he was trying to do; Roosevelt was often able to suggest a clear and forceful line of policy when none in fact existed.

Raymond Moley tells an instructive story of Roosevelt's relations with Hoover in the interim between Roosevelt's election and inauguration. A conference had been arranged between the two men to discuss continuity of policy on the vexing question of foreign debts. Roosevelt, ill-informed on the facts, brought Moley with him as ballast and also carried a set of little cards in his hand as reminders of the questions he wanted to put to Hoover. Hoover talked for some time, revealing a mastery of all facets of the question which profoundly impressed Professor Moley. In contrast with the state of their information was the manner of the two men. Hoover, plainly disconcerted at this meeting with the man who had beaten him in the campaign, was shy and ill at ease and kept his eyes on the pattern of the carpet in the Red Room. Roosevelt was relaxed, informal, and cordial. That he was operating in *terra incognita* did not seem to trouble him in the least.

Roosevelt's admirers, their minds fixed on the image of a wise, benevolent, provident father, have portrayed him as an ardent social reformer and sometimes as a master planner. His critics, coldly examining the step-by-step emergence of his measures, studying the supremely haphazard way in which they were so often administered, finding how little he actually had to do with so many of his "achievements," have come to the opposite conclusion that his successes were purely accidental, just as a certain portion of a number of random shots is likely to hit a target. It is true, it is bound to be true, that there is a vast disproportion between Roosevelt's personal stature and the Roosevelt legend, but not everything that comes in haphazard fashion is necessarily an accident. During his Presidential period the nation was confronted with a completely novel situation for which the traditional, commonly accepted philosophies afforded no guide. An era of fumbling and muddling-through was inevitable. Only a leader with an experimental temper could have made the New Deal possible.

Roosevelt was, moreover, a public instrument of the most delicate receptivity. Although he lacked depth, he had great breadth. A warmhearted, informal patrician, he hated to disappoint, liked to play the bountiful friend. He felt that if a large number of people wanted something very badly, it was important that they be given some measure of satisfaction—and he allowed neither economic dogmas nor political precedents to inhibit him. The story of the W.P.A. cultural projects illustrates his intensely personal methods and the results they yielded. When relief was being organized in the early stages of the New Deal, someone pointed out to him that a great many competent painters were poverty-stricken and desperate. Now, Roosevelt had no taste for painting, very little interest in artists and writers as a group, and no preconceived theories about the responsibility of the state for cultural welfare; but his decision to help the artists came immediately and spontaneously. "Why not?" he said. "They are human beings. They have to live. I guess the only thing they can do is paint and surely there must be some public place where paintings are wanted." And so painters were included in the benefits of C.W.A. Ultimately, under the W.P.A., relief was extended to musicians, dancers, actors, writers, historians, even to students trying to finance themselves through college. A generation of artists and intellectuals was nursed through a trying period and became wedded to the New Deal and devoted to Roosevelt liberalism.

II

James and Sara Delano Roosevelt, Franklin's parents, are reminiscent of secondary characters in Edith Wharton's novels who provide the climate of respectable and unfriendly opinion in which her unfortunate heroines live. James Roosevelt, vice-president of several corporations, was a handsome country gentleman who dabbled in Democratic politics, enjoyed a stable of trotting-horses, and lived in leisure on his Hyde Park estate. Sara Delano, James's second wife, was also from an upper-class family with deep roots in American history; her father had owned copper lands, iron and coal mines, acreage on New York harbor, and a fleet of clipper ships. When they were married Sara was twenty-six and James was fifty-two. Two years later, on January 30, 1882, an entry in James Roosevelt's diary noted the birth of "a splendid large baby boy."

The only child of a fond mother, treated like a grandson by his father, Franklin was brought up with unusual indulgence. He had governesses and tutors; his playmates were from his own class; he owned a pony and a twenty-one-foot sailboat. Eight times before his adolescence he was taken on jaunts to Europe. At fourteen he entered the Reverend Endicott Peabody's Groton School, a little Greek democracy of the elite, which, as its headmaster said, stood for "everything that is true, beautiful, and of good report." The Groton boys, about 90 per cent from social-register families, lived in an atmosphere of paternal kindness and solicitude and swallowed huge gulps of inspiration at Peabody's weekly chapel performances.

From Groton Roosevelt followed a well-beaten path to Harvard. Although he was privileged to hear James, Royce, Norton, Shaler, and other illuminati, his life flowered chiefly outside the classroom. He became a prodigious doer and joiner, with memberships in more than a half-dozen campus clubs and a position on the *Crimson* that won him a good deal of college renown. A large part of his work on the *Crimson* was devoted to petty crusades for campus reforms. At an age when many boys are kicking over the traces, flirting with heresies, defying authority, and incidentally deepening their intellectual perspectives, young Roosevelt was writing exhortations about "school spirit" and football morale. On one occasion he urged in patriarchal fashion that "the memories and traditions of our ancestors and of our University be maintained during our lives and be faithfully handed down to our children in the years to come." His most serious public interest and possibly his first manifestation of sympathy for an underdog was in a college relief drive for the Boers. He left Harvard in

1904; his youth is summed up in his mother's words: "After all he had many advantages that other boys did not have."

Since it had been decided that Franklin should become a lawyer, he entered Columbia Law School. The following year he married his distant cousin Eleanor, to whom he had secretly been engaged, and moved into a home in New York City under the managerial eye of his mother. He was not happy in law school. "I am . . . trying to understand a little of the work," he wrote plaintively to Rector Peabody. Bored by the tenuous subtleties of the law, he failed some of his courses and left school without taking a degree, although he had absorbed enough to pass bar examinations. He joined the well-known New York firm of Carter, Ledyard, & Milburn as managing clerk. In Hyde Park he assumed the public-spirited role that his position required, became a member of the local volunteer fire department, a director of the First National Bank of Poughkeepsie, and a delegate to the 1910 New York Democratic convention.

Peopled by rich gentry and their hangers-on, the Hudson Valley counties were overwhelmingly Republican. Democratic nominations were conventionally given to prominent men of means who could pay the expenses of their campaigns. In 1910 the Democratic Mayor of Poughkeepsie, who had come to like his agreeable young neighbor from up the river, got him the party nomination for state Senator in a district that had elected only one Democrat since 1856. But 1910 was a bad year for Republicans, and Roosevelt, who bore the name of his wife's uncle, the popular twenty-sixth President, conducted a vigorous, unconventional campaign by automobile, ran well ahead of his ticket, and was elected on the crest of a Democratic wave.

In the legislature Roosevelt promptly became a leader among Democratic insurgents who blocked the nomination of Tammany Boss Murphy's choice for United States Senator. He appeared a typical progressive in his voting record, stood for the civil service, conservation, direct primaries, popular election of Senators, women's suffrage, and social legislation. "From the ruins of the political machines," he predicted hopefully, "we will reconstruct

something more nearly conforming to a democratic government."
In 1911 he visited Wilson at Trenton and returned an enthusiastic
supporter. He served well in the 1912 campaign and was rewarded
with the Assistant Secretaryship of the Navy. Just turned thirty-
one, he had had only three years of experience in politics.

From his childhood when he sailed his own knockabout, Roosevelt
had been in love with ships and the sea. He collected ship models
and prints, he read avidly in naval history, particularly Mahan,
and had thought of entering Annapolis. During the Spanish War he
had run away from Groton to enlist in the navy—an escapade cut
short by a siege of scarlet fever. After his appointment Roosevelt
began to campaign for naval expansion in magazine articles and
speeches, revealing a somewhat nationalistic and bellicose spirit.
The United States, he said, could not afford to lose control of the
seas unless it was content to be "a nation unimportant in the great
affairs of the world, without influence in commerce, or in the
extension of peaceful civilization." Although the American people
could look forward to ultimate international limitations of arms,
they must in the present "keep the principles of a possible navy
conflict always in mind." At the time Wilson delivered his war
message to Congress, *Scribner's Magazine* was featuring a moni-
tory article by Roosevelt entitled "On Your Own Heads," which
called for quintupling the navy's personnel. No one could say,
argued Roosevelt, that we were free from the danger of war. "We
know that every boy who goes to school is bound sooner or later,
no matter how peaceful his nature, to come to blows with some
schoolmate. A great people, a hundred million strong, has gone to
school." Later he demanded a system of national conscription for
women as well as men. He believed that service in the navy
smooths out sectionalism and class feeling and teaches equality.
As an administrator Roosevelt was aggressive and efficient, cutting
through red tape with genial disregard for regulations. Against the
advice of most of the admirals he took an important part in
promoting the unprecedented Allied mine barrage in the North
Sea.

In 1920 his party, needing a good name and an effective

campaigner, nominated Roosevelt as James M. Cox's running mate. He made a grand tour of the country, delivering about a thousand speeches. On the primary issue, the League of Nations, he argued effectively, but his enthusiasm was not comparable to his energy. "The League may not end wars," he conceded, "but the nations demand the experiment." During the campaign he made one slip which indicates that his mood was one of imperialistic *Realpolitik* rather than idealistic internationalism. At Butte, answering the argument that the United States would be outvoted by the combined British Commonwealth in the League's Assembly, he said: "It is just the other way . . . the United States has about twelve votes in the Assembly." He went on to explain that Latin-American countries in the projected Assembly looked to his country as "a guardian and big brother," and that it would control their votes.

> Until last week I had two [votes] myself, and now Secretary Daniels has them. You know I had something to do with the running of a couple of little republics. The facts are that I wrote Haiti's Constitution myself, and, if I do say it, I think it a pretty good Constitution.

Immediately the opposition kicked. Roosevelt was simply voicing some of the realities of politics, but the cynicism of his remarks, which smacked so strongly of the bad neighbor, was too open. He covered himself as best he could by saying that he had only meant that the Latin-American countries had the same interests as the United States and would normally vote the same way. For the boast that an alien official had written the Constitution of a neighbor republic there could be no satisfactory explanation.[1]

But it was a campaign in which mistakes did not matter. After Harding's victory Roosevelt, now thirty-eight, became a private citizen for the first time in ten years. He resumed his slight law practice, served as an overseer of Harvard, and took up his old life. A yachting companion, Van Lear Black, gave him a position

---

[1] The boast was untrue as well as unwise. Roosevelt did not write the Haitian Constitution but merely approved a draft submitted to the Navy Department by the State Department.

in the New York office of the Fidelity and Deposit Company of Maryland which carried a salary of twenty-five thousand dollars. But in August, 1921, it appeared that both Roosevelt's public and professional careers were over. After an exhausting spell in the heat of New York City he left for a vacation at his summer home on Campobello Island and soon found himself in the grip of severe pain, unable to move his muscles from the hips down.

III

To be sick and helpless is a humiliating experience. Prolonged illness also carries the hazard of narcissistic self-absorption. It would have been easy for Roosevelt to give up his political aspirations and retire to the comfortable privacy of Hyde Park. That he refused to relinquish his normal life was testimony to his courage and determination, and also to the strength of his ambition. From his bed he resumed as many of his affairs as possible. By the spring of 1922 he was walking on crutches, sometimes venturing to his office, and after 1924, when he found the pool at Warm Springs, he made good progress in recovering his strength. Above his enfeebled legs he developed a powerful torso.

In the long run this siege of infantile paralysis added much to Roosevelt's political appeal. As a member of the overprivileged classes with a classic Groton-Harvard career he had been too much the child of fortune. Now a heroic struggle against the cruelest kind of adversity made a more poignant success story than the usual rags-to-riches theme; it was also far better adapted to democratic leadership in a period when people were tired of self-made men and their management of affairs.

There has been much speculation about the effect of Roosevelt's illness upon his sympathies. Frances Perkins, who writes of him with intelligence and detachment and who knew him before his illness as a pleasant but somewhat supercilious young man, feels that he underwent a "spiritual transformation," in which he was purged of "the slightly arrogant attitude" he had occasionally shown before. She now found him "completely warmhearted," and felt that "he understood the problems of people in trouble." There is a further conclusion, drawn by some fabricators of the legend, that he read widely and studied deeply during his illness and developed a firm social outlook that aligned him forever with the underprivileged. This notion is not sustained by Roosevelt's history during the prosperity of the 1920's. His human capacity, enlarged though it probably was, was not crystallized in either a new philosophy or a heightened interest in reforms.

For anyone of Roosevelt's background and character to have turned to serious social study or unorthodox political views would have been most unusual. From boyhood to the time of his illness he had led an outdoor athletic life, spending his indoor leisure on such diversions as stamp collections, ship models, naval history, and the like, not on sociological literature. His way of thinking was empirical, impressionistic, and pragmatic. At the beginning of his career he took to the patrician reform thought of the Progressive era and accepted a social outlook that can best be summed up in the phrase noblesse oblige.[2] He had a penchant for public service, personal philanthropy, and harmless manifestoes against dishonesty in government; he displayed a broad, easygoing tolerance, a genuine liking for all sorts of people; he loved to exercise his charm in political and social situations. His mind, as exhibited in writings and speeches of the twenties, was generous and sensible, but also superficial and complacent.

Roosevelt's education in politics came in a period of progressive optimism when it was commonly assumed that the most glaring ills of society could be cured by laws, once politics fell into the hands of honest men. If women worked endless hours in sweatshops, if workingmen were haunted by fear of unemployment or stricken by accidents, if the aged were beset by insecurity, men of good will would pass laws to help them. As a state Senator and as Governor this was what Roosevelt tried to do. But the social legislation of the states, however humane and useful, was worked out in provincial theaters of action, dealt more with effects than causes, touched

[2] "Frankness, and largeness, and simplicity, and a fine fervor for the right are virtues that some must preserve, and where can we look for them if not from the Roosevelts and the Delanos?" wrote Franklin K. Lane to Roosevelt, August, 1920.

only the surface of great problems like unemployment, housing, taxation, banking, and relief for agriculture. The generation that sponsored these laws got from them a good deal of training in practical politics and welfare work, but no strong challenge to think through the organic ills of society.

Roosevelt's biographers have largely ignored his life in the twenties except his fight for physical recovery, his role as peacemaker in the faction-ridden Democratic party, and his return to politics as Governor of New York. John T. Flynn, however, has pointed with malicious pleasure to his unsuccessful career in business, which certainly deserves attention, not as a reflection on his ethics or personal capacities, but on his social views during the years of prosperity. The ventures with which Roosevelt was associated—chiefly, one suspects, for the promotional value of his name—were highly speculative, and with one exception they failed. Perhaps the most illuminating of these was the Consolidated Automatic Merchandising Corporation, of which he was a founder and director along with Henry Morgenthau, Jr. This was a holding company, whose promoters were stirred by the typically American idea of a chain of clerkless stores to sell standard goods by means of automatic vending machines. In 1928 the chairman of its board announced that a large store staffed with such machines would soon be opened in New York City. Although it promised fabulous returns to investors, the firm lost over two million dollars within three years and closed its affairs in a bankruptcy court. Since Roosevelt promptly resigned his interest when he became Governor, his connection with it was brief and, in a business way, unimportant; but the social implications of the clerkless store and the jobless clerk, not to mention the loose and speculative way in which the enterprise was launched, do not seem to have troubled his mind.

In 1922 Roosevelt became president of the American Construction Council, a trade organization of the building industry. The council had been conceived in the light of Secretary of Commerce Hoover's philosophy of self-regulation by business, and Hoover presided over the meeting at which Roosevelt was chosen. In his address to the council Roosevelt endorsed the Hoover doctrine:

The tendency lately has been toward regulation of industry. Something goes wrong somewhere in a given branch of work, immediately the public is aroused, the press, the pulpit and public call for an investigation. That is fine, that is healthy . . . but government regulation is not feasible. It is unwieldy, expensive. It means employment of men to carry on this phase of the work; it means higher taxes. The public doesn't want it; the industry doesn't want it.

Seven years later in a Fourth of July speech at Tammany Hall, Governor Roosevelt warned of dangers inherent in "great combinations of capital." But he explained that "industrial combination is not wrong in itself. The danger lies in taking the government into partnership." The chief theme of his address was summed up in the sentence: "I want to preach a new doctrine—complete separation of business and government"—which was an ironic message for the future architect of the New Deal.

Even Mr. Flynn concedes that as Governor Roosevelt was "a fair executive." On social justice and humane reform his record was strong; in matters of long-range economic understanding and responsibility it was weak. He worked earnestly and effectively with a hostile Republican legislature to extend reforms that had been started by Al Smith. He secured a program of old-age pensions, unemployment insurance, and labor legislation, developed a forthright liberal program on the power question,[3] and took the initiative in calling a conference of Governors of Eastern industrial states to discuss unemployment and relief. His state was in the vanguard of those taking practical steps to relieve distress.

[3] Roosevelt believed that the vast potential of the St. Lawrence should be developed to shake down the unreasonable rates of the power companies. He wanted great power sites like the St. Lawrence, Muscle Shoals, and Boulder Dam to be developed by federal or state authority so that they would "remain forever as a yardstick with which to measure the cost of producing and transmitting electricity." This yardstick could be used to test the fairness of private utility rates. He proposed that New York build power structures and market the power they generated through contracts with private companies. If the state failed to get satisfactory contracts it would go into the business of selling power directly to consumers. In 1931 the legislature created the New York Power Authority, embodying his proposals, but the necessary treaty with Canada was first blocked by the Hoover administration and later defeated by the Senate in 1934 when it failed to get the necessary two-thirds majority.

Along with most other Americans, however, Roosevelt had failed to foresee the Depression that began when he was Governor. Six months before the crash he found New York industry "in a very healthy and prosperous condition." In his addresses and messages he ignored the significance of the Depression until its effects became overwhelming. His signal failure was in the realm of financial policy.

On December 11, 1930, the Bank of United States in New York City was closed by the State Superintendent of Banks, in substantial default to 400,000 depositors, mostly people with small savings. It had long been a practice of some New York commercial banks to create special "thrift accounts," which, although much the same as ordinary savings accounts, stood outside the control of state laws regulating savings-bank investments and gave bankers a wide latitude with other people's money. Another device was to create bank affiliates which were manipulated in sundry complicated ways to milk depositors and stockholders for the benefit of insiders.

A few months before the collapse of the Bank of United States, the failure of the City Trust Company had led to an investigation of the State Banking Department, and in Roosevelt's absence Acting Governor Herbert Lehman appointed Robert Moses as investigator. Moses' report roundly condemned many bank practices, especially "thrift accounts" and bank affiliates, and referred to the Bank of United States as an especially flagrant case.

Roosevelt ignored the Moses report and created another commission to study the same subject, appointing as one of its members Henry Pollak—a director and counsel of the Bank of United States! Not surprisingly, the new commission rejected Moses' recommendations. Shortly afterward, when the Bank of United States failed, Roosevelt was self-assured, unabashed, impenitent. To the state legislature he boldly wrote: "The responsibility for strengthening the banking laws rests with you." Insisting that the protection of the laws be extended to depositors in thrift accounts, he waxed righteously impatient: "The people of the State not only expect it, but they have a right to demand it. The time to act is now. Any further delay is inexcusable. . . ."

This incident, particularly Roosevelt's sudden espousal of a reform he had opposed, foreshadows a great part of the history of the New Deal. There is an irresistible footnote to it. When Roosevelt came to power the banks of the nation were in paralysis. In his first press conference he was asked if he favored federal insurance of bank deposits. He said that he did not. His reason was that bad banks as well as good ones would have to be insured and that the federal government would have to take the losses. Nevertheless the Federal Deposit Insurance Corporation was soon created as a concession to a bloc of insistent Western Senators. The FDIC thus took its place among a company of New Deal reforms that add to the luster of Roosevelt's name and will presumably be cited by historians as instances of his wise planning.

When the task of conducting a Presidential campaign fell upon him, Roosevelt's background of economic innocence was dappled by only occasional traces of knowledge. "I don't find that he has read much about economic subjects," wrote Raymond Moley in a family letter, April 12, 1932. "The frightening aspect of his methods is F.D.R.'s great receptivity. So far as I know he makes no efforts to check up on anything that I or anyone else has told him." On occasion his advisers were astounded by his glib treatment of complicated subjects. Once when his campaign speeches on the tariff were being prepared, and two utterly incompatible proposals were placed before him, Roosevelt left Moley speechless by airily suggesting that he should "weave the two together." That "great receptivity" which frightened Moley, however, was the secret of Roosevelt's political genius. He became an individual sounding board for the grievances and remedies of the nation, which he tried to weave into a program that would be politically, if not economically, coherent.

Roosevelt's 1932 campaign utterances indicate that the New Deal had not yet taken form in his mind. He was clear on two premises: he rejected Hoover's thesis that the Depression began abroad, insisting that it was a homemade product, and he denounced Hoover for spending too much money. He called the Hoover administration "the greatest spending Administration in peace time in all our history." The current deficit, he charged, was enough to "make us catch our breath." "Let us have the courage," he urged, "to stop borrowing to meet continuing deficits." And yet he was "unwilling that economy should be practiced at the expense of starving people. Still, he did not indicate how he proposed to relieve starving people. Public works? They could be no more than a "stopgap," even if billions of dollars were spent on them. He was firm in ascribing the Depression to low domestic purchasing power, and declared that the government must "use wise measures of regulation which will bring the purchasing power back to normal." On the other hand, he surrendered to Hoover's idea that America's productive capacity demanded a large outlet in the export market. "If our factories run even 80 percent of capacity," he said (quite inaccurately),[4] "they will turn out more products than we as a nation can possibly use ourselves. The answer is that . . . we must sell some goods abroad."

Roosevelt made several specific promises to the farmers. There was one aspect of Hoover's farm policies that made him especially bitter—the attempt of the Farm Board to organize retrenchment in production, which Roosevelt called "the cruel joke of advising farmers to allow twenty percent of their wheat lands to lie idle, to plow up every third row of cotton and shoot every tenth dairy cow." His own program involved "planned use of the land," reforestation, and aid to farmers by reducing tariffs through bilateral negotiations. Later he backtracked on the tariff, however, promising "continued protection for American agriculture *as well as* American industry."

All Roosevelt's promises—to restore purchasing power and mass employment and relieve the needy and aid the farmer and raise agricultural prices and balance the budget and lower the tariff and continue protection—added up to a very discouraging performance to those who hoped for a coherent liberal program. The

[4] "The United States," concluded the authors [Maurice Leven, Harold G. Moulton, and Clark Warburton] of *America's Capacity to Consume,* "has not reached a stage of economic development in which it is possible to produce more than the American people as a whole would like to consume."

New Republic called the campaign "an obscene spectacle" on both sides.

Roosevelt delivered one speech at the Commonwealth Club in San Francisco, however, which did generally foreshadow the new tack that was to be taken under the New Deal. In this address Roosevelt clearly set down the thesis that the nation had arrived at a great watershed in its development. Popular government and a wide continent to exploit had given the United States an unusually favored early history, he asserted. Then the Industrial Revolution had brought a promise of abundance for all. But its productive capacity had been controlled by ruthless and wasteful men. Possessing free land and a growing population, and needing industrial plant, the country had been willing to pay the price of the accomplishments of the "ambitious man" and had offered him "unlimited reward provided only that he produced the economic plant so much desired." "The turn of the tide came with the turn of the century." As America reached its last frontiers, the demand of the people for more positive controls of economic life gave rise to the Square Deal of Theodore Roosevelt and the New Freedom of Woodrow Wilson. In 1932 the nation was still faced with the problem of industrial control.

A glance at the situation today only too clearly indicates that equality of opportunity as we have known it no longer exists. Our industrial plant is built; the problem just now is whether under existing conditions it is not overbuilt. Our last frontier has long since been reached, and there is practically no more free land. More than half of our people do not live on the farms or on lands and cannot derive a living by cultivating their own property. There is no safety valve in the form of a Western prairie to which those thrown out of work by the Eastern economic machines can go for a new start. We are not able to invite the immigration from Europe to share our endless plenty. We are now providing a drab living for our own people. . . .

Just as freedom to farm has ceased, so also the opportunity in business has narrowed. . . . The unfeeling statistics of the past three decades show that the independent business man is running a losing race. . . . Recently a careful study was made of the concentration of business in the United States. It showed that our economic life was dominated by some six hundred odd corporations who [sic] controlled two-thirds of American industry. Ten million small business men divided the other third. More striking still, it appeared that if the process goes on at the same rate, at the end of another century we shall have all American industry controlled by a dozen corporations, and run by perhaps a hundred men. Put plainly, we are steering a steady course toward economic oligarchy, if we are not there already.

Clearly, all this calls for a re-appraisal of values. A mere builder of more industrial plants, a creator of more railroad systems, an organizer of more corporations, is as likely to be a danger as a help. The day of the great promoter or the financial Titan, to whom we granted anything if only he would build, or develop, is over. Our task now is not discovery or exploitation of natural resources, or necessarily producing more goods. It is the soberer, less dramatic business of administering resources and plants already in hand, of seeking to reestablish foreign markets for our surplus production, of meeting the problem of underconsumption, of adjusting production to consumption, of distributing wealth and products more equitably, of adapting existing economic organizations to the service of the people. The day of enlightened administration has come. . . .

As I see it, the task of government in its relation to business is to assist the development of an economic declaration of rights, an economic constitutional order. . . .

Happily, the times indicate that to create such an order not only is the proper policy of Government, but it is the only line of safety for our economic structures as well. We know, now, that these economic units cannot exist unless prosperity is uniform, that is, unless purchasing power is well distributed throughout every group in the nation.

In cold terms, American capitalism had come of age, the great era of individualism, expansion, and opportunity was dead. Further, the drying up of "natural" economic forces required that the government step in and guide the creation of a new economic order. Thus far Roosevelt had left behind the philosophy of his 1929 Tammany Hall speech. But in the Commonwealth Club speech two different and potentially inconsistent lines of government action are implied. One is suggested by the observation that the industrial plant is "overbuilt," that more plants will be "a danger," that production must be "adjusted" to consumption; the other by phrases like "meeting the problem of underconsumption," making prosperity "uniform," distributing purchasing power, and "an economic declaration of rights." The first involves a retrogressive economy of trade restriction and state-guided monopoly; the second emphasizes social justice and the conquest of poverty. In 1931 the United States Chamber of Commerce's Committee on Continuity of Business and Employment had declared in terms similar to Roosevelt's: "A freedom of action which might have been justified in the relatively simple life of the last century cannot be tolerated today. . . . We have left the period of extreme individualism." The committee then proposed a program very closely resembling the N.R.A. as it was adopted in 1933. It is evident that Roosevelt's premises, far from being intrinsically progressive, were capable of being adapted to very conservative purposes. His version of the "matured economy" theory, although clothed in the rhetoric of liberalism and "social planning," could easily be put to the purposes of the trade associations and scarcity-mongers. The polar opposition between such a policy and the promise of making prosperity uniform and distributing purchasing power anticipated a basic ambiguity in the New Deal.

IV

At one of his earliest press conferences Roosevelt compared himself to the quarterback in a football game. The quarterback knows what the next play will be, but beyond that he cannot predict or plan too rigidly because "future plays will depend on how the next one works." It was a token of his cast of mind that he used the metaphor of a game, and one in which chance plays a very large part. The New Deal will never be understood by anyone who looks for a single thread of policy, a far-reaching, far-seeing plan. It was a series of improvisations, many adopted very suddenly, many contradictory. Such unity as it had was in political strategy, not economics.

Roosevelt had little regard for the wisdom of economists as a professional caste. "I happen to know," he declared in his third fireside chat, "that professional economists have changed their definition of economic laws every five or ten years for a long time." Within the broad limits of what he deemed "sound policy" —and they were extremely broad limits—he understood that his administration would not be politically durable unless it could "weave together" many diverse, conflicting interests. He had built a brilliantly successful career in the Democratic party on his flair for reconciling or straddling antagonistic elements, and he was too practical to abandon a solid bedrock of political harmony in favor of some flighty economic dogma that might be abandoned in "five or ten years." Frances Perkins tells how Lord Keynes, whose spending theories were influential with some New Deal economists, paid a brief visit to the President in 1934 and talked about economic theory. Roosevelt, bewildered at Keynes's "rigamarole of figures," told his Secretary of Labor: "He must be a mathematician rather than a political economist." Keynes for his part was somewhat disappointed, remarking that he had "supposed the President was more literate, economically speaking." The Britisher's mistake is likely to become a model for Roosevelt legend-makers.

Raymond Moley, in his *After Seven Years,* has compiled a fairly long but not exhaustive enumeration of the sharp swerves and tacks in Rooseveltian policy. It will be more simple and profitable to speak only of the two New Deals that were fore-shadowed in the Commonwealth Club speech. In a sense both of them ran concurrently; but it is roughly accurate to say that the first was dominant from Roosevelt's inauguration to the spring and summer of 1935 and that the second emerged during that period and lasted until the reform energies of the nation petered out.

The first New Deal, the New Deal of 1933–1934, was conceived mainly for recovery. Reform elements and humane measures of immediate relief were subsidiary to the organized and subsidized scarcity advocated by the Chamber of Commerce, the Farm Bureau Federation, and the National Grange, and incarnated in the N.R.A. and A.A.A. These great agencies, the core of the first New Deal, representing its basic plans for industry and agriculture, embodied the retrogressive idea of recovery through scarcity.

The A.A.A. was the most striking illustration of organized

scarcity in action. Although successful in raising farm prices and restoring farm income, it did just what Roosevelt had found so shocking in Hoover's Farm Board. To the common-sense mind the policy seemed to have solved the paradox of hunger in the midst of plenty only by doing away with plenty. In an address at Atlanta, in November, 1935, Roosevelt implicitly conceded that the whole policy was geared to the failure of the American economy. He pointed out that the average American lived "on what the doctors would call a third-class diet." If the nation lived on a first-class diet, "we would have to put more acres than we have ever culti-vated into the production of an additional supply of things for Americans to eat." The people lived on a third-class diet, he said candidly, because they could not afford to buy a first-class diet.[5]

The mainspring of the first New Deal was the N.R.A., which Roosevelt called "the most important and far-reaching legislation ever enacted by the American Congress . . . a supreme effort to stabilize for all time the many factors which make for the pros-perity of the nation." Under it business received government sanction for sweeping price agreements and production quotas and in return accepted wage stipulations improving the condition of many of the poorest-paid workers.[6] It is not unfair to say that in essence the N.R.A. embodied the conception of many businessmen that recovery was to be sought through systematic monopolization, high prices, and low production.[7] In spite of the enthusiasm with which its "planned" features were greeted, it retarded recovery, as

[5] The Ever Normal Granary Plan, enacted in 1938, was widely hailed as a more satisfactory policy. Although it promised greater price stability and other benefits, it still involved familiar plans for marketing quotas and the shadow of abundance still hung over it. Its sponsor, Henry Wallace, admitted that "several years of good weather" and good crops would "embarrass" the government.

[6] It may be necessary to say that N.R.A. was not a universal business policy. A poll taken in 1935 showed that Chamber of Commerce members were almost three to one for continuing N.R.A., while N.A.M. members opposed it three to one.

[7] N.R.A. Administrator Hugh Johnson declared in an early press con-ference: "We are going to ask something in the nature of an armistice on increased producing capacity, until we see if we can get this upward spiral started. . . . We are going to plead very earnestly . . . not to use any further labor-saving devices or anything further to increase production for the present."

the Brookings economists concluded, and a strong, sustained advance in business conditions began only after the Supreme Court killed it in May, 1935.[8] Roosevelt was nevertheless slow to give up the N.R.A. idea. In February, 1935, asking for a two-year extension, he said that to abandon its "fundamental purposes and principles . . . would spell the return of industrial and labor chaos."

The initial New Deal was based upon a strategy that Roosevelt had called during the campaign "a true concert of interests," and that meant in practice something for everybody. Farmers got the A.A.A. Business got the N.R.A. codes. Labor got wage-and-hour provisions and the collective-bargaining promise of Section 7 (a). The unemployed got a variety of federal relief measures. The middle classes got the Home Owners' Loan Corporation, securities regulation, and other reforms. Some debtors were aided by inflation. As new discontents developed they were met with new expedients.

Despite all Roosevelt's efforts, however, the nation insistently divided into right and left, and his equivocal position became more difficult to maintain. Pressure from the organized and enheartened Left became stronger; but Roosevelt was also baited into a leftward turn by diehard conservatives. He was surprised and wounded at the way the upper classes turned on him. It has often been said that he betrayed his class; but if by his class one means the whole policy-making, power-wielding stratum, it would be just as true to say that his class betrayed him. Consider the situation in which he came to office. The economic machinery of the nation had broken down and its political structure was beginning to disintegrate. People who had anything to lose were frightened; they were willing to accept any way out that would leave them still in possession. During the emergency Roosevelt had had practically dictatorial powers. He had righted the keel of economic life and had turned politics safely back to its normal course. Although he

---

[8] The end of N.R.A. was certainly not the only factor in the recovery that began in the summer of 1935, but it is beyond argument that the most sustained period of economic advance under the New Deal took place in the two years after the Blue Eagle was laid to rest.

had adopted many novel, perhaps risky expedients, he had avoided vital disturbances to the interests. For example, he had passed by an easy chance to solve the bank crisis by nationalization and instead followed a policy orthodox enough to win Hoover's approval. His basic policies for industry and agriculture had been designed after models supplied by great vested-interest groups. Of course, he had adopted several measures of relief and reform, but mainly of the sort that any wise and humane conservative would admit to be necessary. True, he had stirred the masses with a few hot words about "money changers" and chiselers, but he had been careful to identify these as a minority among businessmen. It was, after all, not Roosevelt but the terrible suffering of the Depression that had caused mass discontent, and every sophisticate might be expected to know that in such times a few words against the evil rich are necessary to a politician's effectiveness.

Nothing that Roosevelt had done warranted the vituperation he soon got in the conservative press or the obscenities that the hate-Roosevelt maniacs were bruiting about in their clubs and dining rooms. Quite understandably he began to feel that the people who were castigating him were muddle-headed ingrates. During the campaign of 1936 he compared them with the old man saved from drowning who berated his rescuer for not salvaging his hat—and again with a patient newly discharged from the hospital who had nothing but imprecations for his physician. Before 1935 Roosevelt had engaged in much political controversy, but he had generally managed to remain on friendly terms with his opponents. Surrounded from childhood with friendship, encouragement, and indulgence, he might have been able to accept criticism offered in the spirit of good-natured banter or the proposal of constructive alternatives (which he would simply have appropriated), but the malice and deliberate stupidity of his critics made him angry, and his political struggle with the "economic royalists" soon became intensely personal. Professor Moley, who in 1932 had admired his lack of "a bloated sense of personal destiny," was saddened to hear him say in 1936: "There's one issue in this campaign. It's myself, and people must be either for me or against me." In public he grew aggressive. He would like to have it said of his second administration, he stated, that in it "the forces of selfishness and of lust for power . . . met their master."

The development of Roosevelt's relation to the Left is of critical importance to the Roosevelt legend. Perhaps no aspect of his public relations has been so quickly forgotten as his early labor policy. At the beginning of his administration Roosevelt was an acquaintance, not a friend, of organized labor. Although he was eager to do something about the poorest-paid workers through the N.R.A. codes, his attitude toward unions themselves was not overcordial. The N.R.A. itself had been rushed into shape partly to head off the strong prolabor provisions of the Black-Connery bill. Section 7(a) of N.R.A., which guaranteed the right of collective bargaining, did not ban individual bargaining, company unions, or the open shop. Workers at first rallied to the N.R.A. with enthusiasm and entered the more aggressive unions by the thousands in response to the plausible but false appeal: "The President wants you to join." But when disputes arose under Section 7(a), General Hugh Johnson and Donald Richberg handed down interpretations that, in the language of the Brookings Institution economists, "had the practical effect of placing the N.R.A. on the side of anti-union employers in their struggle against the trade unions. . . . The N.R.A. thus threw its weight against labor in the balance of bargaining power." Roosevelt stood firmly behind his administrators. Further, his last appointee as N.R.A. administrator was a notorious foe of labor, S. Clay Williams. By early 1935, when there were few in the ranks of organized labor who had any expectation of help from the White House, workers were calling the N.R.A. the "National Run Around." On February 2 William Green threatened that the entire labor movement would oppose Roosevelt.[9]

In the meanwhile another political threat was rising. Huey Long, who had achieved the position of a major leader of mass

[9] An article in *The New York Times,* February 3, 1935, under the heading, "LABOR UNIONS BREAK WITH THE NEW DEAL," reported that labor leaders were "almost in despair of making headway toward union recognition in the face of powerful industrial interests and an unsympathetic administration."

opinion in the hinterland through his demagogic "share-the-wealth" movement, was talking about a third party. In his *Behind the Ballots* James A. Farley recalls that the Democratic National Committee, worried about the 1936 election, conducted a secret national poll to sound Long's strength. They were dismayed at what they learned. "It was easy to conceive a situation," reports Farley, "whereby Long . . . might have the balance of power in the 1936 election." Democrats also had private reports that he would be well financed if he ran. By midspring Professor Moley was horrified to hear Roosevelt speak of the need of doing something "to steal Long's thunder."[10]

It was at this point that the Supreme Court broke the mainspring of the original New Deal by declaring the N.R.A. unconstitutional. Roosevelt, looking forward to 1936, now found himself in a difficult position. The Court had torn up his entire program for labor and industry. Labor seemed on the verge of withdrawing political support. Huey Long's popularity showed the dissatisfaction of a large part of the electorate. And no sign of a really decisive turn toward business recovery had yet come. The result was a sharp and sudden turn toward the left, the beginning of the second New Deal.

In June, 1935, two striking measures were added to the President's list of "must" legislation: the Wagner labor-disputes bill and a drastic new "wealth tax" to steal Long's thunder. By the end of the 1935 legislative session the original New Deal, except for the A.A.A., was scarcely recognizable. In place of the N.R.A. codes and the masquerade of Section 7(a) there was now a Labor Relations Board with a firm commitment to collective bargaining. A strong holding-company act and a stringent wealth tax stood on the books. None of these measures as they were finally enacted had been contemplated by Roosevelt at the beginning of the year. In the W.P.A. a new relief program had been organized, with larger expenditures and a better wage scale. A Social Security Act had been passed. And at the close of the year the chief executive told Moley he was planning a "fighting speech" for his next annual

[10] The Townsend old-age pension movement was a menace of comparable importance, although it had not taken political form.

message to Congress because "he was concerned about keeping his left-wing supporters satisfied."

Roosevelt's alliance with the Left had not been planned; it had not even grown; it had erupted. The story of the Wagner Act, the keystone of his rapprochement with labor, and in a sense the heart of the second New Deal, is illustrative. The Wagner Act had never been an administration measure. It had been buffeted about the legislative chambers for more than a year without winning Roosevelt's interest. His Secretary of Labor recalls that he took no part in developing it, "was hardly consulted about it," and that "it did not particularly appeal to him when it was described to him." Nor did he altogether approve of the vigorous way in which it was later administered by the N.L.R.B. Miss Perkins recalls that he was "startled" when he heard that the Board had ruled that no employer was to be able to file a petition for an election or ask the Board to settle a jurisdictional dispute. Yet under the stimulus of recovery and the protection of the N.L.R.B., unions grew and flourished and provided the pressure in politics that gave the second New Deal its dynamic force. "A good democratic antidote for the power of big business," said Roosevelt.

Since Roosevelt was baited and frustrated by the Right and adopted by the Left, his ego was enlisted along with his sympathies in behalf of the popular point of view. During the formative period of the second New Deal he seems to have begun to feel that his social objectives demanded a crusade against the "autocracy." Early in 1936 at a Jackson Day dinner he made an elaborate and obvious comparison between Jackson and himself in which he observed of Jackson's hold on the common people: "They loved him for the enemies he had made." It is doubtful whether, even in Jackson's day, there had ever been such a close feeling of communion between a President and the great masses of the people as in the 1936 campaign. One incident that Roosevelt recalled for reporters touched him especially. He was driving through New Bedford, Massachusetts, when a young girl broke through the Secret Service guards and passed him a pathetic note. She was a textile worker. Under the N.R.A. she had received the minimum of eleven dollars a week, but had recently suffered a 50 per cent wage cut. "You are the only man that can do anything about it," her note ended. "Please send somebody from Washington up here to restore our minimum wages because we cannot live on $4 or $5 or $6 a week."[11] Here was common ground: the "resplendent economic autocracy" that imposed such a pitiful wage scale was the same interest that was flaying the President. Without design by either, and yet not altogether by accident, Roosevelt and the New Bedford girl had been thrown together in a league of mutual defense.

Roosevelt's Second Inaugural Address was a lofty and benign document in which he remarked with satisfaction on the improvement of "the moral climate of America," declared that the proper test of progress is "whether we provide enough for those who have too little," and called attention to "one-third of a nation, ill-housed, ill-clad, ill-nourished." In the first two years of his second administration he sponsored, in addition to the controversial Supreme Court reform bill, four new reform measures of broad economic importance: the Housing Act of 1937, the Fair Labor Standards Act, the Farm Security Act, and an unsuccessful proposal to set up a national string of seven TVA's. But the New Deal was designed for a capitalistic economy that, as Miss Perkins says, Roosevelt took as much for granted as he did his family. For success in attaining his stated goals of prosperity and distributive justice he was fundamentally dependent upon restoring the health of capitalism. The final part of the New Deal story can be told not only in political battles and reform legislation but in jagged movements on the business-cycle graphs.

Early in 1937, administration circles, watching the rapid rise of the business index almost to 1929 levels, became fearful of a runaway boom. Federal Reserve officials put a brake upon credit, Roosevelt called upon Congress for economies, and W.P.A. rolls were sliced in half. Roosevelt had never publicly accepted spending as a permanent governmental policy; although he had operated upon yearly deficits, he had always promised that when the

[11] See Samuel I. Rosenman, ed., *The Public Papers and Addresses of Franklin D. Roosevelt* (New York, 1938–1950), V, 624.

national income reached a satisfactory level he would return to balanced budgets. But events proved that he had become a prisoner of the spending expedient. As Alvin Hansen has characterized it, the 1935–1937 upswing was a "consumption recovery," financed and spurred by huge government outlays. When government expenditures were cut, a sharp downward trend began, which reached alarming dimensions early in 1938. Just at this time the National Resources Committee, an executive fact-finding agency, placed upon the President's desk a careful survey of consumer incomes for 1935–1936. The committee estimated that 59 per cent of the families in the land had annual cash incomes of less than $1,250, 81 per cent less than $2,000. When this report reached him, Roosevelt knew that business conditions had again declined. There were still about 7,500,000 workers unemployed. Plainly something fundamental, something elusive, was wrong.

The New Deal had accomplished a heart-warming relief of distress, it had achieved a certain measure of recovery, it had released great forces of mass protest and had revived American liberalism, it had left upon the statute books several measures of permanent value, it had established the principle that the entire community through the agency of the federal government has some responsibility for mass welfare, and it had impressed its values so deeply upon the national mind that the Republicans were compelled to endorse its major accomplishments in election platforms. But, as Roosevelt was aware, it had failed to realize his objectives of distributive justice and sound, stable prosperity.[12]

In April, 1938, Roosevelt adopted two expedients that signalized the severity of the crisis in the New Deal: one was a return to spending on a large scale, the other a crusade against monopoly. The first expedient solved the immediate crisis: Congress readily appropriated new funds, business conditions responded quickly, and the "Roosevelt recession" was soon liquidated. Henceforth Roosevelt took it for granted that the economy could not operate

---

[12] Cf. the comment of Professor Tugwell in *The Stricken Land:* "It was in economics that our troubles lay. For their solution his progressivism, his new deal, was pathetically insufficient. . . . I think . . . that he will be put down as having failed in this realm of [domestic] affairs."

without the stimulus of government funds. In his memorable budget message of 1940 he finally accepted in theory what he had long been doing in fact, admitted the responsibility of government retrenchment for the recession, credited the revival of spending for the revival in business, and in general discussed the problem of the federal budget in Keynesian terms.[13]

The second expedient, the call for an attack upon monopoly, was a complete reversal of Roosevelt's philosophy of 1933 and the N.R.A. policy. The message to Congress in which the crusade was announced—and which led to the fruitful TNEC investigations— was one of the most remarkable economic documents that have ever come from the White House. Roosevelt viewed the structure of economic and political power in broad social perspective. "Private power," he declared, was reaching a point at which it became "stronger than the democratic state itself." In the United States "a concentration of private power without equal in history is growing," which is "seriously impairing the effectiveness of private enterprise." "Private enterprise is ceasing to be free enterprise and is becoming a cluster of private collectivisms." A democratic people would no longer accept the meager standards of living caused by the failure of monopolistic industry to produce. "Big business collectivism in industry compels an ultimate collectivism in government." "The power of the few to manage the economic life of the Nation must be diffused among the many or be transferred to the public and its democratically responsible government."

Like Wilson, Roosevelt saw the development of big business and monopoly as a menace to democratic institutions, but like Wilson and all other politicians who touched upon the so-called trust problem, he was equivocal about how this menace was to be controlled. Although his argument carried to the brink of socialism, it was not socialism that he was proposing. Nor did he propose to reverse the whole modern trend of economic integration by trying to dissolve big business, a course of action the

[13] The Hoover administration, which Roosevelt had accused of extravagance in 1932, was now criticized for having failed to spend enough to fight the Depression.

futility of which had been demonstrated by almost fifty years of experience. The economists whose guidance he was following believed that the rigid price structure of the semimonopolized heavy industries was throwing the whole economy out of gear. Presumably antitrust measures were not to be used to break up big corporations but to discipline their pricing policies. How the reformist state was to police the corporations without either destroying private enterprise or itself succumbing to the massed strength of corporate opposition was not made clear. Roosevelt did not tackle such problems in theory, and events spared him the necessity of facing them in practice.

Roosevelt's sudden and desperate appeal to the ancient trust-busting device, together with his failure in the fall elections of 1938 to purge the conservative elements in his party, augured the political bankruptcy of the New Deal. The reform wave had spent itself, and the Democratic party, divided by the Supreme Court fight and the purge and hamstrung by its large conservative bloc, was exhausted as an agency of reform. Always the realist, Roosevelt rang the death knell of the New Deal in his annual message to Congress on January 4, 1939. "We have now passed the period of internal conflict in the launching of our program of social reform," he declared. "Our full energies may now be released to invigorate the processes of recovery in order to preserve our reforms." Almost three years before Pearl Harbor his experimentation had run its course. "The processes of recovery" came only with war. "Our full energies" were never successfully released for peacetime production. What would have happened to the political fortunes of Franklin D. Roosevelt if the war had not created a new theater for his leadership?

V

When the Second World War elevated Roosevelt to a position of world importance, he had no consistent history of either isolationism or internationalism. Having begun his career in national politics as a strong navalist, an admirer of Mahan, who believed that every nation like every schoolboy was bound to come to blows with its fellows, he had turned about in the 1920 campaign to defend the League of Nations; but even then the Haiti incident revealed that he was thinking more in the lines of *Machtpolitik* than highflown internationalism. As the tide of isolationism rolled higher in the 1920's and his party dropped the League, Roosevelt went along with the trend, refusing to expose himself by defending an unpopular cause in which he had no vital interest. In 1932 he became the first Democratic candidate who explicitly repudiated the League: when William Randolph Hearst demanded a disavowal from Roosevelt in an open letter threatening to use his powerful newspaper chain against any internationalist, Roosevelt quickly capitulated. He had no regrets, he said, for his work in behalf of the League in 1920. But now the League was no longer the instrument Wilson had designed. Instead of working for world peace, it had become a mere agency for the discussion of European affairs. Had the United States entered at the beginning, the League might have become what Wilson wanted, but since it had not, "I do not favor American participation." The statement was an intense disappointment to internationalists. "Roosevelt," wrote Henry F. Pringle in the *Nation,* "hauls down banners under which he has marched in the past and unfurls no new ones to the skies."

In spite of Cordell Hull's reciprocal-trade program, New Deal economics was based essentially upon playing a lone hand. It was Roosevelt's campaign thesis that recovery must be based upon independent domestic action rather than world arrangements, and it was he who killed the London Economic Conference of 1933 with a message minimizing the importance of international monetary agreements and affirming the intention of the United States to go its own way. Busy with domestic affairs, he showed no interest in international action up to the fall of 1937, except for an unsuccessful attempt to get Congress to affiliate with the World Court. His overt policy may not have reflected his private convictions. (In 1933 he had implicitly endorsed the "Stimson doctrine" of nonrecognition of Japanese penetration of China,[14] and his intimates heard him expressing a desire in the spring of 1935 "to

---

[14] When Moley and Tugwell objected, the President referred to the fact that his ancestors had been active in the China trade. "I have always had the deepest sympathy with the Chinese. How could you expect me not to go along with Stimson on Japan?"

do something" about Hitler.) But he was in no mood to try to remold the dominant isolationist and pacifist feeling of the country. Although he was opposed to its mandatory embargo provision, he signed the isolationist Neutrality Act of 1935. The Spanish war showed how unwilling he was to lose domestic support or take the slightest risk of foreign conflict to embark upon a crusade against fascist aggression. Since the Spanish war was a civil war, the mandatory embargo on war supplies did not apply to it, but the administration tried to maintain an informal embargo against both sides. When two American exporters insisted on their legal right to sell to the Spanish Republican government, Roosevelt asked Congress to amend the Neutrality Act to cover civil wars, and the Spanish government was definitively cut off from American markets.[15] This move not only violated American diplomatic precedent and what is known as international law, but also breached the 1902 Treaty of Madrid between the United States and Spain. After Franco's victory the Roosevelt administration quickly gave official recognition to his government.

Roosevelt's first sign of a swing toward collective security came on October 5, 1937, when he proposed to "quarantine" aggressor nations and asserted that "there is no escape" for the United States from international anarchy and instability "through isolation or neutrality." It remains a matter of conjecture what caused this turnabout. Hitler's power had already become imposing and, not long before, Japan had resumed its invasion of China. Hostile critics also charged, without more than circumstantial evidence, that Roosevelt was trying to distract attention from the developing

---

[15] Editing his public papers in 1941, Roosevelt insisted that it was "useless to argue" that Spain was the proper place for the European democracies to have stopped the aggressor nations. As for the United States, its people were unwilling to risk "the slightest chance of becoming involved in a quarrel in Europe which had all the possibilities of developing into a general European conflict." Further, he said, the fascists had more shipping than the Republican government, and if American goods had been available to both sides the fascists would probably have bought more. This was a shifty argument. The United States was not limited to the alternative of selling to both sides or neither. It would have been more consistent with American precedent, "international law," and American treaty obligations to continue normal economic relations with a government recognized *de jure* and to embargo shipments to a revolutionary faction.

business recession. What is certain is that the "quarantine speech" produced no sharp turn in public sentiment; almost a year later, in September, 1938, the Gallup Poll showed that only 34 per cent of American voters favored selling arms and ammunition to England and France in case of a war with the Axis. Within seven months Hitler violated the Munich agreement and took Prague and Memel, and the figure went from 34 to 68 per cent.

During this period a deep fissure appeared in the American public mind. The typical American was afraid that if Germany overwhelmed the Western democratic powers, the United States would ultimately have to face the military might of fascism alone. But he was also desperately anxious to stay out of war. When war began he wanted to aid the Allies, to become a silent partner against the Axis, and yet to avoid hostilities. Roosevelt's foreign policy had always been shaped with due regard to the state of domestic opinion, and now his public statements closely reflected this ambiguity in American intentions. "We know," he said to Congress in January, 1939, "what might happen to us of the United States if the new philosophies of force were to encompass the other continents and invade our own." When the war began, however, he said: "I hope the United States will keep out. . . . Every effort of your government will be directed toward that end." On January 3, 1940, he noted that "there is a vast difference between keeping out of war and pretending that this war is none of our business." The fall of France, which broke down all pretense of American "neutrality," did not end the general hope that actual involvement could be avoided. In 1940 Roosevelt and Willkie and their party platforms promised aid to countries fighting the Axis; both promised again and again that they would not take the country into war. Shortly after the campaign was over, Roosevelt said: "Our national policy is not directed toward war. Its sole purpose is to keep war away from our country and our people." In the same speech, however, he described the United States as "the great arsenal of democracy," and stated that "no dictator, no combination of dictators," could weaken American determination to aid Britain. During 1940 and 1941 he sponsored many meas- ures that flouted neutrality, including the trade of destroyers for naval bases, the Lend-Lease Act, occupation of Greenland and Iceland, patrolling the waters between the United States and Iceland, and constructing a naval base in Northern Ireland. In September, 1941, hostilities took place between a German submarine and an American destroyer. The following month the President announced in a Navy Day speech that "America has been attacked," and "the shooting has started." The nation was already engaged in undeclared naval hostilities, but the final public reluctance to wage open warfare made decisive use of national resources impossible. Roosevelt was in a difficult position, but the Japanese attack at Pearl Harbor did for him what the Confederate attack on Sumter had done for Lincoln.

Roosevelt died before the practical direction of his postwar policies became clear. He left a good deal in words, promises, and statements of general objectives, but not much to tell how they were to be translated into action. Since 1935 he had become accustomed to appeal to a liberal audience at home, and presumably to think in the popular humanistic language of the progressive tradition. During the 1944 campaign he talked of guaranteeing broad security and welfare to the people through an "economic bill of rights," of which the most vital was "the right of a useful and remunerative job." But lest anyone imagine that this involved a drastic reconstruction of economic life going far beyond the New Deal, he also spoke of "full production and full employment under our democratic system of private enterprise, with Government encouragement and aid whenever and wherever that is necessary." "I believe in free enterprise and always have," he reiterated. "I believe that private enterprise can give full employment to our people." Abandoning the "matured economy" theory of his Commonwealth Club speech, he spoke hopefully of "an expansion of our peacetime productive capacity that will require new facilities, new plants, new equipment—capable of hiring millions of men." With the economy operating at full speed under wartime conditions it was easy for him to forget the incompleteness of recovery under the New Deal and to refer proudly to the manner in which "we . . . fought our way out of the economic crisis."

He showed a like optimism about foreign relations. In January,

1945, he told Congress that the misuse of power could no longer be a controlling factor in international life. "Power must be linked with responsibility and obliged to defend and justify itself within the framework of the general good." He spoke of "a people's peace" based upon independence and self-determination, and expressed his intention that the United Nations should have "the power to act quickly and decisively to keep the peace by force, if necessary." Returning from Yalta shortly before his death, he said cheerfully of his relations with Churchill and Stalin: "We achieved a unity of thought and a way of getting along together." The Crimean Conference spelled "the end of the system of unilateral action and exclusive alliances and spheres of influence and balance of power and all the other expedients that have been tried for centuries and have always failed."

That Roosevelt ever had deep faith in the United Nations as an agency of world peace is doubtful. His original and spontaneous reaction was to seek for peace and stability not through a general concert of all the nations but rather through a four-power establishment of the United States, Great Britain, Russia, and China, which was to police the world. Cordell Hull reports that in the spring of 1943 Roosevelt wanted all other nations, including France, to be disarmed. "He believed," says Hull, "in the efficacy of direct personal contact between Churchill, Stalin, Chiang Kai-shek, and himself, and he thought that this direct relationship among the chiefs of the four nations would result in efficient future management of the world." Rather than an over-all world organization he favored regional organizations, which were to leave all questions of peace and security to the four great powers. Once when Secretary Hull and some internationalist visitors who wanted a world organization asked him: "Aren't you at least in favor of a world secretariat?" he laughingly replied: "I'll give you the Pentagon or the Empire State Building. You can put the world secretariat there." By the summer of 1943, however, he had accepted the idea of world organization and in the fall he approved the draft of the four-nation declaration adopted at the Moscow Conference of that year, which called for "a general international organization . . . for the maintenance of international peace and security."

Roosevelt has often been criticized for a tendency to think that a clash of interests or principles can be resolved by bringing together two representatives of opposing forces and persuading them to shake hands and be convivial. It was natural to his mode of thought to rest his hopes for future peace upon personal amenability and personal understandings among the leaders of the great powers. In this sense his philosophy of international relations, however democratic as to ends, was far from democratic as to means. In the case of Russia he seems at one time to have had the curious idea that dealing with a dictatorship might be easier than dealing with a parliamentary democracy. "What helps a lot," Vice Admiral Ross T. McIntire remembers him saying, "is that Stalin is the only man I have to convince. Joe doesn't worry about a Congress or a Parliament. He's the whole works."[16] His position between Churchill and Stalin was that of a compromiser and mediator, in the spirit of "weave the two together," and he evidently felt that it would continue to be necessary to "referee" between Britain and Russia. As he had once stood between the Al Smith men and the rural Protestant Democrats, later between the N.A.M. and William Green, and still later between Jesse Jones and Henry Wallace, he now felt that he stood between Soviet and British imperialisms.

How did he propose to deal with these imperialisms? The answer is clearer in the case of England and the other Western European imperial powers. Roosevelt was moved by the plight of the colonial peoples,[17] he hoped to better their condition, and felt that it would be necessary to loosen the bonds of the British,

[16] Arthur Bliss Lane, in *I Saw Poland Betrayed,* comments on Roosevelt's "exaggerated confidence in the power of his charm to persuade diplomatic and political adversaries of his point of view. He seemed to feel that this charm was particularly effective on Stalin."

[17] In a memorandum to Cordell Hull, January 12, 1944, he wrote concerning the plight of Iran that 99 per cent of its people were in bondage to the other one per cent and "do not own their own land and cannot keep their own production or convert it into money or property." "I was rather thrilled," he added, "with the idea of using Iran as an example of what we could do by an unselfish American policy. . . ." Not long afterward he wrote to Hull of his conviction that Indo-China should become independent, rather than revert to France. "France has had the country—thirty million inhabitants—for nearly one hundred years, and the people are worse off than they were at the beginning."

French, and Dutch empires; he believed that the British and French were informally leagued together to sustain each other's colonial possessions. Further, the United States was handicapped in its conduct of the war in the East by the keen resentment of British imperialism among Oriental peoples. During the war American influence was thrown on the side of the colonial peoples, and ultimate independence for India, Burma, Syria, and Lebanon were proposed. At one time Roosevelt said to his son Elliott that postwar discussions should take up the status of India, Burma, Java, Indo-China, Indonesia, the African colonies, Egypt, and Palestine. Secretary Hull records, however, that Britain, France, and the Netherlands were not pressed at any time for an immediate grant of self-government to their colonies. This, it was expected, "would come in time."

Roosevelt's opposition to the colonial empires was not simply altruistic; American commercial interests—for instance, the vast oil concessions that had been made to American companies in Saudi Arabia—were much in his mind. Although he believed that "imperialists"—he used the word as an epithet—had been short-sighted in taking a purely exploitative view of the colonies and that much greater potentialities lay in them if the welfare of the colonial peoples were taken into account, he was also aware of the possibilities for American trade in an economic revivification of the colonial areas under American encouragement. Elliott Roosevelt pictures him talking with the Sultan in Churchill's presence about concessions for American firms in Morocco, and promising Chiang Kai-shek that if Chiang came to terms with the Chinese Communists and democratized his government he would support him in trying to terminate the special rights of the Western empires in Hong Kong, Shanghai, and Canton.

Roosevelt appears to have believed that the ruthless imperialism of the older colonial powers might be replaced by a liberal and benevolent American penetration that would be of advantage both to the natives and to American commerce.[18] He believed that

---

[18] During the nineteenth century Britain had played some such role in Latin America and southern and eastern Europe, supporting nationalism and independence for oppressed peoples and reaping trade advantages from the disintegration of other empires.

British and German bankers had had world trade "pretty well sewn up in their pockets for a long time," to the disadvantage of the United States. Arguing that "equality of peoples involves the utmost freedom of competitive trade," he appealed to Churchill to open markets "for healthy competition" and to dissolve the British Empire trade agreements.[19]

All this seems characteristic—the quick sympathy with oppressed colonials, the ideal of liberation and welfare, and yet the calculating interest in American advantage. Just as the Chamber of Commerce's N.R.A. idea had been clothed in the language of the liberal social planners and had brought gains to the most hardridden sections of the working class, so a new American conquest of world markets might well go forth under the banner of international welfare work.

It was not as evident during Roosevelt's life how critical American-Russian relations would be, and in this sphere his conceptions were not so sharply defined. In February, 1940, at the time of the Russo-Finnish war, he had said that Russia, "as everybody who has the courage to face the facts knows, is run by a dictatorship as absolute as any other dictatorship in the world." But when he met the absolute dictator at Teheran he found him "altogether impressive." "I'm sure we'll hit it off," he said to Elliott, and later remarked that he liked working with Stalin because there was "nothing devious" about his talk. He seemed to think that he had impressed upon Stalin that the United States and Britain were not allied in a bloc against the Soviet Union. "If I can convince him," he said to Vice Admiral McIntire, "that our offer of cooperation is on the square and that we want to be comrades

---

[19] Roosevelt was by no means indifferent to the coming postwar problems of Great Britain's economy. He was much concerned with maintaining Britain's export market, which he felt should be done at Germany's expense. His dominating conception was that Britain's economic fortunes were inverse to Germany's. Although he privately repudiated the idea expressed in the Quebec Conference of making Germany an "agricultural and pastoral nation," he did feel that postwar control of the German economy should be so managed as to work to Britain's advantage. The British Empire must not be permitted to collapse while Germany built up her exports and a new armaments capacity. "The real nub of the situation," he wrote to Hull, "is to keep Britain from going into complete bankruptcy at the end of the war."

rather than enemies, I'm betting that he'll come in." If Roosevelt ever outlined a specific strategy to cope with an aggressive Soviet imperialism, it has not yet been published. At the time of his death the pattern of the "cold war" was only beginning to emerge. Certainly he had no magic formula for getting along with the Russians. James F. Byrnes has taken pains to blast "the legend that our relations with the Soviet Union began to deteriorate only after his death," by revealing that Stalin charged the Anglo-American allies with making separate and secret peace arrangements with Germany in the spring of 1945 and that he angered Roosevelt by questioning the truthfulness of Roosevelt's denials. On the day of his death Roosevelt sent a message to Churchill advising that in a forthcoming speech to the House of Commons "the general Soviet problem" should be minimized. He added: "We must be firm, however, and our course thus far is correct."

It was an ambitious plan of action that Roosevelt outlined in the last year of his life—to lead the nation toward full production and full employment, to realize a sweeping bill of economic rights under private enterprise, enlarge American trade abroad, serve as a diplomatic buffer between Britain and Russia and between China and all the powers that harassed her, dissect the great colonial empires, and bring sanitation, justice, and freedom to the colonial underdogs. This combination, as motley as the various undertakings of the early New Deal, has come to seem even less feasible in the few years since Roosevelt's death than it did during his lifetime; but the world of 1942–1945 has been transformed, and it is idle to project too far into the future the plans of such a changeable statesman. To take his statements literally, to look upon them as anything more than a rhetorical formulation of his preferences, would be a mistake; there seems no more reason to take his words as a literal guide to his projected action than there would have been to expect him to fulfill both his 1932 pledges to balance the budget and give adequate relief to the unemployed.

Roosevelt seems a more flexible and a cleverer politician than Wilson, much his superior in the craft of maneuver, but less serious, less deliberate, and less responsible. What we know of his conduct at the international conferences with Stalin and Churchill compares unfavorably in moral tone if not in practical effect with Wilson's at Versailles. It is hard to imagine Wilson trying to smooth over a conflict between Stalin and Churchill over the prospective treatment of captured Nazis with a joke about the precise number that would have to be killed. It is almost as hard to imagine Roosevelt expressing any such poignant understanding of the human consequences of the war on the home front as Wilson expressed to Frank Cobb, or straining as desperately at Yalta or Teheran as Wilson did at Paris for detailed factual understanding, for intellectual consistency and moral responsibility.

Roosevelt's reputation, however, will remain greater than Wilson's, and in good part because the circumstances of his martyrdom were more auspicious. Wilson died only after his defeat was a matter of historical record; Roosevelt died in the midst of things, and it is still possible for those under his spell to believe that everything would have been different if only he had survived to set the world on the right path in the postwar period. Further, the very lack of confidence in the American future and of a positive program of ideas increases popular faith in the wonder-working powers of the great man. Roosevelt is bound to be the dominant figure in the mythology of any resurgent American liberalism. There are ample texts in his writings for men of good will to feed upon; but it would be fatal to rest content with his belief in personal benevolence, personal arrangements, the sufficiency of good intentions and month-to-month improvisation, without trying to achieve a more inclusive and systematic conception of what is happening in the world.

MORTON J. FRISCH

✪

Roosevelt the Conservator:
A Rejoinder to Hofstadter

All political life concerns itself with preservation or change, that is, with the very practical business of deciding what to preserve and what not to preserve. Hence it is always salutary to be provided with critical comments on our traditions for criticism surely points in the direction of remedies. But, more important, criticism forces us to think seriously about what we hold worthwhile as a nation, or to re-evaluate our traditions. Richard Hofstadter presents his study *The American Political Tradition and the Men Who Made It* as a "reinterpretation of our political traditions," and as a guide for the future (p. vii).[1] As he indicates, especially at a time when "the traditional ground is shifting under our feet," it is imperative to gain "fresh perspectives" on our traditions (p. x). And this means gaining fresh perspectives on the men, or the careers of the men, who made those traditions. Hofstadter himself has a sense of the failure of the tradition. He sees the liberal tradition as "rudderless and demoralized." What is needed is a "new conception of the world" to replace "the ideology

[1] Richard Hofstadter, *The American Political Tradition and the Men Who Made It* (New York: Alfred A. Knopf, 1948).

Reprinted from *Journal of Politics*, Vol. XXV, No. 2 (May 1963), pp. 361–372, by permission of Journal of Politics. Copyright © 1963 by Journal of Politics.

of self-help, free enterprise, competition, and beneficent cupidity"
(p. vii). Certainly Hofstadter is right in suggesting that a properly
ordered democracy requires something more than beneficent cupidity or covetousness. But we seriously wonder whether his reduction
of the tradition or rather the public leaders who made that tradition to their lowest common denominator points in the direction of
the democratic realism which he seeks.

The particular leaders whom Hofstadter selects for his "studies
in the ideology of American statesmanship" were chosen because
they best represented or reflected the tradition (p. x). Presumably
therefore he understood the tradition before he made his selection.
His last essay entitled "Franklin D. Roosevelt: The Patrician as
Opportunist" contains a discussion of a remarkably representative
leader. Roosevelt achieves particular relevance as a statesman, in
Hofstadter's understanding, by virtue of his being sensitively at-
tuned to the play of political forces around him. He is characterized as a "warmhearted, informal patrician" who believed that
"if a large number of people wanted something very badly, it is
important that they be given some measure of satisfaction" (p.
317). And we are told that "although the influence of great men is
usually exaggerated, Roosevelt must be granted at least a marginal
influence on the course of history. No personality has ever expressed the American popular temper so articulately or with such
exclusiveness. . . . [He had] a sharp intuitive knowledge of
popular feeling. Because he was content in large measure to follow
public opinion, he was able to give it that necessary additional
impulse of leadership which can translate desires into policies"
(pp. 315–316). In other words, Roosevelt helped to influence, but
especially reflected the American popular temper.

To measure Roosevelt as a statesman means to measure how he
influenced as well as how he *reflected* the American popular
temper. And if there were parts of our popular temper which he
really influenced or fashioned, he could not at the same time have
reflected them. But Hofstadter does not preserve this distinction
and therefore what was in the popular temper or mind and what
was in the mind of Roosevelt becomes blurred. In his introductory
essay, Hofstadter explains that this study aims to analyze "men of

action in their capacity as leaders of popular thought, which is not their most impressive function." It is less important, he continues, "to estimate how great our public men have been than to analyze their historical roles" (pp. x, xi). But unless we examine what makes our leaders great or influential leaders, how will we be able to learn what happened to their aims and principles in the course of American history? In other words, how would we know what their historical roles really were?

Hofstadter has conceded that "the New Deal marked many deviations in the American course" and that Roosevelt must be granted at least a marginal influence on the course of American history (pp. x, 315). But what is the character of these marginal influences and deviations? The New Deal, says Hofstadter, had left "upon the statute books general measures of permanent value." And we may reasonably assume that he has in mind such measures as the Social Security Act, the National Labor Relations Act, and the Fair Labor Standards Act, all of which are mentioned in the Roosevelt essay. Hofstadter further states that the New Deal had established "the principle that the entire community through the agency of the federal government has some responsibility for mass welfare, and it has impressed its values so deeply on the national mind that the Republicans were compelled to endorse its major accomplishments in election platforms" (p. 340). Here, as Hofstadter himself admits, Roosevelt had put something into, or impressed something upon, the national mind, and in this sense his statesmanship constituted something more than a mere expression or reflection of the national mind.

Hofstadter's emphasis on the representative rather than creative character of our public leaders reveals itself in his first essay entitled "The Founding Fathers: An Age of Realism." Consider, for example, his statement, that "despite their keen sense of history, [the Founding Fathers] felt that they were founding novel institutions and glorified in the newness of what they were doing" (p. vi). Apparently the Founding Fathers were not founding novel institutions at all. According to Hofstadter, what they wanted was known as "balanced government," an idea "at least as old as Aristotle and Polybius," and this "ancient conception" had received "new sanction in the eighteenth century" (p. 7). This notion of balanced government, Hofstadter continues, was most clearly elaborated by John Adams who believed that "the aristocracy and the democracy must be made to neutralize each other" and that "each element should be given its own house of the legislature" (p. 10). Presumably the point of view of the Founding Fathers which Adams was reflecting was that the Senate was meant to be *aristocratic* and the House of Representatives *democratic,* and that these aristocratic and democratic elements would neutralize each other. But was the Senate really intended to be an aristocratic institution? And did the Founding Fathers really mean to secure a mixed or balanced republic, that is, to secure a balance between aristocratic and democratic elements within the confines of a republic?

Hofstadter would be correct in suggesting that the Founding Fathers conceived of the Senate as a safeguard for property rights. But *safeguarding* property rights is not the same thing as *representing* property rights. As Madison understood the distinction: "The senate there [meaning the House of Lords], instead of being elected for a term of six years, and of being unconfined to particular families or fortunes, is an hereditary family of opulent nobles."[2] But membership in the Senate required no property qualification, and Senators were to be appointed or elected in a manner prescribed by the state legislature which, in turn, were elected by the people. Hence the Senate, as it was actually proposed in the Constitution, was intended to operate only in a way (and these are Madison's own words) that would be consistent with "the genuine principles of republican government."[3] It was not intended as an aristocratic body.

Obviously the English Parliament provided the Founding Fathers with the model of a divided legislature. But the intention of a divided legislature in the English Parliament was to secure a balance between aristocratic and democratic elements. And this was connected with the premodern preference of Aristotle and Polybius for a mixed or balanced government. For Aristotle and

[2] *The Federalist,* No. 63.
[3] *Ibid.,* No. 62.

Polybius, the mixture of forms within the framework of a single government contributed to its stability, for the defects of the simple forms would be canceled out, and hence it would last longer than any of the simple forms. But the parceling out of different kinds of powers to different branches and sub-branches of government, installed by the Founding Fathers, had a decidedly different emphasis than the arrangements contemplated by Aristotle and Polybius and operative in the English Constitution. The Founding Fathers had no notion whatsoever of introducing an aristocratic element into their system through the mechanism of divided legislative power. Their concern was far more with the liberty of the individual than with the security of the state, or at least they tended to see the maintenance of republican institutions as the means of safeguarding individual liberties. Separation of powers was intended to prevent the concert of representatives in any scheme of oppression against the liberties of the people. Hofstadter's failure to separate the intent of the mixed government of the English Constitution from that of separation of powers in the American Constitution could only result in the depreciation of the innovations of the Founding Fathers. He does concede that the debates over the Constitution were carried on "at an intellectual level that is rare in politics, and that the Constitution itself is one of the world's masterpieces of practical statecraft" (p. 5). But as a whole the innovations of the Founding Fathers are scrupulously deemphasized as is the creative statesmanship of Roosevelt.

The main thrust of Hofstadter's criticism of Roosevelt and the New Deal is that the President failed to think through the organic ills of society and therefore achieve a more realistic conception of what was happening in the world (pp. 324, 352). For example, Roosevelt saw the development of big business and monopoly as a threat to democratic institutions, but he was "equivocal" about how the threat was to be controlled. Hofstadter continues: "Although [Roosevelt's] argument carried to the brink of socialism, it was not socialism he was proposing. . . . How the reformist state was to police the corporations without either destroying free enterprise or itself succumbing to the massed strength of corporate opposition was not made clear. Roosevelt did not tackle such problems in theory, and events spared him the necessity of facing them in practice" (pp. 341–342). But the alternatives, as Roosevelt well understood, need not be socialism or the corporate state. In recommending the regulation of public utility holding companies to Congress in 1935, the President explained: "I am against private socialism of concentrated private power as thoroughly as I am against governmental socialism. The one is equally as dangerous as the other; and destruction of private socialism is utterly essential to avoid governmental socialism."[4] Perhaps Hofstadter is somewhat impatient with the moderate Rooseveltian answer to the problem of big business and monopoly, namely, government regulation. And government regulation, if properly guided prevents the destruction of private enterprise. Roosevelt made precisely this assumption. We must recognize that Roosevelt was a statesman, and that he was trying to get certain things done. And therefore he had to make some very practical decisions as, for example, whether at a given time a particular enterprise should or should not be regulated or whether there should be more or less regulation in certain industries. But in order to measure his performance as a statesman, as Hofstadter suggests, we would need to consider whether he thought very deeply about what he was trying to get done as well as the practical wisdom of his actions.

What about the President's proposal to reform the Supreme Court in 1937? Was he able to place that proposal in some broader political perspective? Or was he simply caught up in the immediate issues of that controversy? In a later work, entitled *The Age of Reform, from Bryan to F.D.R.,* Hofstadter argues that his fight with the Supreme Court was begun "not in the interest of some large democratic principle," but because the Court's decisions made it impossible for him to achieve "a managerial reorganization of society." Roosevelt's first concern was not that judicial review was "undemocratic," but that the federal government had been stripped of its power to deal effectively with economic problems. If he had opened up the whole question of the

---

[4] Samuel I. Rosenman, ed., *The Public Papers and Addresses of Franklin D. Roosevelt,* 13 vols. (New York, 1938–1950), IV, 101. Cited hereafter as FDR, *PPA.*

propriety of judicial review in a democratic society, Hofstadter continues, he would have been following a more "high-minded approach." But instead Roosevelt offered the pretense that the advanced age of the justices prevented them from performing their judicial duties. And it remained for Senator Burton K. Wheeler, whom Hofstadter describes as a "principled man," to propose an amendment to the Constitution permitting Congress to override judicial vetoes of its own acts.[5] Roosevelt's approach was presumably *unprincipled,* that is, unrelated to some large democratic principle.

Soon after the Court plan was announced, Arthur Krock of *The New York Times* interviewed the President, and the latter made it clear in that interview that the issue was in his estimation "but part of a larger problem." As Krock relates the interview: The President sees a future "far more dangerous if he is balked of his solutions than if they are adopted. He sees a growing belief among the underprivileged that judicial supremacy is certain to cancel the progressive and humanitarian efforts of Congress and the Executive. He sees this belief easily firing into desperate conviction; and he does not happen to doubt, should this happen, a leader will arise to tread down democracy in the name of reform." And Krock continues: "The President has not forgotten Huey P. Long. While he does not say so in precise words, he entertains the opinion that one important reason why the Louisiana Dictator was not able to extend his dominion further during his lifetime was because he was fortunately co-existent with wiser and more sincere remedies for the conditions which produced Long." And had public opinion against the Hoover Administration "not been sufficiently formed by the election of 1932, and had Mr. Hoover therefore been reelected, the President believes that Huey Long would immediately have become a menace to the democratic process."[6] But Hofstadter understands the President's opposition to Long primarily in terms of his threat to the Democratic ticket in 1936. A secret poll

[5] Richard Hofstadter, *The Age of Reform, from Bryan to F.D.R.* (New York, 1956), p. 309n.
[6] *The New York Times,* February 28, 1937, p. 33.

had been taken in 1935, and the Democratic National Committee was concerned about the Louisiana Governor's strength. And Hofstadter relates that Raymond Moley was "horrified" to hear Roosevelt speak about the need for doing something "to steal Long's thunder" (p. 337). But what Hofstadter has not considered is the fact that Roosevelt, even before he became President, referred to Long as "one of the two most dangerous men in the United States" and at that time indicated the need for doing something about him.[7]

We must not forget that Franklin Roosevelt and Adolf Hitler came to power within a few months of each other. Hitler actually became German Chancellor in January, 1933. And Roosevelt never overlooked the possibility of a similar occurrence in the United States. One of the original Brain Trusters, Rexford Guy Tugwell, relates a conversation in 1932 which reveals Roosevelt's uneasiness: "There was latent, he thought, not far below the uneasy surface of our disrupted society, an impulse among a good many . . . men used to having their own way, mostly industrialists who directed affairs without being questioned, a feeling that democracy had run its course and that the totalitarians had grasped the necessities of the time. People wanted strong leadership; they were sick of uncertainty, anxious for security, and willing to trade liberty for it."[8] In his 1940 annual message to Congress, the President declared "that dictatorship—and the philosophy of force that justifies and accompanies dictatorship—have originated in almost every case in the necessity for drastic action to improve internal conditions in places where democratic action for one reason or another has failed to respond to modern needs and modern demands."[9] Roosevelt continually emphasized the lesson of history "that dictatorships do not grow out of strong and successful governments, but out of weak and helpless ones."[10] As the experience of the present time, not to mention that of the

[7] Rexford G. Tugwell, "The Progressive Orthodoxy of Franklin D. Roosevelt," *Ethics* (October 1953), p. 18.

[8] Tugwell, *The Democratic Roosevelt* (New York, 1957), p. 349.

[9] FDR, *PPA*, IX, 1.

[10] *Ibid.*, VII, 242.

recent past, serves to show, in southeastern Asia and elsewhere, the dictatorship of the proletariat is considered preferable to the status quo if the status quo means disease and starvation. And in such circumstances any change is regarded as a change for the better. One of the President's favorite quotations was: "The most dreadful failure of which any form of government can be guilty is simply to lose touch with reality, because out of this failure all imaginable forms of evil grow."[11] It was his considered opinion that the Supreme Court majority in its opposition to crucial New Deal reforms had simply lost touch with the economic realities of the period.

Hofstadter seems to take it for granted that the principle of judicial review, which the President did not seek to circumscribe, is "undemocratic." But as the Founding Fathers well understood (not to mention Woodrow Wilson and Franklin Roosevelt), a democratic regime requires certain checks or controls on the mechanism of majority rule in order to maintain itself because every regime has within itself the seeds of its own destruction. Needless to say, the practice of judicial review is very much a part of our democratic tradition, and it was recognized as such by the President despite his charges, during the course of the court fight, that the Supreme Court had been misconstruing the Constitution. Surely, challenging the Court's interpretation of the Constitution is not the same thing as restricting the right of the Court to interpret the Constitution. The President was not willing to do the latter. He properly characterized Senator Wheeler's proposed amendment that Congress be permitted to override judicial vetoes of its own acts as "an attack upon the very function of the Court and upon the legitimate exercise of that function." And he went on to say that he was not prepared, nor did he consider it advisable, to undermine "one of the foundations of our democracy."[12] In a letter to Joseph M. Patterson, written before the court plan was ever presented, the President expressed the hope that "the problem created for the Nation by the Supreme Court" could be faced and

[11] *Ibid.*, V, 387.
[12] *Ibid.*, VI, lxiii.

solved "without getting away from our underlying principles."[13] And "without getting away from our underlying principles" required, as far as the President was concerned, the retention of the principle of judicial review.

Certainly, as Hofstadter states, the President's first concern was that "the federal government had been stripped . . . of its power to deal with economic problems." But surely the preservation of a democratic regime, or the ability of a democratic regime to deal with its own crises, economic or political, is in line with "large democratic principles" which give to that regime its "democratic" character. Prior to the announcement of the court plan, the President stated that "we have come to realize that a nation cannot function as a healthy democracy with part of its citizens living under good conditions and part forced to live under circumstances inimical to the general welfare."[14] The democratic society which then existed was essentially a good society, but in the President's estimation many improvements still needed to be made. And if these improvements were not made, there existed the possibility of that society degenerating to the point of collapse, and fascism emerging in its wake. The President believed that there was a real danger to the nation if the Supreme Court majority persisted in its attempt to invalidate crucial New Deal measures. Indeed, his struggle with that Court was begun in the interest of some large democratic principle, and that was the preservation of our democratic institutions. And he chose to accomplish this objective without altering the traditional power of the Supreme Court which in fact would have amounted to a change in the Constitution in the broader sense. Therefore he *was* able to see the court plan in its broader political perspective and realize its central significance in the politics of the New Deal period.

Hofstadter states that his studies have convinced him that more emphasis needs to be placed on the "common climate" of American opinions within our political tradition. But, as he observes, the existence of this climate has been obscured by "the tendency [of

[13] Elliott Roosevelt, ed., *F.D.R.: His Personal Letters, 1928–45*, 2 vols. (New York, 1950), I, 625.
[14] FDR, *PPA*, V, 685.

historians] to place political conflict in the foreground of history."
The conflicts are constantly reactivated, while the commonly
shared convictions are most of the time neglected (pp. vii, ix). But
how could the study of history and especially political history
properly be separated from political conflict? Is not political
conflict, or the struggle between competing groups within the
political community, the very crux of political history? And how
can Roosevelt be understood apart from political conflict when it
is in political conflict or crisis that his superbly realistic statesmanship makes its appearance? We must read Roosevelt, as well as our
other influential political leaders, not primarily as representatives
of the public mind, but for what we can learn about how they
influenced the course of our national political life. It is important
to estimate or measure how influential our public men have been.
But in order to make such an estimate, we must examine, in the
case of Roosevelt, the important political conflicts or crises of his
career; for it is in political crisis, acting under the pressure of
events, that the President was drawn to "the depths of the problem," and it is here that his highest thought emerges.

Hofstadter has characterized Roosevelt as "a public instrument
of the most delicate receptivity" and thus arrives at the conclusion
that his successes as a statesman were based almost wholly upon
his responsiveness to what the people wanted, and his ability to
translate those wants into public policies. He was a more flexible
and cleverer politician than Wilson, but "less serious, less deliberate, and less responsible" (pp. 317, 351). But as Roosevelt's
handling of the crisis of the Great Depression showed, he understood very well what it means to be *responsible* for as well as
responsive to the public interest or need. He once suggested that
most of the great accomplishments in American history had been
made by Presidents who so "truly" interpreted the "needs" and
"wishes" of the people that they were supported in their great
tasks by the people.[15] But of course "needs" are not the same as
"wishes" and are sometimes opposed to wishes. What the people
wish for may fall far short of their needs, and in fact may be

[15] Basil Rauch, ed., *Franklin D. Roosevelt: Selected Speeches, Messages,
Press Conferences and Letters* (New York, 1957), p. 37.

detrimental to or even destructive of their needs or necessities. If the people as a whole were always able to determine what their needs really are, there would be little conflict between needs and wishes. And sometimes needs are more easily discernible or more visible as, for example, in a crisis. As Roosevelt observed: "It is only in a crisis that we look back to our common concerns. The stress of a vast emergency rudely awakes us all from our local concerns and turns us to wider [or public] concerns."[16] But at other times the needs will appear less obvious and hence the conflict between needs and wishes. To interpret the needs and wishes of the people, as Roosevelt suggested, would require pointing the wishes of the people in the direction of their needs. Indeed, to convince the people to wish for what they really need is the Herculean task for the democratic statesman. And this task is made especially difficult by the fact that a democratic people are the ultimate judges as to what constitutes their needs. What Roosevelt did was to point the American Democracy in the direction of its needs within the most difficult context of democracy.

The epigraph at the beginning of Hofstadter's introductory essay reads: "In times of change and danger when there is a quicksand of fear under men's reasoning, a sense of continuity with generations gone before can stretch like a lifeline across the scary present" (p. v). But this quotation does not really reflect his understanding of our present situation for our sense of continuity with generations gone before, as he sees it, would be a very *inadequate* lifeline indeed. This quotation comes from a chapter in John Dos Passos' *The Ground We Stand On* entitled "The Use of the Past." But Hofstadter's epigraph contains only part of the sentence. The last part, which is omitted, reads: ". . . and get us past that idiot delusion of the exceptional." As it appears in Dos Passos, the full sentence is: "In times of change and danger when there is a quicksand of fear under men's reasoning, a sense of continuity with generations gone before can stretch like a lifeline across the scary present and get us past that idiot delusion of the exceptional."[17] In other words, a sense of the tradition has

16 FDR, *PPA*, I, 631.
17 John Dos Passos, *The Ground We Stand On* (New York, 1941), p. 3.

salutary effects, not the least important of which is ridding ourselves of that "idiot delusion" that our times are "exceptional"
times. And Dos Passos states also: ". . . our problem is not so
very different now [from that of the Founding Fathers]."[18] As
the full statement suggests, Dos Passos is recommending the
recovery of a tradition not for the sake of transcending it, but for
the sake of *using* it. And, as he advises, if we fail to cope with the
problem of adjusting the industrial machine to human needs, "it
won't be for the lack of the political tradition."[19] That is, he
believes we already have a satisfactory political tradition from
which to work and our failing is the neglect of that tradition.

As we have previously indicated, the whole burden of Hofstadter's thesis, the introductory essay notwithstanding, is that
Americans need a new conception of the world or a clearly
articulated break with the traditional or inherited faith, and *not* a
sense of continuity with generations gone before (pp. vii, 324,
352). But Dos Passos says that the "worldpicture" which the
Founders had was one of "the grandest and most nearly realized
worldpictures in all history."[20] And therefore, "in times like ours,
when old institutions are caving in and being replaced by new
institutions not necessarily in accord with men's preconceived
hopes, political thought has to look backwards as well as for-
wards."[21] Certainly, Dos Passos continues, we would need to
know "which realities of our life yesterday and our life today we
can believe in and work for," but the permanent basis for the
worldpicture into which we can fit our present lives is afforded by
the traditions and habits of the Founding Fathers.[22] Hofstadter
says that Americans have found it more convenient to see where
they have been than where they are going (p. v). But Dos Passos
says that we need to know what kind of "firm ground" other men,
belonging to generations before us, have found "to stand on."[23]

18 *Ibid.*, p. 13.
19 *Ibid.*, p. 8.
20 *Ibid.*, pp. 11, 12.
21 *Ibid.*, p. 3.
22 *Ibid.*, p. 11.
23 *Ibid.*, p. 3.

Hofstadter actually reverses the Dos Passos thesis for he recommends a *break* with the tradition. But we never learn what the character of that break should be like or in what direction that break should move. It would then appear that Hofstadter's impatience with Roosevelt is based upon Roosevelt's failure to found wholly new modes and orders and *our* question is whether Roosevelt's or Hofstadter's understanding of the importance of continuity is the better.

✪

History's Bone of Contention: Franklin D. Roosevelt

The title of this chapter is intended to suggest that a definitive, not to say final, evaluation of Franklin D. Roosevelt cannot appear for generations. That is not because of any difficulty in mobilizing the facts, nor is it because of the complex character of the man. It is because his personality, appeal and policies so divided people that those who loved him will hear no evil, and those who hated him will tolerate no praise. In such an atmosphere, calm and judicial evaluations are lost.

Perhaps this is because he was so good for so many and so bad for so many others. His major achievements cut deeply into the social structure of our country. Since 1933 there has been a revolutionary shift in the economic strata. Those who have benefited will revere Roosevelt's memory. Those who were dispossessed will revile it. And children and children's children will inherit those conflicting judgments.

It is not for me in this space to contribute to that debate. For the reasons stated above, it would be futile. It would take volumes to do it. And it would be foreign to the purpose of this book.

For that reason, I may disappoint two kinds of reader: Those in

Reprinted from *27 Masters of Politics* (New York: Funk and Wagnalls Co., 1949), pp. 30–45, by permission of the author.

whom there is a lust to probe the motives and lacerate the reputation of anyone who speaks anything but praise of Roosevelt; and those who seek in every contemporary discourse on Roosevelt some new revelation of his duplicity or failure.

I am writing about people who had something to teach about politics, and Roosevelt had a great deal. I shall therefore set down some considerations and judgments of Roosevelt only as a politician. In that role he was a master—an immensely successful one. His capacity and conduct in the fields of economic and social reform, in the reaches of human affairs embraced by the Presidency will be considered only in so far as they throw light upon Roosevelt the politician.

Roosevelt's career will remind us once more that success in politics demands more than casual interest or belated addiction. It is no profession to be taken up in later life, like golf or bridge, after success in business or in a profession. It demands long experience, constant attention and, what is most important, a radical adaptation of mental processes. It demands personal and environmental advantages denied to most. It is a jealous art and can tolerate only slight time for other human concerns. Roosevelt had most of the necessary advantages and paid the price and the penalties.

We need not speculate about why or when he decided to give his life to politics, because such decisions are seldom knowingly made. The circumstances of his early environment, as well as the nature of his mind and character dominated his course.

The environment into which he was born and spent his early life is a familiar story. Economic security, association with eminent people of his time, the historical memories of the Hudson Valley and the prestige and name of his distant cousin, Theodore, were among his advantages. Roosevelt himself once wrote the following rule for a beginner contemplating the vicissitudes of a political career:

"I think we can lay down a rule covering a political career entered into with the highest purpose of serving one's community or one's country. Either the individual should have enough money of his own safely invested to take care of him when not holding office . . . or else he should have business connections, a profession or a job to which he can return from time to time."

His personality lent further advantages and incentives. He was unusually attractive in physique and in manner. He liked people, and most people liked him. His mind tended to discursiveness, except when politics was concerned. He was what highbrowism lists as activist. He did not quarrel with life as he found it. The world into which he was born was something to be worked with and to provide him with satisfactions.

His mentality was perfectly suited to the life he was to lead in pursuit of political eminence and power. His academic record at Harvard and at the Columbia Law School was mediocre. There is no evidence of even a mild interest in history, theoretical politics, psychology or economics. This is the more remarkable because in his day Harvard and Columbia offered the unparalleled incentive of courses in those fields given by brilliant and distinguished men. In this respect, his absorption of those offerings was markedly inferior to that of T.R., who avidly devoured whatever was within reach at Harvard and later at Columbia.

We are almost shocked at the contrast between F.D.R.'s casual interest in fine thinking and classical culture and the prodigious industry of Jefferson at William and Mary, of Madison at the College of New Jersey, of Woodrow Wilson in his father's study and at Davidson, Princeton and Johns Hopkins, or the mastery of the few books within Lincoln's reach.

Roosevelt simply was not reflective or philosophical. He had little patience with the abstractions of mathematics and economics and, so far as I was ever able to discern in five years of association, he was quite ignorant of such political classics as are the primary reading of the younger students at Oxford, Cambridge, or the best of American universities.

Even Bryan had manifested an interest in ameliorative and reformist literature, although he neglected basic information. But Roosevelt as a young man showed none of that broad interest in economic pain-killers which developed in his Presidential years, and even then his interest was in their adaptation to the exigencies of politics.

One can hardly recommend this sort of preparation for statesmanship, but it had immense reward for Roosevelt. It freed his mind for intense, almost passionate concern with matters which most serious people regard as the escapist pastimes of idle hours. And these, when pursued with intense concentration, are invaluable in politics.

Roosevelt's lack of capacity for fruitful and revealing reflection, his meager scholarly interests, his frail delvings into complex economic problems and his juvenile off-hour interests were positive advantages to him as a politician. They were understandable by the generality of people, whose interests were similar.

To a philosopher, a scientist or a great lawyer, the preoccupations of a politican seem to be the interests of a person too lazy to apply himself to serious things. This is a gross underestimation of the politician's job. For beneath the surface he is applying his mental faculties to exceedingly complex subject matter, and if he is to be successful he must labor with incessant energy and meticulous care. For political genius is the capacity to give continuous, undivided and sedulous attention to matters that to most serious people seem too trivial to bother with.

Whether Roosevelt chose law as the most convenient avenue to a political career or as a serious vocation is not clear. What we do know is that his residence at the Columbia Law School was not marked by unusual work and that he left before the course was finished. After admission to the bar, he worked casually and briefly in a big law office and, in 1910, turned to active politics, as a candidate for state Senator in his heavily Republican home district.

This was a most orthodox beginning. T.R. had trod the same road nearly thirty years before. And F.D.R.'s campaign showed real capacity for a rookie politician. He adopted a plan which became immensely significant and unfailingly successful in 1928, 1930 and 1932. He neglected the cities in his district, because by tradition they had Democratic tendencies, and saved all his energies for winning the rural Republican votes. Thus, he wasted no time on those who needed no conversion.

He also recognized that it was essential to get attention by spectacular means. He threw his attractive personality at his prospective constituents, driving about in a shiny red automobile in a whirlwind man-to-man canvass of the backroads.

Once in the Albany legislature, he made another shrewd move. He established a home which was pleasant diversion for colleagues wearied by hotel routine and restaurant food.

And most notable of all, Roosevelt, realizing his political inexperience, his previous lack of contact with the press and his shortcomings as a writer of speeches and papers, enlisted as an assistant and tutor a veteran political reporter, Louis Howe, who was destined to remain a sort of political equerry for a quarter of a century.

Later, he seized the opportunity to ally himself with those who hated and distrusted machine politics, the emblem and embodiment of which was Tammany Hall. Thus, by the simple means of selecting a common enemy, he garnered widespread recognition and approval.

Those who called themselves the better people of New York have always had mixed reasons for opposing Tammany. The reasons which they do not express are that Tammany suggests alien ancestry, religious affiliations antagonistic to those of most native Americans, and generally the "lower" and poorer element. The reasons expressed are the corruption, the misgovernment and the autocracy of the machine. These latter evils are not to be minimized. The former, however, are important and pervasive. In any event, opposition to Tammany has made national reputations for Democrats and Republicans alike—from Tilden to Dewey.

Roosevelt's defeat of Charles E. Murphy's Tammany candidate for the United States Senate, Blue-Eyed Billy Sheehan, made him a national figure at small cost. For with his Republican constituency behind him and a national field of action before him, he needed Murphy only as the "heavy" in his play.

The feat, together with his active advocacy of Woodrow Wilson in the 1912 pre-convention fight, brought him favorably to the notice of the new President and, again following the T.R. pattern, Roosevelt received as his reward the Assistant Secretaryship of the Navy.

In 1914, according to Roosevelt's own account, at Wilson's

specific request he ran for the Senate as an independent Democrat. Although it was a futile gesture, it was nevertheless good public relations. The war, the prominence of the navy and Secretary Daniels' unpretentious façade provided an unusual opportunity for the Assistant Secretary. Moreover, it offered a zestful indulgence in the affairs of ships and the sea. The evidence is clear that he did his job well. His nomination and candidacy for the Vice-Presidency in 1920 was, like the 1914 candidacy for the Senatorship, productive of good will.

His subsequent illness was a tragic personal blow. I leave to others the resolution of the question whether adversity enriched his character. I have no clear opinion on that. But on the political side, Roosevelt performed magnificently in overcoming the handicap that his illness placed in the way of his ambition. He continued his political interests with the devoted help of Marguerite LeHand, his secretary, and of Louis Howe.

At the very center of his political activity there was always a mighty flow of postal correspondence. This, as was shown by Jefferson and Lincoln, is indispensable to political success. As I note later in connection with Louis Howe, letter writing came to be so voluminous that the dictation and signing of letters flowed beyond both Roosevelt and Howe and was carried on by several assistants. It billowed up during the Governorship until tens of thousands of Americans cherished friendly missives from Roosevelt.

It hardly needs saying that every political omen pointed to a Republican victory in 1928 and that the Democratic nomination would be worthless. Echoing this general belief among experienced people, Will Rogers wrote a full-length magazine article suggesting that it was a shame to waste Al Smith in such a race and that the Happy Warrior should be saved for 1932. But Smith could not afford to wait. The maturity of his career had arrived, and he had no choice.

The effort to induce Roosevelt to run for Governor raised a serious issue. I am willing to let others interpret the personal considerations involved, among which health loomed very large. In any event, Roosevelt's magnificent physical courage always dominated that consideration as it did in 1944. The political question before him was the advisability of running in a year when only a bare chance of election was offered. In a Republican sweep the New York Governorship almost always went with the rest. So it had been in 1920.

But the considerations in favor of Roosevelt's running for Governor were strong. It would restore his standing as a national figure. It would show that his physical handicap was no bar. If he were defeated, he would for many reasons surely run ahead of Smith. Not least among the considerations was the fact that party men respect and admire a person who for the sake of his party runs in the teeth of defeat. And, finally, there was the chance that he might weather the storm. His judgment was abundantly vindicated.

At this point there should be recorded an uncomfortable element in the mind and calculations of Roosevelt. In those years and well into the first years in the White House, Roosevelt entertained a nagging awareness that might easily but incorrectly be called an inferiority complex. He was deeply sensitive to the fact that so many among the people who knew him—particularly among those who belonged in the social stratum in which he was born and lived—believed, for one reason or another, that he lived beyond his intellectual means.

Al Smith and Newton D. Baker held this opinion. So did men like Judge Seabury and other leaders at the bar and in business in New York. This view attained classical expression in Walter Lippmann's famous column in 1932 in which he said, among other things, that Roosevelt was "a pleasant man who, without any important qualifications for the office, would very much like to be President." In cultural and pseudo-cultural circles in New York, this attitude in the years before 1933 was a fashion. It had some ground in the record. But those who shared it overlooked the intense mental effort Roosevelt had given to a career not as blessed by academic or professional prestige but quite as difficult as law, medicine or scholarship.

This opinion hurt Roosevelt, but he braced his determination to overcome it. It may be added that with this effort came a not quite

Christlike tendency to beat down not only the opinion itself but those who held it.

It is not remarkable, therefore, that when he became governor he did not avail himself of Smith's generous tender of help and advice. Smith people were not retained. Roosevelt determined to take things in his own hands. From then on, the die was cast so far as Smith and all and sundry who held Smith's opinion of Roosevelt were concerned. The mighty engine of governmental power was not destined to spare those who once deluded themselves with a notion that Roosevelt was a weak man.

Once established as Governor, Roosevelt began to set up the machinery by which his succeeding steps to the Presidency could be mounted. Louis Howe was established in New York City. He lived in the Roosevelt house on East 65th Street and worked in the office of a rather anomalous set-up called the National Crime Commission. This afforded maintenance for Howe and facilities for contacts with visitors in New York and for correspondence—always correspondence.

In Albany Roosevelt had as his counsel Samuel I. Rosenman, who had grown up in a Tammany environment. Rosenman maintained contacts with New York City politics and with Democratic members of the legislature. He performed valuable service in handling state legislative problems and in helping Roosevelt with speeches in state matters. There was always bitter feeling between Howe and Rosenman, but such was the care with which Roosevelt delegated authority that their clashes were not often serious.

Roosevelt's major staff acquisition was Edward J. Flynn, boss of the Bronx. In his book, *You're the Boss,* Flynn has described the persistent, almost frantic effort of Roosevelt to get him to accept the position of Secretary of State, a near-sinecure of some prestige and a convenient means of establishing at close quarters a man to whom Roosevelt delegated great power as a political deputy. Later, James A. Farley was selected by Roosevelt to be the political drummer of his cause.

In 1931 I came to be actively associated in the scheme of things and in early 1932 was designated to handle for him all matters relating to the issues, speeches and statements of the national campaign—first for the nomination and then for the election.

It is astonishing that Roosevelt so ordered the various divisions of his political activity, so sharply delegated authority and so clearly maintained personal contact with each of us that there was never the semblance of conflict and never an overlapping of function. This was a mark of superb administrative ability in the political field.

I have known something of the administration of Republican campaigns in the four election years that have followed 1932. In every instance, even under the meticulous Dewey, there has been friction, jealousy and lost motion.

I can best illustrate Roosevelt's capacity for political administration through my own case. He made it clear that I was to gather together the people necessary to the background and substance of his national policies and to be responsible for those people. I insisted on a promise that he would work through me exclusively in these matters. He so notified party leaders in the nation in writing.[1] He never deviated from this in the four years that followed. I exercised arbitrary authority in my limited role, but only in that way could chaos be averted.

I am glad to set this down, because one of the most frequent charges against Roosevelt in his administration of government and one of the traits most irritating to the members of his cabinet was his habit of telling two or three people to do the same thing, tactfully refraining in each case from telling either what the other was up to. There was no such muddling in the mind of Roosevelt the politician.

Mrs. Roosevelt scarcely ever participated in the meetings, conferences and general activities of the campaign period or, in post-election days, in such affairs around the White House. Roosevelt never seemed to consult her beyond minor questions of housekeeping or family affairs. Except for her great dependence on Louis Howe and her minor contacts with Farley, she kept out of

[1] For text of letter, see my *After Seven Years* (New York, 1939), p. 45.

our way. Roosevelt seemed to place no reliance on her political judgment and, so far as I know, never permitted her to interfere in major decisions of government. She was generally regarded as a kindly woman who had torrential energy. Certainly, her curious economic and social ideas never crept into our concerns.

I have elsewhere described in some detail the methods followed in preparing speeches, statements and public papers.[2] It is only necessary to repeat here that in the ordinary sense of the word, "ghost writing" was out of the question. Such cheap deceit would have been repugnant to my own sense of workmanship and a disservice to Roosevelt. An important speech needs to be tailored, with many fittings and revisions. The ideas of many people need to be incorporated. The finished product must be a part of the personality and ideas of the speaker. He must feel it as his own.

But F.D.R. wanted help and made no bones about the fact that he received it. Only once in that entire campaign did he depart from the text, and that was when, in Baltimore, he took a swipe at the Supreme Court. The hornet's nest thus opened insured subsequent caution.

After Roosevelt's accession to the Presidency, my relations with him in assisting with speeches, public papers and statements continued for more than three years. The scope of subject matter was enlarged, however, and the methods employed were revised. In the first six months of that period I served as Assistant Secretary of State, a position with no statutory duties, which permitted me to serve Roosevelt directly on a wide variety of subjects. I left that office to assume the editorship of a magazine, but still served Roosevelt unofficially.

In those years it was possible to use officials, Cabinet members and others as sources of material and memoranda, but always Roosevelt used me in the final formulation of speeches and public papers. It would probably be news to the top brass in the State Department of those days, who jealously resented my access to the White House, that during that period Roosevelt always secured from them and submitted to me their memoranda for use as raw material in preparing speeches and annual messages.

[2] *Ibid.*, Chapters I and II, and *27 Masters of Politics*, pp. 149–150.

The country as a whole was unaware of the fact that in about the middle of the year 1935 Roosevelt radically shifted the whole strategy of his political career. In that year he apparently decided that the earlier New Deal was no longer adequate to sustain his power. Consequently, he shifted his appeal to labor, to minority racial groups and to the masses of the cities. This was not only a repudiation of Jefferson's famous dependence upon agriculture and small towns, but it reversed the policy built and carried through from 1910 on by Roosevelt and Louis Howe. In 1932 Roosevelt felt keenly that he was unable or unsuited to evoke the enthusiasm of large city audiences. He once said to me, "Al Smith is good at that. I am not." By 1935 his mood changed, and the whole course of political history was altered.

The proof of this will be apparent to anyone who will note the course of his legislative program. Social Security, the Wagner Act and a revamped W.P.A. came in that year, and the radical Roosevelt tax program was launched. Perhaps he took a lesson from his dreaded enemy, Huey Long; but also he calculated the ease with which this new course could be taken. He was, in short, bartering acreage for population.

He realized that he could—by cementing the labor vote by the privileges and powers of the Wagner Act, by unemployment and old-age benefits, by the liberal use of relief money and by class appeals in his speeches—win the solid support of great masses in the larger cities. He was thoroughly aware of the continuous drift of the population toward cities, partly because of the growth of urban industry and partly because of the mechanization of farms.

Comfortable alliances with such bosses as Kelly of Chicago and Hague of Jersey City through patronage and the use of relief funds were part of the strategy. Advocacy of civil rights helped with the gathering hosts of Negro voters in Northern cities.

To be sure, such a shift would start the return of rural counties and districts to the Republican party. The statistics of subsequent elections show that return. He could also be sure that he would set Southern Democratic leaders on their guard, if he did not stir their opposition. But he could calculate that, while they might cause trouble in Congress, they would be impotent in elections—locked in the one-party system.

Meanwhile, vast majorities were assured in the cities, which would overwhelm Republican majorities elsewhere. This strategy proved itself in his three successive elections. It sufficed for the duration of his life. What will come of it remains to be seen.

His third-term candidacy, I have reason to believe, was fore-ordained. I felt that he intended to try it because of a remark he made in 1933. One morning after Lewis Douglas, then Budget Director, had completed his early morning conference in the Roosevelt bedroom and had left, I said something in his praise. Roosevelt agreed and then added thoughtfully, "In twelve years he would be a good Democratic candidate for President." There are ironic touches to this, considering his subsequent break with Douglas and his own drift far to the left of the Douglas funda-mentalist economics. Roosevelt's statement, I always felt, indi-cated a purpose in his mind, even at that early date, to break tradition and to try for a third term.

In the two years before he "consented" to run in 1940, Roose-velt's zest for subtle mystery was fully satisfied. Indirect but not conclusive suggestions that he wanted to return to Hyde Park were merely to divert speculation and to enable him to choose time and place. He never seriously considered any other candidate. As Farley and others say, he systematically eliminated all other prospects. His casual notations of Harry Hopkins' assets and liabilities, solemnly presented by Robert E. Sherwood in his *Roosevelt and Hopkins* as serious evidence that he favored his good friend, can be discounted. This encouragement was merely a way he had in friendly dawdling with intimates. He knew, as many master politicians have known, that to tell a harsh truth to a friend is dangerous, especially when the truth is certain to hurt. And by nature he hated to inflict hurt—directly and face to face. He knew, and Hopkins should have known, that the idea was preposterous.

Roosevelt's lack of directness and sincerity, so abundantly shown in the record now being made public by those who worked with him, can best be understood by a consideration of the mentality and code of conduct exacted by a lifetime of concentration in the art of politics. If the politician were to live wholly by the code of those whom he dominates, he could not expect to win the mastery to which he aspires. His code of right and wrong, his reactions to stimuli and his conduct cannot conform in their entirety to those patterns which are set up in the copybooks to guide the youth of the land. In this divergence arises much of the conflict of opinion about Roosevelt the man, the politician and the statesman.

This is because to an ultimate degree Roosevelt attained what may be described as the political mind.

I have been asked many times by those who know of my long association with Roosevelt: "Is he"—or was he—"sincere?"

When time permitted, I always answered that sincerity, as a quality known to the generality of people is not fairly applicable to a politician. Or to put it another way, in a category of virtues appropriate to a politician, sincerity occupies a less exalted place than it does among the qualities of a novelist, a teacher or a scientist. And that is in no way damning the politician, for he may exalt virtues such as kindness, understanding and public service far beyond those who sniff at his lack of sincerity.

Perhaps a fairly simple explanation of my meaning can be conveyed by a classical parable written in Plato's *Republic*.

A character in that dialogue describes an underground cave with its mouth open toward the light and, within, a wall facing the light. Inside the cave, and looking toward the wall, are human beings chained so that they cannot turn. From childhood they have seen only the wall and the reflections cast thereupon.

Behind them and toward the mouth of the cave is a fire. Between the imprisoned human beings and the fire men pass with "statues and figures of animals made of wood and stone and various materials."

The objects thus carried are reflected upon the wall—the fire supplies the light. The human beings see the shadows, never the substance. And by manipulation of the objects, those who carry them determine what the enchained human beings conceive to be the reality—the truth.

Roughly translated into the terms of political behavior, the human beings are the public. The carriers of the objects are the politicians, considering not the substance of what they carry but the effect produced upon those who see the shadows.

The politician creates illusions. His words must be selected not because they are the most forceful or descriptive in conveying exact facts and situations, but because they will produce in the minds of hearers or readers the reaction desired by the speaker or writer. What therefore, does sincerity, as we talk this virtue to our children, have to do with the calculations of a politician?

Ultimately, the considerations of a politician are not based upon truth or fact; they are based upon what the public will conceive to be truth or fact.

This produces what is called a "political mind." It is an adaptation enforced by the necessities of environment and survival, just as is the fur of a polar bear or the coloration of a groundhog. A sort of natural selection operates in the political environment which promotes the survival and success of minds capable of what some may call dissimulation and others call insincerity.

The classical definition of a political mind has been provided by Bernard Hart in his great work on psychology. He said:

When a party politician is called upon to consider a new measure, his verdict is largely determined by certain constant systems of ideas and trends of thought, constituting what is generally known as "party bias." We should describe these systems in our newly acquired terminology as his "political complex." The complex causes him to take up an attitude toward the proposed measure which is quite independent of any absolute merits which the latter may possess. If we argue with our politician, we shall find that the complex will reinforce in his mind those arguments which support the view of his party, while it will infallibly prevent him from realizing the force of the arguments propounded by the opposite side. Now, it should be observed that the individual himself is probably quite unaware of this mechanism in his mind. He fondly imagines that his opinion is formed solely by the logical pros and cons of the measure before him. We see, in fact, that not only is his thinking determined by a complex of whose action he is unconscious, but that he believes his thoughts to be the result of other causes which are in reality insufficient and illusory. This latter process of self-deception, in which the individual conceals the real foundation of his thought by a series of adventitious props, is termed "rationalization."

If this be shocking to those unacquainted with the life of politics I hasten to assure them that the public has developed immunities which measurably serve as a sort of protection.

I realize that Roosevelt himself would and Mrs. Roosevelt probably will deny the foregoing evaluation. That, however, would be a logical extension of my argument. For no real politician would wish his words and judgments to be known as political. To eschew political motives is a first rule of politics.

Frederick the Great wrote a discourse refuting Machiavelli's *The Prince*. Someone said that Machiavelli, had he been alive, would have heartily approved Frederick's action in writing the book, because a first consideration in a Prince must be to repudiate the methods by which he actually rules.

To quarrel with this interpretation of a politician, his habits of mind and his motives is to quarrel with human life, and, I may add, with politics as we know it. This suffices to explain the contrast between Roosevelt's words and actions and the verities and results written in the record.

There are, however, in any master of an art shortcomings due to character or failures in judgment.

For reasons that we need not explore, Roosevelt lacked the generosity that would have added to his stature as a politician and a statesman. The truthful but wistful account of Farley reveals how little it might have taken to cement the loyalty of a genuinely susceptible soul. Failure to praise or to acknowledge a real obligation helped in a major way to alienate a powerful lieutenant. This was no isolated case. Marguerite LeHand commented many times to me that it was difficult to get Roosevelt to express gratitude to those who helped him. This is always a major failure in politics. Burke once remarked that "Magnanimity in politics is not seldom the truest wisdom."

Roosevelt unnecessarily and capriciously provoked antagonism. His suspicion denied him the help of many who could have enriched the achievement and distinction of his administration.

He was, in an unusual degree, susceptible to the heady wine of power. In 1932 he was patient, amenable to advice, moderate and smilingly indifferent to criticism. As time went on and victories mounted, he grew impatient of advice, however well intended. He succumbed to the unlovely habit of telling, not asking. He developed self-certitude to the extent that he tended to ascribe self-interest, cowardice or subtle corruption to those who crossed him. He closed, one by one, the windows of his mind. Perhaps this is a disease that haunts the White House. In any event, Roosevelt developed pernicious attacks of it, and this lessened his capacity as a political leader and statesman.

Finally, as Roosevelt's political power came to be more and more personal, there developed under his Presidency little improvement in the unity or coherence in the Democratic party which he dominated. His genius in promoting his own success and in winning elections had no counterpart in a capacity to build organization from the bottom up. Perhaps this is not possible in the Democratic party because of the Solid South. The two wings of the party may always be destined to have antagonistic aims. Meanwhile, it remains to be seen whether organized labor, under American conditions, can ever be assimilated in a party.

It may be a strange anomaly that the achievements of Roosevelt in winning masses of voters by positive benefits, in conducting a war and in the field of diplomacy may live longer than his constructive party activities.

That may well be because his political capacity, which was of a supremely high order, was so largely devoted to his own career. The issues he created, however, and the potent influence of his name will be assets of his party for a long time.

REXFORD G. TUGWELL

✪

The Compromising Roosevelt

I

There is a serious problem of ends and means in political life: nowhere does it focus with more significance than in the American Presidency. Ends tend to become especially enlarged for the President since he seems to be the only agent in the government who is expected to accomplish what has to be done in the general interest, or even to effectuate those policies to which commitment has been made.

Because of this compulsion—which comes to be more and more strongly felt as the President struggles toward shaping a program and meets inevitable opposition in carrying it out—there is constant temptation to resort to the means readiest at hand for getting his way in the exigencies of struggle. There is the further necessity, felt by every President, to perpetuate the policies he has labored to establish; and this turns usually into an urge for re-election, or for the continuation in power of his party and of those in it who will see his policies through.

Short-run tactics are in the usual circumstances a ready resort, irresistibly attractive because of their convenience and relative certainty. Since the President has great ends in view, means he

Reprinted from *The Western Political Quarterly,* Vol. VI, No. 2 (June 1953), pp. 320–341, by permission of the University of Utah, copyright owners.

would not attempt to justify philosophically seem to diminish in significance. Because they cannot be justified, he tends to employ these means either secretly or without linking them into a system related to the body of his principle.

He probably always knows that this often approaches the doubtfully moral, and may be dangerous; but if he has become President it is usually because he has been a supremely successful political strategist. And this implies that he has either joined in the usual political game, or at any rate has been aware that he has been its beneficiary and that it has "worked," by bringing him to a position of power and influence. This tends to blur distinctions between ends and means, between long- and short-run tactics, and even between the public and a personal interest. To a mature man, who has survived and has come to a commanding position in such a system, such means as have accomplished it are likely by then to be regarded as ordinary, often as the only ones available, and certainly as practically effective. As he comes to grips with the exigencies of office, the accepted way of getting things done not only does not seem wrong, it seems to be necessary. There are no ready alternatives.

As difficulties multiply, and he has to rely on subordinates, means are likely to degenerate still further. They are carried out by secondary staff who are given tasks to do—the conduct of enormous administrative agencies, securing legislation, gaining approval for appointments, bargaining for reduction in specific or general opposition—and who are instructed only as to ends. Subordinates are under even more compulsion and have less reason for restraint in making those "deals" and compromises which are the daily stuff of political life.[1]

It is not certain but that this procedure, though not much of it

[1] Marriner S. Eccles, speaking of his role as amateur in government and the difficulties encountered by a subordinate, has remarked: "He is always under pressure to do the expedient thing rather than pursue a course that he believes in the long run is in the public's best interest. He may, in fact, sacrifice his public career if he balks at expediency and chooses instead the unpopular course—not as an expression of a contentious nature, but as the logical application of what he believes is right in principle and fact." *Beckoning Frontiers* (New York, 1951), p. 141.

comes to the surface and is discussed, would generally be approved. The American penchant for practicality conduces to understanding, to forgiveness, even to approval—particularly if the ends sought are approved and if the tactics succeed. If what was wanted is got, the methods for getting it are not too closely examined even for their long-run consequences, to say nothing of their compatibility with professed principle. And when examination is made, say by legislative investigation, very often it is conducted with such partisan bias as to have about it a strong odor of hypocrisy, as if the examiners possessed a quite different code of reference. Political means, however, do have inevitable consequences, even if no exposure brings them to light. They even link up into a system, sometimes; when there is properly hostile exposure there may well be a kind of revulsion among those who accepted gratefully enough the results they achieved, or who, as to any one incident, may have been approving, again with the excuse of necessity; but aside from this possible reaction, the system of consequence takes shape and ultimately has to be reckoned with.

It is not such periodic "exposures" which throw the strongest light on the compromises of politics; it is the verdict of long-run judgment as consequences reveal themselves, assume a kind of pattern, and become history, which furnishes the significant lessons. At such times it is possible to see that the means used—and the approval given—were justified or were not justified. They were wrong because means and ends could not be separated and because means have a way of becoming even more important than ends. Or they were right because both ends and means merged to achieve consequences important to the public interest.

II

When Lincoln rejected the advice of those who said that Grant was a doubtful choice for commander in chief of the Union forces because he was a drunkard, his reply is said to have been that he wished his other generals used the same brand of whisky. That is a story Americans have retold endlessly and with the warmest approval. So long as battles were won it was a small matter that a general should have been a man of doubtful character. But his weaknesses were inevitably registered in the scandals of his administration when he succeeded, as a popular hero, to Lincoln's office. The people approved the man who could win, above others whose integrity was unassailable.

There is something of an analogy, certainly, in President Roosevelt's choice of a running mate in 1944. The sacrifice of Henry Wallace, who had been Vice-President between 1940 and 1944, to the exigencies of compromise, gave the United States at a time of crisis, six years later, an administration tormented with the mean and unnecessary incidents of domestic dishonesty. These had been in the making for a long time and were not by any means a new pattern peculiar to the Truman regime. They went deep into the structure of support with which President Roosevelt had underpinned his domestic, and especially his foreign policy—his ends. To meet the challenge of the Nazi-fascist threat from 1936 on seemed to him so overwhelmingly the most important contemporary objective that compromise of almost any sort, if it was really required, was worth the price.[2]

It may have been worth the price. But only as later events unfolded could it be seen what that price really was—and, of course, its precise measure would never be known because it was possible only to speculate about the kind of President Henry

---

[2] If the writer seems to identify compromise with expediency it is because compromise was so frequently, in the Roosevelt case, made in the interest of expediency—was practical, and involved a giving up of items in an integrated program. This is the way it was: the President and his advisers, facing crises to be surmounted and agreed reforms to be gained, came eventually in each case to the point of dealing with those who must enact enabling legislation. There they met those who knew what opposition would be offered by affected interests; and who, to make their task easier, or perhaps expressing a latent opposition of their own, demanded modifications. The President would be advised, gravely, that not so much could be done; this point and that point would need to be given up or weakened. Coming from legislators like Garner, Robinson, Harrison, Rainey, etc., who in New Deal days were in the strategic positions, these represented urges toward "common sense," and orthodoxy; and the word "practical" was very often used. What businessmen wanted was always "practical." The President knew that these objections had to be met somehow; it was easiest always to make a preliminary "deal," and long-range objectives could be deferred.

Wallace might have been. It was clear, however, that far more was being paid in the early 1950's than was indicated by the minor turpitude in and about the White House and in the executive agencies—the acceptance of gifts and favors for the use of influence. The presence of fixers and influence-peddlers among the entourage of the Presidency constituted evidence of an irresponsible carelessness concerning the dignity and purity of a great office. This carelessness, however, did not involve the Constitution itself. It did show that President Roosevelt's successor had not separated his ends and means as history would require of him, although this carelessness did not involve the nation in controversy concerning more than the proper conduct of that office, a controversy so persistently recurrent as to indicate a continuing dilemma for all its occupants.

It is possible to say that President Roosevelt used doubtful, even sinister, means to achieve his results just as it is possible to assert that he was never injudicious about what he was doing. For such departures, it can be seen or inferred by the serious student, he had well-weighed reasons. If there were bad consequences it was because he had deliberately chosen what he believed to be a lesser evil. His wide experience, his deeply felt responsibility for imperative objectives, may have weighed too heavily in his mind; or his own power to command response and get his way without the particular compromises he made may have been underestimated. But the choices he made can be looked at now with more sympathy because it is so clear, as it was in the case of Lincoln's support of Grant, that what President Roosevelt believed to be the paramount American necessity was successfully achieved. The depression he inherited was overcome; that of 1937 was aborted; and the Nazi-fascist conspiracy to dominate the world by force was defeated. These were the great objectives of his policy.

We are, however, entitled to reassess the situation he faced, to examine the other consequences involved, and to speculate concerning the possibilities of lesser or different compromises. For the consequences of surrender enlarged themselves to frightening size as time went on, and finally involved not lesser deviations from a moral code but the integrity of the Constitution itself.

It was not the minor irresponsibilities of Presidential attachés of the Truman administration, the weaknesses of a regime riddled with small corruptions, which in themselves were so significant, as that these and other signs of degeneration weakened the office itself at a time when leadership was necessary to national survival; and that the minor stigmata were evidences of major failure. Constitutional principles themselves were finally involved.

A President speaking from an impregnable moral position as the chosen leader of his people would not, for instance, have placed his office in jeopardy to legislative aggression and then have allowed his military chiefs to take over the argument pro and con concerning national policy—not military strategy, but high political decision. The controversy between MacArthur and the other generals—Marshall, Bradley, et al., which took place under Congressional auspices in the spring of 1951, ought never to have happened in American life. It was in fact a constitutional disaster.

However, is it not true that such serious occurrences were the direct consequence of Roosevelt rather than Truman choices which even though made under duress, were nevertheless so grave as to raise questions concerning their wisdom? Beyond that, is it not true that the frequency of similar occurrences indicated a weakness in the system in which they recurred? Or does it have to be said, rather, that the American President has to be allowed so much freedom of maneuver that moral judgments are inappropriate, and that the only allowable judgment is as to whether or not the gains outweigh the losses?

III

Two of the compromises made by President Roosevelt were perhaps more serious than others—his reliance on the city machines for political support after 1940, and his acceptance of the business method of preparation for the world conflict which the United States entered in 1941. At the time it was difficult to see how he could have done otherwise since both were necessary in view of the circumstances. Yet it is far from certain that the consequences may not have been more serious than those of other choices he might have made. At least it is interesting to speculate about alternatives.

The road to Presidential office lies inescapably through the ordeal of nomination; and to a degree not understood by the uninitiated this road is controlled by professional politicians. This is far more true of a first term than of a second term. It is usually conceded that any President can be nominated for a second term because he has come into automatic leadership of his party and has been able to place his own men in strategic positions—particularly in the national party offices—and because he has been able to dispose of the many favors necessary to firm organization. During these first four years, time has not been given for party disunity to set in, for dissidence to get well started, and for competing aspirants to establish themselves. It is not strange that President Roosevelt sailed into his second term with hardly any vocal opposition, or even that he was able to strengthen his mandate by aggressive affirmation of his philosophy. There were, of course, the Liberty Leaguers, and the opposition of a large percentage of the business-minded press. But all that counted for rather than against him with the electorate—a matter which, in the heat of contest, it was hard to understand, but which, nevertheless, was obvious. Such opposition was a necessary confirmation in voters' minds that their candidate had been effective.

However, a novel set of circumstances was presented by the problem of nomination for third and fourth terms.[3] In the Roosevelt story these third- and fourth-term experiences have considerable significance. By 1940, disaffection had bitten deep, especially in two directions. The constant hammering of the conservative press had had a certain effect beyond that of confirming the President in the public mind as a progressive leader. The middle-income group had widened with returning prosperity and had taken on conservative color. Its members had, in effect, returned to their natural Republican affiliation. In consequence the professional Democratic politicians were seeking some means of appeasing the demand for an end to the New Deal with its "bold, new

[3] These will not arise again so long as the constitutional amendment limiting Presidential service to two terms remains in effect.

experiments." And this sensitivity was heightened by the growing disaffection among the Southern Democrats, most of whom bitterly hated all those associated with the policies of the past eight years.

Much of this disaffection centered itself in a professed opposition to the departure from custom represented by a third-term bid. What lay beneath it was a welter of resentments, ambitions, fears of defeat and dissent from various items of the Roosevelt policy. The Supreme Court fight of 1937–1938 still rankled, the bitterness remaining from the disestablishment of the National Recovery Administration was still strong; the powerful farm organizations had turned hostile; isolationists were conscious that progress toward European involvement was being pushed from the White House; and businessmen had a deep conviction that the President implacably disapproved the system of government-business reciprocity through which they functioned so successfully.

It was very widely believed, even by many of those close to the President, that he himself would not run again but would exert his influence to insure a like-minded successor. One frustrating difficulty, felt both by New Dealers and by their opponents, was that there was no obvious successor on whom the struggle could have centered. For lack of a more likely Democratic candidate a good deal of attention was centered on a most unlikely person—Secretary of State Hull. This conservative and elderly gentleman from Tennessee would have suited the professionals very well in every respect except the rather vital one that he could not possibly win. The professionals felt that only a candidate could win who would promise to keep labor's gains and who, at the same time, would not offend the conservatives. Since such a man did not exist, only President Roosevelt could win.

The President had not taken the necessary steps to build up a possible successor of his own sort. Mr. Robert H. Jackson, for instance, might have been made Governor of New York in the place of Mr. Lehman; but when James A. Farley—who had unlikely ambitions of his own in the same direction—objected, the matter had not been pushed. There were some indications of a build-up for Harry Hopkins; but if a build-up was intended it obviously did not catch on; and, anyway, no New Dealer but the

President could be forced on the professionals, and he only because of the prospect of victory.

When the 1940 convention approached there was no possibility that a Roosevelt-minded successor could be nominated. The President had either to take the nomination himself or to abandon it to someone like Hull and invite almost certain defeat for the party. Moreover, the situation was complicated by the disaffection of Mr. Farley, the national chairman, whose assiduous cultivation of the professionals had seated him more securely in the party leadership than any chairman before him, and given him large ideas about his own availability. The President was in the position of having to get the nomination in spite of the professionals' reluctance and against the desires of most of those party attachés who may have owed much to him but had never been reconciled to his policies. He had to make some kind of a deal, and he did not have a Farley to manage it for him as had been done at the convention of 1932.

At Chicago, Harry Hopkins, sheer amateur, worked it out for President Roosevelt. It was a deal with the big-city machines, a practical one on both sides. They were to support the nomination and work for the election; and their local power was to be recognized by Washington. Flynn of New York, Hague of Jersey City, Kelly of Chicago—these were the key figures. They abandoned Farley; Flynn was made national chairman, the nomination went through, and the election was won. Henry Wallace for Vice-President was the Roosevelt gambit for the preservation of the New Deal in spite of the city machines. The President found the support necessary for going on into his great years as a war leader and as the nemesis of Nazi-fascist totalitarianism.

It is no service to his memory to pretend that a high price was not paid in that deal. The only question is whether or not the price paid was too much for what was received. This will be an interesting field of exploration for future students. At present we still feel too strongly the fears of aggression, and we realize too strongly the narrow margin of the victories in 1942 and 1943 to have any very calm judgment. The high price was paid first when the machine leaders demanded the sacrifice of Henry Wallace in 1944; but the costs continued to mount. There were a good many shocked reminders of the deals of 1940 and 1944 in the revelations of the Kefauver crime-investigating committee in 1950–1951 and in the other revelations which subsequently multiplied. The Kefauver investigations carried inevitable reminders for all those who were old enough to remember, and for those familiar with social history, of similar revelations in the early years of the century and even of those farther back in the days of Tweed and his infamous colleagues. They recalled, as well, the fairly recent Teapot Dome scandals in Harding's time. The reminder was that civic virtue is an end not won by unvirtuous means. The municipal corruption which Tom Johnson and Brand Whitlock fought and which the muckrakers revealed, was not solved by exposure, but only by municipal ownership of the public utilities the corruptionists would not let alone so long as there was money to be made from them. And the officials did not stay uncorrupted so long as there were favors to sell. All during those decades everyone concerned knew well enough that any means of purification short of the drastic one of public ownership would be insufficient. Yet none of them quite dared to say so or to risk their political futures on so uncompromising a policy. It was not until municipal services became unprofitable that American cities took over—at a good price—the utilities which had been for so long the center of repeated scandals.

Meanwhile the corruptionists had other fields to cultivate—not new ones, but ones which grew fabulously more profitable as America grew fabulously more wealthy. Vice, crime, gambling, and racketeering were the targets of repeated investigation. Many a political reputation—including that of Thomas E. Dewey—was won by exposure and prosecution of the participants although nothing was done to scotch the sources. One of these was well enough known to be the big-city machines which operated by selling the favors delivered by those they maintained in office. It was these machines which President Roosevelt covered with the New Deal mantle when Harry Hopkins made the deals for renomination in Chicago in 1940 and which were confirmed in power when Senator Truman was substituted for Mr. Henry Wallace as Vice-Presidential candidate in 1944. The consequences became available for examination when the Kefauver Committee's report was made.[4]

IV

As President Roosevelt approached World War II, the implementation of his grand strategy required an enormous spurt of industrial productivity. He had to consider how it could be obtained. It is not necessary to review in detail the various phases through which the policy was developed. Some of the story will be found in the accounts of various participants.[5] None of them throws much light on the shaping of the decision to entrust existing business organization with the task. It is taken for granted that no alternative existed and that mobilization was merely a matter of farming out to large organizations appropriate functions and entrusting to them the further task of subcontracting. Perhaps this was the only feasible procedure. It was certainly so in the minds of the President's subordinates, few of whom had gone through the struggles with business which had tormented him in the early days of the New Deal. In view of that struggle, and the influence it must have had on the Roosevelt mind, this interpretation seems a far too simple approach. There must have been a struggle in the President's mind and a deliberate decision to proceed as he did.

When President Wilson was shuddering at the prospect of war in 1917, he said to his Secretary of the Navy, Josephus Daniels:

[4] In Chapter I of *This I Remember* (New York, 1949), Eleanor Roosevelt had this to say: "Franklin was a practical politician. . . . I often heard him discuss the necessity and role of local political organizations, but he recognized that certain of them were a detriment to the party as a whole. He never got over his feeling against Tammany Hall or any boss-ridden organization, though he acknowledged that some were well administered and valuable." Or, she might have gone on to say, "that some were so necessary as to be indispensable."

Other revealing comments on the President's relation to local political organizations will be found in James A. Farley's *Behind the Ballots* (New York, 1938); and Edward J. Flynn's *You're the Boss* (New York, 1947).

[5] *See,* for instance, Donald M. Nelson's *Arsenal of Democracy* (New York, 1946); General H. H. Arnold's *Global Mission* (New York: Harper & Bros., 1949); and Robert E. Sherwood's *Roosevelt and Hopkins: An Intimate History* (New York, 1948).

There are two reasons why I am determined to keep out of war if possible. The first is that I cannot bring myself to send into the terrible struggle the sons of anxious mothers, many of whom would never return home. The second is that if we enter this war, the great interests which control steel, oil, shipping, munition factories, and mines will of necessity become dominant factors, and when the war is over our government will be in their hands. We have been trying, and succeeding to a large extent, to unhorse government by privilege. If we go into this war all we have gained will be lost and neither you nor I will live long enough to see our country wrested from the control of monopoly.

And this Daniels is known to have cited to President Roosevelt at the outbreak of World War II, saying: "If our country should be drawn into this maelstrom, the benefit of your reform measures will be lost and our country will again fall into the same quagmire witnessed in 1921–1933."[6] This passage evokes recollections of Secretary Daniels' valiant opposition during the Wilson administration to these same interests. The purveyors of steel, oil, and other naval materials had firm relationships with procurement officers in the navy and the Secretary's efforts were largely futile; but he did on several occasions reject outrageous identical tenders from steel and oil companies; and he never missed an opportunity to oppose what he believed to be sinister influences on naval policy. Franklin D. Roosevelt was the Assistant Secretary at that time and a little impatient with his chief, who was lumped in his mind with Bryan and others as "dear, good people," but hopelessly unrealistic.[7] The younger man evinced very little concern about the issues which provoked in Daniels such righteous indignation. All his thoughts were centered in the necessity for getting on, for "efficiency," and he was far more under the control of his officers than was Daniels.

[6] These remarks are quoted in Mr. Frank Freidel's biography of President Roosevelt, one volume of which has been published. The original citation is to be found in the Daniels manuscripts in the Congressional library.

[7] This characterization was made in a letter to his wife from Washington, August 2, 1914. It is published in Elliott Roosevelt, ed., *F.D.R.: His Personal Letters, 1905–1928* (New York, 1948). "These dear, good people, like W.J.B. [Bryan] and J.D. [Daniels], have as much conception of what a general European war means as Elliott has of higher mathematics. . . ."

His impatience with his chief, so evident in his private letters at that time, was a source of regret to him later on. He came to see that Daniels' scruples had been justified; and he must have developed in time a rather sorry picture of himself as an injudicious and shortsighted young hothead. When he became President, the older man was made Ambassador to Mexico and was in every way possible shown the honor due to an elder statesman who had proved to be right. For Wilson, quoted so approvingly by Daniels, had been amply justified. The postwar era *was* a "quagmire," and it *did* end in a debacle for which those same interests were solely and inescapably responsible. Franklin D. Roosevelt knew it then.[8]

Still he could see no way to get the nation back on its feet when he inherited the Hoover Depression in 1933 except by restoring business to "prosperity." This was what "recovery" meant. Yet there had to be some admixture of "reform" in the recovery. This was the product of the "dear, good people's" scruples. It did not go far, no further than would make the system operate tolerably. Even this was bitterly resented as every item of "reform" had to be fought for inch by inch; and the fight grew harder as recovery proceeded and the renewed strength of business could be poured into its lobbies, its control of mass-communication media, and its resistance to change of any sort. This resistance perverted N.R.A.; it hindered labor legislation, higher taxes, unemployment relief, and social security. Finally, with some gains registered, the New

---

[8] President Roosevelt had learned to value the older man long before that, and very evidently regretted his earlier criticism. The letter he sent in good-by on August 6, 1920, was affectionate beyond any formal need; it also acknowledged a debt; "You have taught me," he said, "so wisely and kept my feet on the ground when I was about to skyrocket—and in it all there has never been a real dispute or antagonism or distrust. . . . Hence, in part, I will share in the reward for which you *will* get true credit in history. I am very *proud*—but more than that I am very happy to have been able to help . . . please let me keep on coming to you to get your fine inspiration of real idealism and right living and good Americanism." *Personal Letters,* Chapter 11. The attitude of Secretary Daniels toward his assistant secretary is very cautiously approached in the volume of his reminiscences titled *The Wilson Era* (Chapel Hill, N.C., 1946). But of course these were written after the Roosevelt Presidency in which Daniels had served as Ambassador to Mexico. Daniels was a kindly man and he had something like a fatherly attitude toward his younger colleague.

Deal was brought to a full stop as the price of adequate preparation for an obviously oncoming world conflict. The epitaph was
provided when "Dr. Win-the-war" was acknowledged to have
taken over from "Dr. New Deal." The occasion was the press
conference in December, 1943.

All this Daniels watched from his post in Mexico; and when he
warned the President, reminding him of Wilson's fears and of how
they had been justified by events, he must have raised in the
President's mind not only recollections of the means used for
victory in World War I but also the many intervening events which
would buttress such a warning. The President must have recalled,
for instance, the incidents associated with the minor economic
recession of 1937. Even after the events of 1929–1933 and the
subsequent partial recovery through government action, the big
businessmen had learned nothing. Neither, it seemed, had some of
the cabinet members. Messrs. Farley and Morgenthau in particular
were bitterly opposed to "compensatory spending," largely because
it seemed unorthodox to businessmen. Their suggestions for recovery were the same ones which had proved inadequate before;
but they were just as determined to try them again as if the failure
were not of record. As a consequence of this official advice, it was
to the "restoration of confidence" that the President addressed
himself in his special message to the Congress on November 15,
1937. He had been reluctant. Mr. Morgenthau had said to him:
"What business wants to know is: Are we headed toward state
socialism or are we going to continue on a capitalistic basis?" And
the President had answered, wearily, "I have told them again and
again." But he did consent, with whatever reluctance, to reiterate
once more the futile formula. Subsequently, as Mr. Morgenthau
admits, even he was shaken when, a few days later, he spoke to the
Academy of Political Science and was received with open skepticism and hostility:

> On each side of me sat a Morgan Company partner. The audience
> was filled with the wealthiest and most conservative businessmen in
> New York City. . . .
> I told the audience of businessmen: "We want to see capital go into
> productive channels of private industry. We want to see private

business expand. We believe that much of the remaining unemployment will disappear as private capital funds are increasingly employed in productive enterprise. We believe that one of the most important ways of achieving these ends at this time is to continue progress toward a balance of the federal budget."

The reception of my New York speech almost convinced me that he was right. The audience of leading businessmen openly tittered and hooted when I tried to set forth the Administration policy. . . .[9]

Mr. Morgenthau was not the only member or friend of the administration to be thus humiliated. The President himself was not immune. "Confidence" was not restored. Recovery from incipient depression required policies not approved by the businessmen. As a result of the campaign of 1940, when Dewey headed the Republican reaction, the split between the "monopolists" and the President's followers was opened wide. They were his enemies and the enemies, as he believed, of American progress. How, then, could the President subsequently have contemplated calmly the entrusting to big businessmen of the preparations for war, with all the opportunity this would offer for consolidating their power over the economy? He must have had the gravest misgivings.

Yet that is what, finally, he felt compelled to do; and when he died, as the war was ending, the enemies of American progress remained in all the strategic places of power. From those places of power they proceeded at once to oust from the administration all the remaining New Dealers, to institute a new "red hunt," and in general to drive into political exile all those who might furnish any opposition.

V

If President Roosevelt had been asked directly at any time during the war what he felt the future position of Germans and Japanese

---

[9] Henry Morgenthau, "The Struggle for a Program," *Collier's,* October 4, 1947, pp. 20 ff. It might be noted that Secretary of the Treasury William G. McAdoo in Wilson's cabinet was treated in much the same way by the New York financial fraternity. The story of his struggle to gain their consent to the Federal Reserve legislation in 1913 is told in his *Crowded Years* (New York, 1931), pp. 240 ff. But business confidence did not bulk so large in McAdoo's estimation as in Morgenthau's.

in the world ought to be, it seems certain that he would have spoken for their reinstatement in the family of nations. There might be difficulties. Some guarantees were certainly due France and China, he would have said; and some were due also the long-suffering victims of dictatorship. But he would neither have lost his Christian conviction that the vanquished ought to be saved for civilization nor subscribed to the theory that all Germans and Japanese were involved in the guilt of the ruling groups.

Yet it is difficult to see how these ends could be conceived as implicit in some of the means adopted to achieve military victory. The same question did—and still does—arise over the Darlan incident in connection with the African invasion. But longer consequences attach themselves to certain other decisions, such as that for the terrible mass bombings of both nations, for unconditional surrender, and finally for the use of the atomic bomb at Hiroshima and Nagasaki. Looked at in sequence, all these constitute a kind of progression. One more terrible means followed another until the genocidal weapon was finally adopted. The world did not soon recover from these abandonments of moral scruples. At best they left a deep wound in the armor of Western principle and made it impossible for the Christian nations to occupy the position which traditionally ought to be theirs as they confront the wholly "practical" Russian colossus.

As time goes on the conclusion seems more and more inescapable that the means resorted to in achieving the immediate end of victory very seriously compromised the further ends of organization for peace. There are echoes, in the Rooseveltian "unconditional surrender," of Wilson's "force, force to the utmost"; and there is the further suggestion that Roosevelt's United Nations, like Wilson's League, may have been thought of as an overriding concept which would wipe out the consequences of doubtful means. Perhaps that may turn out to be the case; perhaps, also, the war could not have been won without the use of doubtful means. This last appears now not to be true. On the contrary, unconditional surrender, mass bombing of civilians, and the use of the atomic bomb, seem now either to have contributed much less to victory than was at first thought, or actually to have prolonged the conflict. This is true of "unconditional surrender," as was almost immediately seen by many, since it bolstered the resolution of the bombed population and deepened their sense of identity with their rulers instead of contributing to the divisiveness which might have weakened the enemy. It is least true, perhaps, of the atomic bomb which did put an end to wavering Japanese resistance. Even in this case, in spite of the Stimson justification, it is doubtful whether the full-scale invasion of the home islands, with its consequent million American casualties, would actually have been necessary. Besides, as can be said, this was not Roosevelt's but his successor's final choice. However, since it was merely the last in a long train of contributing decisions, the wartime President must bear some of the responsibility. The decision to use the bomb was partly, although not wholly, implicit in the almost completed preparations for using it. From April to August in 1945 nothing really important occurred except the tests at Alamogordo which determined the practicality of the bomb.

It may be said that the choices in all these instances have to be judged as they must have presented themselves at the time and not as they appear in the light of subsequent events. Of course, this is true. Yet each of these—with the exception of mass bombing, which was taken under great provocation—was a decision which seems to have come from a source other than strict necessity. Unconditional surrender was presented as the United Nations' aim at about the same juncture in World War II as was Wilson's Fourteen Points program in World War I, and it stands against the latter in dramatic contrast. Unconditional surrender could not have been thought of as a strategic concept; it must have been adopted with a view to the situation after the victory, which, in fact, made the situation more difficult, and was recognized by many dissenters at the time as likely to make it more difficult.

While Assistant Secretary of the Navy in World War I, the future President had felt that easy treatment of the aggressor would be a mistake. There is a passage in one of his letters[10] written before the declaration of war in Europe in 1914, which seems to foreshadow the "unconditional surrender" of 1943.

[10] Dated August 2, 1914, written to his wife, *Personal Letters,* Chapter 6.

"Rather," he said, "than long drawn-out struggle I hope England will join in and with France and Russia force peace *at Berlin.*" He was very evidently possessed of a deep conviction that humiliation was necessary, a wounding of German pride and a destruction of the will to conquer. The peace of 1918 had not been forced at Berlin. This had been a mistake which ought not to be repeated. At Casablanca the United Nations were committed to the avoidance of mistakes made in 1918. This decision must be associated with the whole line of reasoning prominently identified at that time with Lord Vansittart, who claimed to have the only practical solution of the German question. This, of course, began with the premise that all Germans were equally responsible, along with Hitler and his Nazi associates, for degenerate national behavior, and proceeded to the conclusion that they must be exterminated. Short of extermination, the indication was for such severe punishment as would forever be recalled in situations of similar temptation to aggressiveness. The other possible source would seem to lie in the Old rather than the New Testament. An eye for an eye was an understandable demand of many of the Jews who had suffered so terribly from Nazi persecution; but it was questionable as public policy. And President Roosevelt did, later on, lend himself to the so-called Morgenthau plan for reducing Germany to a peasant country without the industrial potential for further war making. There would thus seem to be a kind of pattern. And it could be argued that the same pattern persisted through the decision to break up the territory into three occupation zones, and even into the establishment in West Germany of an atomized and therefore weak federal government.[11]

[11] Professor J. L. Kunz, in a discussion of the status of occupied Germany (*Western Political Quarterly,* December 1950, pp. 538 ff.), has shown how little doubt there can be that the destruction and dismemberment of Germany was considered in American administration councils a necessary course. There was, of course, the "Morgenthau Plan" outlined in the first pages of *Germany Is Our Problem* (New York, 1945) by Henry J. Morgenthau himself; but also Sumner Welles, in *A Time for Decision* (New York, 1944) advocated dismemberment. And that these ideas were entertained— although they were perhaps moderated on reflection—by President Roosevelt, was shown by his proposal at Teheran for partition of Germany into five "autonomous" states and two internationally controlled areas. Actually a Commission for the Dismemberment of Germany was set up. Secretaries

At any rate the consequence of the wartime slogan of unconditional surrender was the destruction of German cities and industries to such a degree that a successor government was impossible to establish even if it had been desired. By sheer necessity there followed the costly and inept Allied military occupation. Not only occupation—soon recognized as a mistake—was involved in the destruction of the whole German state, but so also was the power vacuum, into which the Soviet government at once tried to rush. It is certainly arguable that if a conditional surrender had been arranged, as in 1918, and a successor government established, the worst of all the sources of conflict between the Russian and American imperia might have been avoided.

VI

Another instance of a compromise rather than an ideal solution of difficulty is furnished by the course taken to meliorate the fiscal crisis of 1933. At the outset it should be said that most of those who have studied the events of that period have not felt that President Roosevelt could have done other than he did. What was done has been described as inevitable by Mr. Moley and others who took part in it. Even Professor Laski argued that to have adopted an alternative would have been practically impossible because so foreign to American practice. I do not share this interpretation. Judged by the long test of consequence it will become clearer that the humiliating compromises concluded during this era with the financiers were mistakes.

It seems that those who argue against the existence of alternatives minimize the discredit into which the system had then fallen and the readiness of a paralyzed people to accept drastic solutions offered by a trusted leader. Even if the hypothetical character of this argument is admitted, it is worth asking what the alternative was and what the consequences of *its* adoption might have been. The financial collapse of 1933 could have been approached by two general means of attack. One was the nationalizing of the banking

---

Stimson and Hull were opposed, however; and so was Stalin. President Roosevelt lost his enthusiasm; but Germany was in effect dismembered, and West Germany was provided with the weakest possible central government.

system and the other was the use of national credit as a balancing mechanism. I argued for these alterations although I was excluded from actual decision making in financial matters, as policy was adopted in early New Deal days. The banking system was never nationalized, although the Banking Act of 1935 tended in that direction and Mr. Eccles whose counsel this writer had strongly recommended to the President was largely responsible for its shape; but orthodox handling of the government's credit did finally, even if reluctantly, give way to the balancing concept.

If President Roosevelt, rejecting Baruch's, Ballantine's, Harrison's, and others' comparable advice, had asked at once in 1933 for a new banking act, he could have got it then as well as in 1935; if he had abandoned the dogma of annually balanced budgets and had used more effectively the taxing power, there would not have been more disaffection in the business community than occurred anyway. But he was persuaded to follow "practical" advice. His confidence that it was the right advice was shaken in the fall of 1933 when it became obvious that people's resolution not to fear fear itself was not enough. Again, there was "practical" advice from Professor Warren, abetted by Mr. Morgenthau, then the Secretary of the Treasury; and the futile experiment of gold purchase was undertaken. Not until after the visit of John Maynard Keynes in 1934 and the appointment of Mr. Eccles to the chairmanship of the Federal Reserve Board did fiscal policy become really effective for public purposes. In this case the alternatives had been thoroughly weighed; the practical course had been followed; gradually and embarrassingly it had had to be abandoned. Inflation was doubtless better than stagnation. If we could not have planned rebalancing, inflation was a possible recourse, although it was a dangerous national habit to acquire. Mr. Eccles was opposed to N.R.A. thus proving more realistic than those who expected too much of it. But he would have taken more immediate measures for rebuilding purchasing power and for reorganizing the credit system.

The confusion, the delay in recovery, and the suffering of the unemployed and their families in the years immediately following cannot be measured. They were, however, very great. And they must be charged to the "practicality" of the business leaders as against the "radicalism" of those of us who would have acted differently even if we did not precisely agree. Our general remedy had in the end to be accepted, even if in modified form, and with an admixture of noxious inflation. Much of the story is told in Mr. Eccles' *Beckoning Frontiers.* Indeed, the story offers a really illuminating instance of compromise with "common sense" and "orthodoxy" on the advice of practical men, a course which proved to be the worst possible resort if measured by long-run necessities.

VII

One of the most striking reversals in political history is certainly that associated with the American attitude toward collective security. The League of Nations was rejected after World War I; but after World War II, the United Nations was embraced with a good deal of enthusiasm. This dramatic change is largely attributed to President Roosevelt. It usually is said to have been made possible by an empirical handling of the political situation. Certainly results were got which President Wilson altogether failed to achieve. It could hardly be said that Wilson was not willing to compromise at the Peace Conference. He knew that the Treaty of Versailles was unworkably vindictive in many respects. He traded expensively for his League and got it. But he lost it at home because he would not compromise with the Senate as he had with Lloyd George and Clemenceau. President Roosevelt, on the other hand, got his United Nations without that kind of a bargain. The United Nations was accepted without any peace treaty. Yet it would not be true to say that no compromise was made at Dumbarton Oaks in preparation for San Francisco. In fact, President Roosevelt did approve a Charter created in the pattern of the League of a quarter-century past when he was well enough aware that it ought to have been drafted in accordance with a pattern a quarter-century in the future. The consequences seem likely to be as serious for the world as those which followed for the United States from the compromises of 1787.

It is arguable that President Roosevelt learned too much from the Wilsonian failure; and that his United Nations was cast in a too-acceptable mold in the effort to forestall opposition in the Senate. By 1945, the League, under another name, had decades of argument behind it; and as a result the United Nations was hardly opposed at all. To have proposed something nearer world government, requiring some sacrifice of sovereignty, would have involved a tour de force similar to that of Wilson. It might very well not have carried in the Senate. Yet it cannot be said categorically that a more advanced concept would not have been supported. The United Nations, even if useful, has not been able to function as a center of collective security. In a very large sense, the United Nations was hardly worth doing except as it might furnish a point of departure for some further, more effective organization.

What seems much more certain is that a stronger Charter would not have been accepted by the Soviet Union. The predominance of Anglo-Americanism in all the preliminaries had reinforced the isolationist feeling of the Soviet government, and their suspicion that the intention was to carry out a subversive attack on the Communist system became very strong. Their demand for complete national integrity without any possibility of outside interference would doubtless have prevented a stronger emphasis on centralization. Whether events could have been shaped so that these suspicions might have been allayed is difficult to say. But it is obvious that compromise with the Soviet government was of equal importance with conciliation of the American Senate; the two together, and President Roosevelt's unwillingness to force the issue, were responsible for the shaping of a Charter very little different from that of the League.

It was a practical Charter, which furnished an over-all framework for all those international efforts already in existence and some others for which the time had obviously come. Even for this purpose the Russians, although they seemed ready to accept the Charter, were unwilling to use its facilities; and beyond joining in the discussions of its publicity forum, the Assembly, they were to establish a virtual boycott of its activities. Since this boycott was effective over half the world, the Soviet government and its followers turned the work of the United Nations into a kind of travesty.

President Roosevelt obviously thought of the United Nations in peace as an extension of the united nations which had been developed for war. He had had less difficulty with Stalin at Teheran and Yalta than he had encountered with Churchill. He perhaps was justified in regarding Britain as still "on the make" imperially, since he could not anticipate the immediate victory of the Labour party after the war. He may well have underestimated postwar difficulties which would so weaken Britain as a Great Power. He did not therefore anticipate the vacuum in Europe and the inrush of the Soviets which would, because of Britain's weakness, push America into the support of Britain in her historic role as the counterweight to the vast amorphous mass of Russia. Nor did he anticipate the alliance through Communism of China with Russia.

The United Nations was not capable of reaching the necessary arrangement, because the division of the world into two parts instead of five was not recognized in the Charter of the United Nations, and it was therefore incapable of dealing with the real issues. So, in 1952, the American government would still be countering Soviet invitations to big-power conferences with reminders that such discussions must be centered in the United Nations. This was a literal and legalistic position which could be maintained because it had reference to a "practical" institution which, in fact, was anachronistic and therefore supremely impractical. But it did stand in the way of negotiation, an ideological barrier the West could not or would not abandon. The world's need was for an arrangement for coexistence between the two great antagonistic power systems. That too was the goal of American policy as defined by the President and the Secretary of State. It could hardly be arrived at without discussion between the principals.

VIII

All these are illustrations of the operating method inherent in give-and-take policies. President Roosevelt is often spoken of admiringly as a supreme practitioner of that art of compromise, and those most qualified to speak are the most admiring. There are often instances to which reference might be made. One is the decision to administer social security through state agencies, with consequences which have run far beyond the mere ineffective administration of the system itself. This was a "practical" decision, one which lessened objection of vested political interests to the institution of the system itself. Again, it seems certain that even if a federal regionalized administrative organization had been decided on as public policy seemed to require, the Act would have passed. The time had come for that kind of thing; it could not have been resisted.

Still another instance which may be cited is the course followed in the development of the Tennessee Valley Authority. Here was an opportunity for a spectacular demonstration in rehabilitation. The land was exhausted; the people were deep in rural and urban poverty; and all this had proceeded from remediable causes. Nothing lay heavier on President Roosevelt's conscience than this degeneracy of America's land and people. He had studied and experimented in New York State with methods of attack on the problem. When he assumed the Presidency, the way had been prepared by years of discussion for such an adventure as he proposed. There was opposition—open from the power interests who were his old enemies, and latent from local interests who wanted no disturbance of the status quo—but there were powerful allies, too, among progressives like Senator Norris who for years had fought to preserve the resources of the Tennessee Valley for the people there and for the nation. When the dramatic announcement of the plan came, it was received with very general acclaim and with only muted and cautious disapproval from those who were opposed. The bill passed; the administration was set up; and then degeneracy set in. The decline of the TVA is a long, involved, and sad story of compromise in practice which went a long way to defeat the announced intentions of conservation and rehabilitation.[12] The compromises were practical ones intended to appease

[12] Further explored by R. G. Tugwell and E. C. Banfield, "Grass Roots Democracy—Myth or Reality," *Public Administration Review* (Winter 1950), pp. 47 ff.

the disaffected and to reduce objection. They ended by making the TVA little more than a public corporation for the production of hydraulic power. The wider intentions of rehabilitation were very largely lost, so that the TVA stood finally, if measured by the original objectives, as a far less significant demonstration than it might have been. What the cost of the necessary support for a firmer policy would have been is, as usual, difficult to say; but a study of each crisis and its settlement would not show that the sacrifices were necessary except in the most grossly expedient sense.

These illustrations lead one to conclude that expediency usually resulted in immediate success, a smoothing out of difficulties. Success, however, must be measured against the possibility of a harder resistance to compromise and the possible results of that harder policy. In the case of the TVA, as in the other cases, judgment will differ, varying perhaps a good deal because of firm or weak belief in the intention. There are those who do not believe that the TVA was a good idea, just as there are those who do not believe in a system of social security. So far as they are concerned, any degree of emasculation is so much to the good. But it was President Roosevelt's intention to shape a strong means for an intended end in both cases; and in both cases, compromise went some way to attenuate the means and so to defeat the ends.

We have to consider always the Presidency; and the extreme complexity of the everyday maneuvers which must center there. Matters do not present themselves singly or simply. It is often necessary—or it seems necessary—to sacrifice the lesser for the greater. That this may degenerate into the making of choices for momentary convenience is true: and some decisions have to be forgiven out of sheer sympathy for the harassments of office. But others are made to secure ends often known only at the central deciding point, and the process of choosing does not have any record which can later be subjected to examination.

Later critics have attempted assessment about every President, especially those who have been fated to preside over national crises. Yet, it is very rarely that these critics possess sufficient information to make their analyses with any certainty. How impor-

tant was it in early New Deal days—in 1934–1935—to relieve
Senator Harrison's mind about a possible challenge from his rival
politico, Bilbo, at home in Mississippi? Harrison was an important
majority leader; there was legislation to be achieved in which
Harrison did not believe but which he would support in return
for favors. So Bilbo was given a useless job in Washington and
kept away from the hustings at home while Harrison went along
with the administration. It was a humiliating—even an immoral—
arrangement; and it did no more than postpone the Bilbo crisis.
However, it did secure a flank of the administration forces for the
movement.

Another example showing the humiliating price of political
compromise, which so often remains unknown to later critics, is
close at hand since it relates to the writer of this article whose
confirmation by the Senate as Undersecretary of Agriculture had
been requested by President Roosevelt in 1934. It was clear that
the appointment to a higher post, just created, would raise a first-
class storm of protest against the author of the "Tugwell bill" for
the stricter regulation of the trade in food and drugs; against one
of the authors of A.A.A. and N.R.A.; against the earnest advocate
of more generous relief to be paid for by higher taxes; and beyond
these offenses, against an influential member of the "brain trust."
I thought and said that my usefulness was too slight to justify the
expenditure of any political capital. Yet the President chose to
invest a good deal in my promotion. Before it was over, I had
become even more notorious, having been subjected to Senatorial
inquisition and having been publicly castigated by a dozen Democratic Senators. Mr. Farley had had to be put to work. When it was
over, the President said to me: "You will never know any more
about it, I hope; but today I traded you for a couple of mur-
derers." I do not to this day know precisely what the deal was with
what strategic Senator. I could guess; but I have spent much more
thought on considering whether the compromise was worth the
price.

The President is in a position to know better than anyone else
the virtues of the merit system. No one suffers so much as he from
the divided loyalties which arise from Congressional control of

jobs in the administrative services. Nevertheless he is also bound to use his powers to secure the embodiment of his program in law and to perpetuate the administration which is pledged to its continuance. If he is to be stopped from using patronage he loses an easy hold on legislative leaders and a convenient means for consolidating his support. President Wilson gave in to the arguments of his Postmaster General, Burleson, who was the political boss of that administration, in the interest of his legislative program. And other Presidents had always done the same thing. President Roosevelt, being a master of political finesse, deliberately withheld the distribution of jobs during his first hundred days, much to the anguish of Mr. Farley,[13] and then rewarded the faithful when the first batch of laws had been passed. He must have had second thoughts when he saw how thoroughly the discipline was broken once the hungry were fed, and the price he had to pay even for small favors. Evidently—though on such matters he did not comment—the President thought the results worth the cost, for he continued to use the same methods even when they were far less effective. Mr. Farley who administered the system had no doubts: when the system failed it had merely been badly used. It is possible to believe that if patronage based on political considerations should be outlawed by extensions of the merit system, the American Presidency might be deprived of a very necessary weapon, one vital to the conduct of the office.

This possibility, however, has to be weighed against consequences which are seldom of record but which are very real. It may be that the Presidency loses more than it gains. It seems that this was true in the Roosevelt case. For, in spite of sedulous cultivation of political means and their skillful use by a masterly team, power slipped from the President's hands at crucial times and compromises of substance had continually to be made. The New Deal had finally to be abandoned in a grand finesse to gain consent to strengthening the military in preparation for war. The political method was not enough; in the end domestic reform had to be traded for national security. That was when TVA was attenuated,

---

[13] As is frankly recounted in that engaging account of Mr. Farley's *Behind the Ballots.*

when conservation and rehabilitation were given up, when the fatal concessions, so feared by Josephus Daniels, were made to the "monopolists." Even this deal was successful only by the slimmest margin. In 1940, the draft bill was renewed in the House by one vote; and when the crisis came there were two years of war during which the margins of victory were terrifyingly slim.

IX

There exists a great interest among Americans—and, for that matter, among other people—about President Roosevelt. It is an interest which grows rather than declines. Along with the simple sorrow of those who lent themselves to his leadership, who trusted him to be their better selves and gain their better ends, there prevails a much more sophisticated interest which has its center in the place prepared by the President himself at Hyde Park. There are gathered not only the mementos of his personal life—the ice boat he used on the Hudson, the *choiserie* from his desk, his various extraordinary collections, even his favorite furniture—but also the mountains of paper out of which, sifted and compared and analyzed, political historians will try to learn something of how a man gets to be President and how he manages the Presidency. This last, no less than the uncritical reverence of ordinary folk, will go on and on. It will not develop any certainties, perhaps not even much wisdom, for future statesmen. It has begun to dispel some myths which could be of no service to a great man's memory—such, for instance, as that of a kind of infallibility, which some of his uncritical followers would perpetuate if they could.

What is emerging from this just-beginning analysis is the portrait of a man who maneuvered endlessly for political preferment, learned his trade in professional fashion, rose to the greatest office in America, and then had to struggle just as endlessly, with the means he had and understood, to gain for his people the ends he saw as imperative to their future. The struggle was a political one; it was neither clean nor pretty. His opponents were unscrupulous, powerful, and determined. He had to gain his people's victories against odds, often, and always against potentially powerful opposition. They—the people—judged that he succeeded. The methods he used they were not aware of; mostly they were not interested. He had no support for niceness and scrupulosity; if he adhered to such standards it was because another course offended something inside himself, not because he feared any disapproval. He had those scruples. They came from his parents, his school, his church. But all his experience taught him that they had to be compromised in politics. Fire had to be fought with fire. When he died he had been through perhaps the most sublime ordeal of contemporary humanity. If he could speak to those who remain behind him, he would be the last to gloss over the ordeals he underwent, to belittle the baseness of the struggles he often had to carry on, or to claim that his ends were not more noble than his means. He would say that perhaps he had been mistaken, but that with what he had at the time, he had done his best.

American Intervention: 1941

In the still short history of World War II historiography, there are superficial resemblances to patterns after World War I. During and shortly after the war, accounts appeared praising American intervention as just, wise, and realistic. Two reporters, Forrest Davis and Ernest K. Lindley, published *How War Came* (New York: Simon & Schuster, 1942). As they recast the situation, the United States had faced three powers, Germany, Italy, and Japan, all committed to totalitarian philosophies and bent on conquering the globe. After June, 1940, when Germany overcame France and Japan moved into French Indo-China, the United States had to commit its strength against them. The task of the American government was to overcome isolationist obstruction and accomplish, step by step, whatever was necessary to check and ultimately overthrow the Axis aggressors. President Roosevelt and the majority of his advisers hoped that the dispatch of new expeditionary forces would not be necessary. They tried to defeat Germany by giving economic aid to Britain and to restrain Japan by diplomatic pressure. The latter proved inadequate. Japanese forces struck Pearl Harbor, and Germany and Italy declared war. Like Page and House after World War I, these newspapermen saw almost no way in which blame could be attached to the United States.

Reprinted from Publication number 30, Service Center for Teachers of History, American Historical Association, pp. 11–14, by permission of the author.

Another school arose, however, to condemn the intervention of 1941, much as Grattan, Millis, and other disillusionists had condemned that of 1917. Charles A. Beard published two volumes, the thin *American Foreign Policy, 1932–1940* (New Haven: Yale U. Press, 1946) and the fatter *President Roosevelt and the Coming of the War, 1941* (New Haven: Yale U. Press, 1948). He advanced two principal theses. First of all, he charged Roosevelt and his aides with having deliberately misled public opinion. From 1932 through 1941, he said, they had consistently reassured the people that they meant to avoid war. In 1940, Roosevelt sought and won a third term by pledging, "Your boys are not going to be sent into any foreign wars." Yet he deliberately abandoned neutrality, promising aid to Britain in June, 1940, trading destroyers to Britain in September, asking billions for Lend-Lease in early 1941, and later ordering the escort of convoys and actual attacks on German commerce raiders. In each instance, he defended the policy before the public as a means of avoiding war. Critics pointed out probable consequences which administration spokesmen either denied or belittled. In debate over Lend-Lease, for example, opponents contended that if the act passed, American ships would inevitably have to escort convoys. Members of the administration knew very well that this was true, but they refused to admit it publicly until after the act passed. The American people, Beard argued, wanted no war. Roosevelt and a handful of interventionists acted on the undemocratic assumption that they were wiser than the majority, and they lied the United States into an undeclared war with Germany.

Beard's second thesis was that the administration deliberately provoked Japan into attacking, presumably so that public resistance to war would finally crumble. Some active opponents of intervention, including several members of Congress, had felt suspicion about Pearl Harbor from the beginning. As soon as the war ended, a joint House-Senate committee began a massive investigation to determine who had been responsible for the Pacific Fleet's unreadiness, and some of the questioners sought information about the whole background of the attack. Thirty-nine volumes of testimony, documents, and reports were published by the committee, and it was from fragments of this evidence that Beard reconstructed his case.

It ran as follows: The United States, having broken Japan's most secret code, knew, in the first place, that the Japanese were desperately anxious for some pride-satisfying end to their four-year-old war with China and, in the second place, that Japan faced crucial shortages of oil and other raw materials. The President and the State Department demanded, as a precondition for any détente, that the Japanese accept humiliating terms in China. In addition, they clamped embargoes on oil and other exports from the United States. They left Japan little alternative except to strike out for resource-rich conquests in Southeast Asia, and they refused even to offer the hope of a compromise. When Premier Prince Konoye, at the risk of his own life, asked Roosevelt to meet him in mid-Pacific, the President coldly refused. By late November, 1941, the administration knew that Japan was about to open hostilities. The Secretary of War noted in his diary, after a cabinet meeting on November 25, "the President . . . brought up the event that we were likely to be attacked perhaps (as soon as) next Monday, for the Japanese are notorious for making an attack without warning, and the question was what we should do. The question was how we should maneuver them into the position of firing the first shot." Neither he nor the Secretary of the Navy gave adequate warning to the commanders at Pearl Harbor, where the American fleet lay concentrated. On the morning of Sunday, December 7, the chief officials of the government absented themselves from their offices. When news of the attack was received, they expressed relief that the suspense was over. As Beard and others have argued this case, the administration deliberately provoked the Japanese and sacrificed the obsolescent battle fleet bunched at Pearl Harbor.

This second thesis of Beard's has been the more popular of the two. Tansill has argued both of them, with some variants of his own, in *Back Door to War* (Chicago: Regnery, 1952), a much more intemperate and unbalanced book than his study of World War I. And Tansill has gone beyond Beard in arguing explicitly that the Axis powers had legitimate grievances and that the United States could have arrived at satisfactory understandings with Hitler if the administration had not been irrationally Anglophile. But most of the widely read writing of this school has focused on American-Japanese relations. The case outlined above is argued with great vehemence in George Morgenstern, *Pearl Harbor: The Story of the Secret War* (New York: Devin-Adair, 1947), and Rear Admiral R. A. Theobald, *The Final Secret of Pearl Harbor* (New York: Devin-Adair, 1954), the latter a study originally printed in *U. S. News and World Report.*

★

Did Roosevelt Start the War?:
History Through a Beard

I

About twenty years ago, Oliver Wendell Holmes in a letter to his friend Sir Frederick Pollock had something to say about Charles A. Beard's *Economic Interpretation of the Constitution*. Beard, said Holmes, argued that "the Constitution primarily represents the triumph of the money power over democratic agrarianism and individualism. Beard . . . went into rather ignoble though most painstaking investigation of the investments of the leaders, with an innuendo even if disclaimed. . . . Belittling arguments always have a force of their own, but you and I believe that high-mindedness is not impossible to man."

That famous book came out in 1913. The "innuendo" that Holmes alluded to has been disclaimed by the author more than once, and his penultimate work, *The Enduring Federalist* (1948), might have pleased Alexander Hamilton. But his latest, *President Roosevelt and the Coming of the War* (1948), may also be characterized as a "rather ignoble though most painstaking investigation." It is a coldly passionate argument, posing as objective

Reprinted from *Atlantic Monthly,* Vol. CLXXXII (August 1948), pp. 91–97, by permission of Curtis Brown, Ltd. Copyright © 1948, by The Atlantic Monthly Company, Boston, Massachusetts, 02116.

history, to prove that Franklin D. Roosevelt planned to pull his country into World War II shortly after it commenced, deceived the American people into re-electing him a second time by swearing to keep them out, plotted with Winston Churchill to provoke some incident which he could call an "attack" by Germany; and, when Hitler refused to fall into the trap, "maneuvered" Japan into hitting the Pacific Fleet at Pearl Harbor.

Nobody can laugh Beard off. He is, by any standards, an important historian and a fine man. Born in Indiana seventy-three years ago, he went through the regular mill for professional historians, rose to be full professor at Columbia, and taught students effectively for several years. His *Rise of American Civilization,* which appeared twenty-odd years ago, is still, in my opinion, the most brilliant historical survey of the American scene ever written; a delight to read, so clear, stimulating, witty, and revealing. He has been president of the American Historical Association. His *American Government and Politics* has been a standard text for almost forty years.

As a man, Beard is and should be an object of admiration. His resignation from Columbia University in 1917, as a protest against the dismissal of Professors Cattell and Dana, was a noble and a courageous gesture. No American since John Fiske had been able to earn a living by writing history, apart from an academic milch cow. But Charles and Mary Beard, the forthright lady whom he had married in 1900, preferred four-legged cows to the academic variety. They established themselves on a hilltop farm in New Milford, Connecticut, created a successful dairy farm, and continued to write books which have been no less profitable. Farmer Beard has been a good neighbor and a power in his community, while Dr. Beard has performed countless acts of kindness and encouragement to younger students, including myself. I won't pretend that I hate to write what follows, for I enjoy controversy quite as much as does the Sage of New Milford; but my esteem for Beard the man far outweighs my indignation with Beard the historian.

No more rugged individualist exists than Charles Austin Beard. Since his salad days he has belonged to no party and joined no sect. He takes a puckish delight in shocking the smug and the complacent; but he also enjoys letting down with a thump any group of liberals who claim him as their own. At the present moment he is the darling of the McCormick-Patterson Axis, but I doubt whether he enjoys their patronage. Beard is no joiner, his name never appears on those long letterheads that spill down the margins, and he is always one jump ahead of the professional patrioteers. On rare occasions when a Legionnaire goes after Charles, or a D.A.R. after Mary, the assailant retires howling from the scene, like a jackal that attacks a lion; for Beard keeps a blunderbuss loaded with facts and figures at his barn door.

II

One of the amusing if unamiable devices of Beard's historical method is an effective use of innuendo. A typical one, in *The Rise of American Civilization* (II, 83), describes how "on one occasion" during the American Civil War, "Gladstone, whose family fortune contained profits from the slave trade . . . virtually acknowledged southern Independence." Admiral Mahan, anathema to Beard, makes his bow in *A Foreign Policy for America* (p. 39) as "the son of a professor and swivel-chair tactician at West Point," who "served respectably, but without distinction, for a time in the navy," and "found an easy berth at the Naval War College." In the Roosevelt book (p. 254), referring to a constitutional opinion that he dislikes, written by the Assistant Solicitor General, Beard remarks, "Mr. Cox, with a B.A. acquired at Christ Church, Oxford, England, whose knowledge of the American Constitution may have been slighter than his knowledge of the English Constitution. . . ." Mr. Cox spent three years at Oxford as a Rhodes Scholar, after graduating from the University of Nebraska, and for several years before his government appointment, practiced law in New York. With equal unfairness I might write, "Mr. Beard, whose favorable reception in Japan many years ago predisposed him to favor that country rather than his own in 1941."

Another trait that runs through Beard's writings is a disbelief in the Great Man. One looks in vain for any appreciation of Washington, Hamilton, Jefferson, Jackson, Clay, Webster, Lee, or Cleveland as men. Their intellectual qualities may be praised, not their moral stature. Some are treated with subtle disparagement; others appear as wan products of economic forces. In all his work I can remember but three clear, well-rounded pictures of eminent personalities: Lincoln in the *Basic History,* Theodore Roosevelt and Jonathan Edwards in the *Rise;* and even T.R. is described as a natural product of a bourgeois background. Jonathan Edwards appears to be one of Beard's few objects of admiration—an instructive parallel might be drawn between his theology and Beard's historiography. If Charles could only have moved to Connecticut two centuries earlier, how he and Jonathan would have lambasted each other from rival pulpits!

A third constant in Beard's work is his attitude toward war and those who fight and direct wars. Since his youth, when he tried to get into the summer frolic of 1898, Beard has detested war and has done his best to ignore war, to minimize its results and to deride military men. Now, one may share Beard's detestation of war as a barbarous survival; but one must admit that American liberty, union, and civilization would never have been unless men had been willing to fight for them. Whether well directed or not, an immense amount of American effort has gone into preparation for war, making war, and paying for war; and to leave war out of any general history of the United States, whether it be called Basic, Political, Constitutional, or Cultural, is an evasion of essential truth. Beard, aloof on his Connecticut hilltop, was unofficial high priest for the thousands of churchmen, teachers, and publicists who promoted disarmament in a world where adventurers of various countries were substituting guns for butter, and who prepared the younger generation for everything but the war that they had to fight.

The clue to Beard's inconsistencies and tergiversations is furnished by the historical method he has consciously adopted and consistently preached. This method, spread at large in several articles and books,[1] is well known to the profession but hardly to the public, who have no reason to suspect that his standards of truth and objectivity differ from those of any other professional historian. He starts with a negative, the denial of Ranke's classic dictum to write history "as it actually happened" (*wie es eigentlich gewesen ist*). Nobody, says Beard, can do that, since history, conceived as the sum total of human activity, is so multifarious and multitudinous that nobody could possibly put it all down in writing; and if he did, nobody would read it. (Of course that is not what Ranke meant, but never mind.) The historian therefore tries to make sense out of the totality of history by selecting facts that to him are significant. Consciously or not, he selects and arranges these facts according to some "frame of reference" as to what is socially desirable for the time, place, and circumstances in which he writes. "The historian who writes history . . . performs an act of faith, as to order and movement. . . . He is thus in the position of a statesman dealing with public affairs; in writing he acts and in acting he makes choices, large or small, timid or bold, with respect to some conception of the nature of things, and the degree of his influence and immortality will depend upon the length and correctness of his forecast" (*American Historical Review,* XXXIX, 226).

G. M. Trevelyan reminds us that "the object of history is to know and understand the past on all its sides"; but Beard will not have it so. The object of history, according to him, is to influence the present and future, in a direction that the historian considers socially desirable. The ordinary, dumb, as-it-really-happened historian admits he has some frame of reference; but he does not consciously go about polishing one up before he starts writing, or reject facts that do not fit the frame. He believes that he has an obligation to keep himself on the alert for facts that will alter any tentative conclusions with which he starts. Moreover, an historian conceives it to be his main business to illuminate the past in the light of his acquired knowledge and skill; not to use the past to

[1] "Written History as an Act of Faith," *American Historical Review,* XXXIX (1934), 226. *The Nature of the Social Sciences* (1934) and *The Discussion of Human Affairs* (1936).

project the future. He may wish to influence the future, but that should not be his main preoccupation. I naturally hope, through my naval history, to help persuade the American people not to scrap their navy; but that is incidental. My real task is to tell what the navy did in World War II, mistakes and all.

History fitted to a consciously set frame, with the historian's sights set for the future, not the past, is really a kind of preaching. However noble or generous the objective set by such a writer, his product could only by exception be history in any modern or reputable meaning of that word. It would ordinarily be in a class with the violent sectarian histories of past centuries, or with those in which Communist historians throw the "party line" into the past.

When Beard set himself up as preacher and prophet, he was lost as an historian. One may quote against him the lines that James Russell Lowell wrote on himself:

> There is Lowell, who's striving Parnassus to climb
> With a whole bale of *isms* tied together with rhyme;
>
> .   .   .   .
>
> His lyre has some chords that would ring pretty well,
> But he'd rather by half make a drum of the shell,
> And rattle away till he's old as Methusalem,
> At the head of a march to the last new Jerusalem.

Beard's last new Jerusalem is a socialized, collectivist state in isolation. "Does the world move, and if so, in what direction?" he asked in 1933, after both Hitler and Roosevelt were in power. "Does it move forward to some other arrangement which can be only dimly divined—a capitalist dictatorship, a proletarian dictatorship, or a collectivist democracy? The last of these is my own guess. . . ." And in an article, "The World as I Want It," which he wrote for the *Forum* in June, 1934, he showed clearly that by "collectivist democracy" he meant a "workers' republic" without poverty or luxury; "a beautiful country . . . labor requited and carried on in conditions conducive to virtue." A fair vision indeed, such as his Fabian friends had dreamed of at the turn of the century.

Within two years, however, there appeared a disturbing shadow, the threat of war. While Beard was not a pacifist in the strict meaning of the term, he felt he had been sold by Woodrow Wilson and the Treaty of Versailles. Although he had time and again urged students to get behind the documents and discover the reality, he swallowed the famous Nye Report complete, without believing it was the whole truth. He supported disarmament and cast ridicule on the generals and admirals who opposed stripping the national defense.

III

Beard realized, however, that mere criticism was not enough. Hating war, yet faced with a world where Japan and Germany were arming feverishly, he conscientiously sought a way out. And in a series of publications he presented a positive program which he believed would let America live in peace and prosperity even if the rest of the world went to hell.[2] The United States should evacuate the Philippines, renounce all "engines of war and diplomacy," and apply its entire political thought and energy to a super New Deal directed by a super TVA, the "Standard of Life Authority." Foreign trade would be controlled by a National Trade Authority with an eventual purpose of attaining complete economic isolation. Immigration must cease, except for students and tourists; the merchant marine must be allowed to sink, and the navy be reduced to a submarine or coast-defense force.

"Continental Americanism," as Beard called this blueprint for the future, made no headway. It looked too much like that which the Chinese Empire had followed for some five hundred years, the end product of which was not alluring. It also had a disquieting resemblance to the economic autarchy practiced by Hitler. His friends wondered how a scholar of Beard's knowledge and experience could propose anything so extravagant. Perhaps the answer is

---

[2] Especially *The Open Door at Home, a Trial Philosophy of National Interest* (1934). My quotations from Samuel F. Bemis's review in *American Historical Review*, XL, 541–543; *Giddy Minds and Foreign Quarrels* (1939); *A Foreign Policy for America* (1940).

that isolation breeds isolationism. In a university there is an intellectual rough-and-tumble that one lacks on a hilltop. You get more back talk even from freshmen than from milch cows.

This pacifistic super-isolationism has apparently become Beard's frame of reference for recent history. In a thoughtful letter to the *Saturday Review of Literature* (August 17, 1935), answering an article by Julian Huxley, he declared that there was an objective test for every system of economics or sociology; namely, "its continuing appropriateness for life and thought amid the remorseless changes of human affairs in time—which is the subject of historical inquiry." In other words, did the prophet make good? One would suppose that if Hitler and Hirohito had not convinced Beard that a Chinese policy was inappropriate for America, the atomic bomb would. On the contrary, the whole Roosevelt book falls within that same frame. Beard is trying to show that Roosevelt dragged the nation into an unnecessary war. He is trying to revive the same masochistic state of public opinion into which he and most of the American people fell at the end of World War I. Wilson then, Roosevelt again, sold us down the river; watch out that Truman does not try it a third time.

Indeed, Beard is so firmly and emotionally enmeshed in this new frame of reference that he has smashed his earlier ones. Time was when history through a Beard moved with the sweep of relentless, dynamic forces. The American Revolution and the Civil War were forcordained by economics; the concept of the former as a quarrel caused by George III and his ministers "shrinks into a trifling joke"; the latter "was merely the culmination of the deep-running transformation that shifted the center of gravity in American Society. . . ." In a little book of 1936, entitled *The Devil Theory of War,* he again stressed dynamic economic-social forces, and reserved his most devastating sarcasm for the "childish" theory that "wicked politicians, perhaps shoved along by wicked bankers," marshaled innocent people into war; that the politician "is a kind of *deus ex machina,* . . . making the people do things they would never think of doing otherwise."

Yet, note how the *deus* (or rather *diabolus*) *ex machina* emerges ten years later. Franklin D. Roosevelt, personally, without any dynamic forces or interests behind him, completely changes the orientation of his country in *American Foreign Policy in the Making, 1932–1940* (1946); and now appears in full diabolic array, with Stimson, Hull, Knox, Stark, and Marshall as attendant imps.

The premise of both books is stated in the opening sentence of the second: "President Roosevelt entered the year 1941 carrying moral responsibility for his covenants with the American people to keep this nation out of war—so to conduct foreign affairs as to avoid war. Those covenants, made in the election campaign of 1940, were of two kinds. The first were the pledges of the Democratic Party. . . . The second were his personal promises. . . .

"The anti-war covenants of the Democratic Party . . . were clear-cut: 'We will not participate in foreign wars, and we will not send our Army, naval or air forces to fight in foreign lands outside the Americas, except in case of attack. . . . The direction and aim of our foreign policy has been, and will continue to be, the security and defense of our own land and the maintenance of its peace.' "

This is the first time, to the writer's knowledge, that any historian has honored a party platform with the old Puritan name of "covenant." As Beard is a great stickler for semantics, the use of so solemn a word for flimsies like party platforms and campaign promises is astonishing. Yet, even if we concede that a party platform is a promise binding the candidate, all promises have implied predicates. If Farmer Beard promises to sell twenty heifers on a certain date for a certain price, it is understood that if in the meantime the heifers die or the other party goes bankrupt, or if he dies and his widow needs the heifers for her support, the promise no longer binds. So, political promises imply no important change of conditions that will make their implementation contrary to the public interest. A party platform is a party platform, not the supreme law of the land. The Presidential oath of office—that the President will, to the best of his ability, "preserve, protect and defend the Constitution of the United States"—must override any campaign promise. Moreover, that platform had a saving clause, "except in case of attack." Not that that daunts Beard! Off he goes, like Don Quixote, to prove that the Japanese did not attack us at Pearl Harbor; F.D.R. attacked them.

IV

The main object of foreign policy is not peace at any price, but the defense of the freedom and security of the nation. It is clear that Beard still firmly believes that nothing that the European Axis or Japan did or could do endangered the freedom or security of the United States, which he holds no less dear than does any citizen. His argument for the faithlessness of President Roosevelt to his "covenant" is carried out in a sort of dialectic isolationism, as if the issue of peace or war, the most momentous the nation had to face since 1861, was merely a matter of debate and negotiation between the two ends of Pennsylvania Avenue, Washington, D.C., with Charles A. Beard of New Milford, Connecticut, in the role of God Almighty delivering the last judgment. If all books on the war before 1942 but Beard's should perish from the earth, the curious reader in the far future would have to infer that a dim figure named Hitler was engaged in a limited sort of war to redress the lost balance of Versailles; that Japan was a virtuous nation pursuing its legitimate interests in Asia; and that neither threatened or even wished to interfere with any legitimate American interest.

Beard would answer, maybe the Nazis and Japs were devils too, but what the hell? Adopt my Chinese foreign policy and America is safe. Those responsible for American foreign policy naturally did not see it that way. Unlike the Sage of New Milford they lacked the imagination to suppose that American freedom could be defended if Japan was allowed to bring half the world's population under her hegemony, and Hitler controlled most of the other half.

Even his stoutest supporters will not deny that President Roosevelt failed to take the American people into his complete confidence or that he attempted to build up national defense without clearly indicating what the dangers were. Mr. Stimson was evidently troubled by this and still believes that Theodore Roosevelt by sounding the trumpet earlier and more frequently would better have prepared the people psychologically for war. Mr. Sherwood in his articles based on the Harry Hopkins papers regrets that the President had to utter soothing phrases in 1940 in order to be re-elected. No one can be certain whether they are right or not. Let the reader, however, cast his mind back to 1940, or read a few newspapers or magazines of that year, and he will recall or ascertain a climate of opinion which compelled the President to do good by stealth. The American people were still bogged down in the most pacifistic or antiwar phase of their history since 1806. Disillusionment as to the results of World War I, the Nye Report, the appeasement of Hitler by Neville Chamberlain, the Communist propaganda against an "imperialist war," and the speeches and writings of hundreds of able men, of whom Beard was one of the best, had brought about a state of opinion that regarded American entry into World War II as unthinkable. During the first half of 1940 men of good will, leaders in business and the professions, journalists and crossroads philosophers, were virtually united in the belief that the European war was "no concern of ours," that to stop Hitler was not worth the life of one American, that the oceans were a sure defense of the United States, and that if Hitler tried any monkey business in South America, the American nations could stop him without aid from anyone. The fall of France and of the Low Countries and the expected attack on Britain shook this complacency but failed to break it.

Thus, the essential problem of the administration was to support Great Britain (and after June, 1941, Russia) as much and as far as Congress and public opinion would permit, to build up American armed strength, and to keep Japan quiet by diplomacy; hoping by measures "short of war" to prevent an Axis victory or, if that did not suffice, to come into the war prepared to win it. There is no distinction of kind, in a world at war, between measures that a neutral takes to prevent being involved, and measures taken to win if finally involved; only a difference of degree. As James Madison once wrote: "The means of security can only be regulated by the means and the danger of attack. They will, in fact, be ever determined by these rules and by no others."

Exactly when President Roosevelt and his advisers decided that "short of war" would not suffice may never be known. It is improbable that they knew, themselves. As the fortunes of war fluctuated in Europe, it seemed one day that with Lend-Lease and indirect aid Britain and Russia would win; then would come a sudden blitz in North Africa or Crete or elsewhere that dashed Allied hopes. Under those circumstances, inconsistency appeared between the administration's words and its deeds. It is an easy matter to draw a brief of Rooseveltian "hypocrisy." Other great men under similar circumstances, puzzled and baffled under myriad pressures, have been subject to the same accusation. James Monroe published in 1797 a furious diatribe against Washington's inconsistent conduct of foreign affairs; Lincoln was accused of vacillating over the issue of secession; Sir Edward Grey lay under the same charge in 1914; even Winston Churchill was not quite so consistent as he makes out in his *Memoirs*.

V

Now for a few sordid details on *President Roosevelt and the Coming of the War,* a book so full of *suppressio veri* and *suggestio falsi* that it would take one of almost equal length to expose every error, innuendo, or misconception. The book is divided into three parts, "Appearances," "Unveiling Realities," and "Realities as Described by the Pearl Harbor Documents"; but there is a rather confusing interplay of the three.

Beard taunts Roosevelt with doing nothing to help Britain until he got re-elected; but the destroyer-naval bases deal, the first "short of war" aid, was consummated on September 2, 1940.[3] An entire chapter, "Patrols as Appearances," is vitiated by Beard's confusion of the Neutrality Patrol, set up as early as September 5, 1939, and approved by the Act of Panama on October 2, with escort-of-convoy operations; nor does he distinguish between escorting ships to occupied Iceland and escorting ships to belligerent

[3] See my *Battle of the Atlantic,* pp. 33–36. Statements of fact hereinafter made may largely be verified from that book and *The Rising Sun in the Pacific,* Vols. I and III of my *History of United States Naval Operations in World War II.*

Britain. The first Lend-Lease Act was passed by Congress March 11, 1941; Iceland was occupied by United States forces on July 7; and the navy was ordered to escort convoys to Iceland only a few days later. The first transatlantic convoy to be assisted by the U.S. Navy sailed from Halifax September 16; and until war was formally declared, the American escort dropped such convoys at a mid-ocean meeting point. The President's denials in April that the navy was escorting British ships to Britain were true and not false, as Beard contends; and the reference Beard gives on page 98, note 16, to prove the contrary only shows that the Atlantic Patrol was being augmented at the expense of the Pacific Fleet.

Part II, "Unveiling Realities," affords Beard a marvelous opportunity, by quoting all manner of gossip, slander, Congressional snipings, and the like, to build up in the reader's mind an impression of frightful iniquity on the part of the administration. For instance, David Lawrence is quoted on pages 289–290 as asking a number of rhetorical questions, such as: "Why were all our battleships in harbor in Hawaii on December 7, 1941, instead of out at sea, and who in Washington gave the orders to keep them there?" But Beard never gives the answer: that they were there by Admiral Kimmel's order, in accordance with normal peacetime routine, after he had received the "war warning" message of November 27.

Again, Lawrence is quoted to the effect that Admiral Richardson protested in 1940 against concentration of ships in Pearl Harbor on the ground that it "was dangerous and offered the Japanese a chance to destroy much of the Navy at a single blow." But Beard, after combing through the Richardson testimony, is not candid enough to state that the Admiral expressly disclaimed danger as motive for his protest, which was based entirely on logistic grounds—the difficulty of supply and the deprivation of leave and liberty to naval personnel.

The "Realities as Described by the Pearl Harbor Documents" are of course "realities" only in the Beardian sense; namely, such selections from the multitude of available facts as fit his conscious frame of reference, to the effect that President Roosevelt was a villain and the war was unnecessary. Unfortunately the average reader, unacquainted with Beard's private conception of reality, does not know this, and expects an objective exposition, which he does not get.

An important insinuation against "the management of the Congressional Committee" (probably meaning its counsel, Mr. Seth Richardson) appears in a note on page 420. The "management" is accused of leaving out of the printed record, "for reasons of its own," a letter of Admiral Stark, dated April 3, 1941, to the commanders in chief of the three fleets, in which Stark says, "The question of our entry into the war now seems to be *when* and not *whether.*" "Students of history" are pompously warned by Beard to be "on guard" against such omissions. Now, it should be obvious to anyone who has combed through the records, that the Committee omitted this letter because it contained nothing important that was not in other letters which it did print. For instance, the Committee printed Stark's private letter to Kimmel of April 4, in which he says, "Something may be forced on us at any moment which would precipitate action, though I don't look for it as I can see no advantage to Mr. Hitler in forcing us into the war, . . . On the surface, at least, the Japanese situation looks a trifle easier, but just what the Oriental *really* plans, none of us can be sure." This does not, of course, fit the Beard frame of reference.

Beard concludes his handling of Stark with another unjustified sneer. "Perhaps it was for this 'indiscretion,' " he says—said indiscretion being the generous submission of his private correspondence file to the Congressional Committee—"that Admiral Stark, after services in the war for which he was awarded high honors, was cashiered by Secretary Forrestal, . . ." (p. 585). Admiral Stark was never "cashiered," and the reproof by Admiral King and Secretary Forrestal, to which Beard refers, is dated over a year before the Admiral gave his testimony.

By harping on a rather unfortunate use of the word *maneuver* in the diary of Secretary Stimson, who, unlike Beard, is no expert in semantics, the author tries to prove that Japan was prodded and pushed into the attack on Pearl Harbor. Mr. Stimson, recording the so-called war cabinet meeting of November 25, 1941, noted (p. 516) that the President predicted "we were likely to be attacked perhaps next Monday. . . . The question was how we should maneuver them into the position of firing the first shot without allowing too much danger to ourselves." Why should this caution be regarded as iniquitous? Throughout modern history Western nations in danger of war choose to await the first blow rather than give it. If Beard is right, American history will have to be rewritten; Captain Parker who at Lexington Green said, "Stand your ground. Don't fire unless fired upon, but if they mean to have a war let it begin here," was a warmonger.

VI

Although Beard gives the chronology of the approach of war well enough, and makes accurate summaries of the voluminous notes that were exchanged, he gives so little of what the Japanese were doing as to provide a distorted picture. And it is strange that an historian so identified with economic influences should almost wholly ignore the significance of oil. The assets-freezing order of July 26, 1941, which included complete stoppage of oil exports to Japan, is mentioned as a provocation without observing that it was an answer to the Japanese occupation of French Indo-China. Roosevelt is criticized for not publishing his next warning, of August 17, 1941, that if Japan took any further steps against "neighboring countries," America would adopt all measures "necessary" to safeguard "legitimate rights and interests of the United States" (p. 488). But anyone who knows Japan would realize that the publication of this stern warning would infuriate the Japanese government and defeat the object of the note.

Again (p. 496), Roosevelt is attacked for his secrecy as to Prince Konoye's proposed personal conference in September; but Beard fails to inform his readers that the secrecy was urgently requested by the prince premier, because he knew that if the proposal leaked, the Tojo crowd would throw him out—which is exactly what happened. We now know from Japanese sources, published by the Joint Committee, that Konoye promised us one thing and Tojo another, which is exactly what Hull suspected.

Beard gives the Japanese a break by describing their proposals of November 20 as a *modus vivendi* (pp. 506 ff.). They were not that, but (as the Japanese foreign minister said) an ultimatum; Japan's last alternative to making war on us and the British and the Dutch. They required the United States to cease reinforcing the Philippines and sending naval vessels into the South Pacific; but Japan was to be free to pour more troops into French Indo-China. The United States must unfreeze Japanese assets, restore the flow of oil and other strategic materials, and stop all aid to Chiang Kai-shek. The only thing Japan promised to do in return for these concessions, appropriate for a nation defeated in war, was to move troops from southern Indo-China into northern Indo-China (whence she was planning to cut the Burma Road) and to evacuate that French colony after forcing China to conclude peace. Such is the proposed Japanese settlement which Beard considers fair and equitable, and the rejection of which by Hull and Roosevelt "proves" that they were bent on war at any price.

As for Pearl Harbor, Beard carries over from the minority report of the Joint Congressional Committee the insinuation that Washington knew all along that the Japs were going to strike, and where. What Washington knew, as early as November 25, was that Japanese forces were moving southward and that something was going to happen soon, without a declaration of war. But everyone made two grave errors in evaluating the information at hand. They believed the Japanese to be incapable of more than one major operation at a time; and they assumed Tojo's government had more sense than to arouse America by a sneak attack. No fact was more conclusively brought out by the Joint Congressional Committee than that nobody in authority at Washington, civil or military, anticipated Pearl [Harbor].

Perhaps the most indecent of Beard's numerous innuendoes in this book are those respecting the Roberts Commission. Mr. Stimson suggested Justice Roberts to head the Pearl Harbor Commission not only because of his personal integrity but as a Republican appointed to the Court by President Hoover, and as an experienced lawyer who had investigated the Teapot Dome scandal. Nevertheless, Beard insinuates (p. 380) that Justice Roberts' appointment was part of a triple play to put Kimmel and Short "out," and conceal the iniquities of F.D.R. and Stimson in a cloud of dust. He creates suspicion by declaring (p. 378) that the appointment of a Justice of the Supreme Court to head an investigating commission was improper, unprecedented, and unconstitutional. That is pure nonsense. In *Hayburn's Case,* to which Beard refers, the Supreme Court under Chief Justice Jay refused as a Court to accept the additional duty of passing on pension claims, but at the same time declared that individual Justices might do it. Chief Justice Hughes served as chairman of President Taft's committee to determine postal rates to be paid by newspapers; Justice Reed and others have recently served on civil service commissions. Even if Justice Roberts were the man to accept the dishonorable role imputed to him, how could he have played it, with two generals and two admirals, one a former commander in chief of the fleet, as colleagues?

Since the discrediting of the Roberts Report is necessary for Beard's case, the Justice is pursued into the Congressional investigation with clubs and brickbats. Beard's three charges against him on page 362—that he had been uninformed on vital matters, that Senator Brewster forced him to concede error on a "crucial point," and "unbecoming levity"—are not supported by the Justice's testimony to which he refers. The point was not crucial, the matter was not relevant to the scope of his inquiry; and why criticize the Justice for keeping his sense of humor under the badgering to which he was subjected by Senators Ferguson and Brewster? The Roberts Commission was only concerned with the question whether American military authorities had shown "derelictions of duty or errors of judgment" on the basis of the information they then had; and the Commission's findings as to the shortcomings of Admiral Kimmel were amply sustained both by the Navy Court of Inquiry and the Joint Congressional Investigating Committee. Beard's statement (p. 604) that Kimmel was "exonerated by the Navy Board" is incorrect. Admiral King's endorsement on the report of that board, dated November 6, 1944, and without which the report is incomplete, brackets Stark with Kimmel as committing "derelictions" which were "faults of omission rather than faults of commission," indicating a lack of "superior judgment." The "official thesis," as Beard calls the Roberts Report, never has been "undermined," except by partisan Congressmen or so-called historians who are unwilling to face the facts fairly.

In concluding, I wish long life and much happiness to Charles the Prophet and to Mary his wife, who have done so much in the past to illuminate American history. May they rise above the bitterness that has come from brooding over their lost horizon of a happy, peaceful, collectivist democracy insulated from a bad world. May Dr. Beard recast his frame of reference once again, raise his sights a little higher than the Connecticut hills, and apply his erudition, wit, and craftsmanship to writing history without innuendo, history tolerant of mistakes that men make under great stress; may he try to understand rather than to blame and to sneer, and even discover before he dies "that highmindedness is not impossible to man."

ISAIAH BERLIN

✪

Roosevelt Through European Eyes

It is an undeserved honor for me to be allowed to commemorate so great a man; especially as I cannot claim any special connection with him—I never met him, and although I spent more than three years in Washington during the war, I never even saw him. I regret this, for it seems to me that to see and, in particular to hear the voice of someone who has occupied one's imagination for many years, must modify one's impression in some way, and make it more concrete and three dimensional. However, I never did see him, and I heard him only over the radio. Consequently, I must try to convey my impression without the benefit of personal acquaintance, and without, I ought to add, any expert knowledge of American history or of international relations. Nor am I competent to speak of Mr. Roosevelt's domestic or foreign policies, nor of their larger political or economic effects. I shall try to give only a personal impression of the general impact of his personality on my generation.

When I say that some men occupy one's imagination for many years, this is literally true of Mr. Roosevelt's effect on the young men of my own generation in England, and probably in many parts of Europe, and indeed the entire world. If one was young in the thirties and lived in a democracy, then, whatever one's politics, if

Reprinted from *Atlantic Monthly,* Vol. CXCVI (July 1955), pp. 67–71, by permission of Curtis Brown, Ltd. Copyright © 1955, by The Atlantic Monthly Company, Boston, Massachusetts, 02116.

one had human feelings at all, or the faintest spark of social idealism, or any love of life, one must have felt very much as young men in Continental Europe probably felt after the defeat of Napoleon during the years of the Restoration: that all was dark and quiet, a great reaction was abroad, and little stirred, and nothing resisted.

It all began with the great slump of 1931, which undermined the feeling, perhaps quite baseless, of economic security which a good many young people of the middle classes then had. There followed the iron thirties, of which the English poets of the time—Auden, Spender, Day Lewis—left a very vivid testament; the dark and leaden thirties to which, alone of all periods in history, no one in Europe wishes to return, unless, indeed, he laments the passing of fascism. There came Manchuria, Hitler, the hunger marchers, the Abyssinian war, Spain, the peace ballot, the Left Book Club, M. Malraux's political novels, an article by Virginia Woolf, least political of writers, in the *Daily Worker,* the conversions of idealistic young liberals and radicals to Communism or to strong sympathy with it, often for no better reason than that it seemed the only force firm enough and strong enough to resist the fascist enemy effectively. Such conversions were sometimes followed by visits to Moscow, or by fighting in Spain and death on the battlefield or else bitter and angry disillusionment with Communist practice; or, particularly after the Soviet political trials and purges, by some desperate and unconvinced choice between two evils of that which seemed the lesser.

The most insistent propaganda in those days declared that humanitarianism and liberalism and democratic forces were played out, and that the choice now lay between two bleak extremes, Communism and fascism—the red or the black. To those who were not carried away by this patter the only light in the darkness was the administration of Mr. Roosevelt and the New Deal in the United States. At a time of weakness and mounting despair in the democratic world, Mr. Roosevelt radiated confidence and strength. He was the leader of the democratic world, and even today upon him alone, of all the statesmen of the thirties, no cloud has rested —neither on him nor on the New Deal, which to European eyes still looks a bright chapter in the history of mankind. It was true that his great social experiment was conducted with an isolationist disregard of the outside world, but it was psychologically intelligible that America, which had come into being in reaction against the follies and evils of a Europe perpetually distraught by religious or national struggles, should try to seek salvation undisturbed by the currents of European life, particularly at a moment when Europe seemed about to collapse into a totalitarian nightmare. Mr. Roosevelt was therefore forgiven by those who found the European situation tragic for pursuing no particular foreign policy—indeed for trying to do, if not without any foreign policy at all, at any rate with a minimum of relationship with the outside world; for that was to some degree part of the American political tradition.

II

His internal policy was plainly animated by a humanitarian purpose. After the unbridled individualism of the twenties which had led to economic collapse and widespread misery, he was seeking to establish new rules of social justice. He was trying to do this without forcing his country into some doctrinaire straitjacket, whether of socialism or state capitalism or the kind of new social organization which the fascist regimes flaunted as the New Order. Social discontent was high in the United States; faith in businessmen as saviors of society had evaporated overnight after the famous Wall Street crash, and Mr. Roosevelt was providing a vast safety valve for pent-up bitterness and indignation, and trying to prevent revolution and construct a regime which should establish greater economic equality, social justice and happiness, above all, human happiness—ideals which were in the best tradition of American life—without altering the basis of freedom and democracy in his country.

This was being done by what, to unsympathetic critics, seemed a haphazard collection of amateurs, college professors, journalists, personal friends, freelances of one kind or another, intellectuals, ideologists—what are nowadays called eggheads—whose very appearance and methods of conducting business or constructing policies irritated the servants of old established government institutions in Washington and tidy-minded conservatives everywhere. Yet it was clear that the very amateurishness of these men, the fact that they were allowed to talk to their hearts' content, to experiment, to indulge in a vast amount of trial and error, that relations were personal and not institutional, bred its own vitality and enthusiasm.

Washington was doubtless full of quarrels, resignations, palace intrigues, perpetual warfare between individuals and groups of individuals, parties, cliques, personal supporters of this or that great captain, which must have maddened sober and responsible officials used to the slower tempo and more normal patterns of administration. As for bankers and businessmen, the feelings of many of them were past describing; but at this period they were little regarded, since they were considered to have discredited themselves too deeply, and indeed forever.

Over this vast, seething chaos presided a handsome, charming, gay, intelligent, delightful, very audacious man, Mr. Franklin Delano Roosevelt. He was accused of many weaknesses. He had betrayed his class; he was ignorant, unscrupulous, irresponsible. He was ruthless in playing with the lives and careers of individuals. He was surrounded by adventurers, slick opportunists, intriguers. He made conflicting promises, cynically and brazenly, to individuals and groups and representatives of foreign nations. He made up, with his vast and irresistible public charm and his astonishing high spirits, for a lack of virtues considered more important in the leader of the most powerful democracy in the world: the virtues of application, industry, responsibility.

All this was said and some of it may indeed have been just. What attracted his followers were countervailing qualities of a rare and inspiring order. He was large-hearted and possessed wide political horizons, imaginative sweep, understanding of the time in which he lived and of the direction of the great new forces at work in the twentieth century—technological, racial, imperialist, anti-imperialist. He was in favor of life and movement, the promotion of the most generous possible fulfillment of the largest possible

number of human wishes, and not in favor of caution and retrenchment and sitting still. Above all, he was absolutely fearless.

He was one of the few statesmen in the twentieth or any other
century who seemed to have no fear at all of the future. He
believed in his own strength and ability to manage, and to succeed,
whatever happened. He believed in the capacity and loyalty of his
lieutenants, so that he looked upon the future with a calm eye, as
if to say, "Let it come, whatever it may be, it will all be grist to
our great mill. We shall turn it all to benefit." It was this, perhaps,
more than any other quality, which drew men of very different
outlooks to him. In a despondent world which appeared divided
between wicked and fatally efficient fanatics marching to destroy,
and bewildered populations on the run, unenthusiastic martyrs in
a cause they could not define, he believed in his own ability, so long
as he was in control, to stem the terrible tide.

He had all the character and energy and skill of the dictators,
and he was on our side. He was, in his opinions and public actions,
every inch a democrat. All the political and personal and public
criticism of him might be true; all the personal defects which his
enemies and some of his friends attributed to him might be real;
yet as a public figure he was unique. As the skies of Europe grew
darker, in particular after war broke out, he seemed to the poor
and the unhappy in Europe a kind of benevolent demigod who
alone could and would save them in the end. His moral authority,
the degree of confidence which he inspired outside his own country
—far more beyond America's frontiers than within them at all
times—has no parallel. Perhaps President Wilson in the early days
after the end of the First World War, when he drove in triumph
through the streets of London and Paris, may have inspired some
such feeling; but it disappeared quickly and left behind it a terrible
feeling of disenchantment. It was plain even to his enemies that
President Roosevelt would not be broken as President Wilson had
been. For to his prestige and to his personality he added a degree of
political skill—indeed virtuosity—which no American before him
had ever possessed. His chance of realizing his wishes was plainly
greater; his followers would be less likely to reap bitter disappointment.

Indeed he was very different from Wilson. Indeed they represent two contrasting types of statesmen, in each of which, occasionally, men of compelling stature appear. The first kind of statesman is essentially a man of single principle and fanatical vision. Possessed by his own bright, coherent dream, he usually understands neither people nor events. He has no doubts or hesitations, and by concentration of will power, by directness and strength, is able to ignore a great deal of what goes on outside him. His very blindness and stubborn self-absorption, in certain situations, enables him to bend events and men to his own fixed pattern. His strength lies in the fact that weak and vacillating human beings, themselves too insecure or confused to be capable of deciding between alternatives, find relief and peace and strength in submitting to the authority of a single leader of superhuman size to whom all issues are clear, and who marches toward his goal looking neither to right nor to left, buoyed up by the violent vision within him.

Such men differ widely in moral and intellectual quality, and, like forces of nature, do both good and harm in the world. To this type belong Garibaldi, Trotsky, Parnell, de Gaulle, perhaps Lenin too—the distinction I am drawing is not a moral one, not one of value but one of type. There are great benefactors, like Wilson, as well as fearful evildoers, like Hitler, within this category.

The other kind of effective statesman is a naturally political being, as the simple hero is often explicitly antipolitical and comes to rescue men, at least ostensibly, from the subtleties and frauds of political life. The second type of politician possesses antennae of the greatest possible delicacy, which convey to him, in ways difficult or impossible to analyze, the perpetually changing contours of events and feelings and human activities around him. He is gifted with a peculiar political sense fed on a capacity to take in minute impressions, to integrate a vast multitude of small, evanescent, unseizable detail, such as artists possess in relation to their material. Statesmen of this type know what to do and when to do it, if they are to achieve their ends; which themselves are usually not born within some private world of inner thought or introverted feeling, but represent the crystallization of what a large number of their fellow citizens are thinking in some dim, inarticulate, but nevertheless persistent fashion. In virtue of this capacity to judge their material very much as a sculptor knows what can be carved out of wood and what out of marble, and how and when, they resemble doctors who have a natural gift for healing which does not directly depend upon (though it could not exist without) that knowledge of scientific anatomy which can only be learned by observation or experiment or from the experience of others.

This instinctive, or at any rate incommunicable, knowledge of where to look for what one needs, the power of divining where the treasure lies, is something common to many types of genius, to scientists and mathematicians no less than to businessmen and administrators and politicians. Such men, when they are statesmen, are acutely aware of the direction in which the thoughts and feelings of human beings are flowing, of where life presses on them most heavily; and they convey to these human beings a sense of understanding their inner needs, of responding to their own deepest impulses—above all, of being alone capable of organizing the world along lines for which the masses are instinctively groping.

To this type of statesman belong Bismarck and Abraham Lincoln, Lloyd George and Thomas Masaryk, perhaps to some extent Gladstone, and to a minor degree Walpole. Roosevelt was a magnificent virtuoso of this type, and he was the most benevolent as well as the greatest master of his craft in modern times. He really did desire a better life for mankind. The great majorities which he obtained in the elections in the United States during his four terms of office, despite the mounting hostility of the press and perpetual prophecies on its part that he had gone too far and would fail to be re-elected, were ultimately due to an obscure feeling on the part of the majority of the citizens of the United States that he was on their side, that he wished them well, and that he would do something for them. And this feeling gradually spread over the entire civilized world. He became a legendary hero—they themselves did not know quite why—to the indigent and the oppressed far beyond the confines of the English-speaking world.

III

As I said before, he was, by some of his opponents, accused of betraying his class; and so he had. When a man who retains the manners, style of life, the emotional texture and the charm of the old order, of some free aristocratic upbringing, revolts against his milieu and adopts the ideas and aspirations of the new, socially *révolté* class—and adopts them not from motives of expediency but out of genuine moral conviction, or from love of life—inability to remain on the side of what seems to him narrow, corrupt, mean, restrictive—the result is fascinating and moving. This is what makes the figures of such men as Condorcet or Charles James Fox, or some of the Russian, Italian, and Polish revolutionaries in the nineteenth century, so attractive; for all we know, this may have been the secret also of Moses or Pericles or Julius Caesar. It was this gentlemanly quality, together with the fact that they felt him to be deeply committed to their side in the struggle and in favor of their way of life, as well as his open and fearless lack of neutrality in the war against the Nazis and fascists, that endeared him so deeply to the British people during the war years.

I remember well in London, in November, 1940, how excited most people were about the result of the Presidential election in the United States. In theory they need not have worried. Mr. Willkie, the Republican candidate, had expressed himself forcibly and sincerely as a supporter of the democracies. Yet it was absurd to say that the people of Britain were neutral in their feelings vis-à-vis the two candidates. They felt in their bones that Mr. Roosevelt was their lifelong friend, that he hated the Nazis as deeply as they did, that he wanted democracy and civilization, in the sense in which they believed in it, to prevail, that he knew what he wanted, and that his goal resembled their own ideals more than it did those of all his opponents. They felt that his heart was in the right place, and they did not, therefore, if they gave it a thought, care whether his political appointments were made under the influence of bosses, or for personal reasons, or thoughtlessly; whether his economic doctrines were heretical; whether he had a sufficiently scrupulous regard for the views of the Senate or the House of Representatives, or the prescriptions of the United States Constitution, or the opinions of the Supreme Court. These matters were very remote from them. They knew that he would, to the extent of his enormous energy and ability, see them through.

There is probably no such thing as long-lived mass hypnotism; the masses know what it is that they like, what genuinely appeals to them. What most Germans thought Hitler to be, Hitler, in fact, largely was; and what free men in Europe and in America and in Asia and in Africa and in Australia, and wherever else the rudiments of free political throught stirred at all—what all these felt Roosevelt to be, he, in fact, was. He was the greatest leader of democracy, the greatest champion of social progress, in the twentieth century.

His enemies accused him of plotting to get America into the war. I am not competent to discuss this controversial issue, but it seems to me that the evidence for it is lacking. I think that when he promised to keep America at peace he meant to try as hard as he could to do so, compatibly with helping to promote the victory of the democracies. He must at one period have thought that he could win the war without entering it, and so, at the end of it, be in the unique position, hitherto achieved by no one, of being the arbiter of the world's fate, without needing to placate those bitter forces which involvement in a war inevitably brings about, and which are an obstacle to reason and humanity in the making of the peace.

No doubt he trusted too often in his own magical power of improvisation. Doubtless he made many political mistakes, some of them difficult to remedy. Some say he was disastrously wrong about Stalin and his intentions and the nature of the Soviet state; others, with equal justice, point to his coolness to the Free French movement, his cavalier intentions with regard to the Supreme Court in the United States, his errors about a good many other issues. He irritated his staunchest supporters and most faithful servants because he did not tell them what he was doing; his government was highly personal and it maddened tidy-minded officials and humiliated those who thought that his policy should be conducted in consultation with and through them. His anti-imperialism at times (in Yalta, for example) assumed gaily irresponsible forms. He vastly oversimplified many issues. He overestimated his own capacity to build a new world by the sole use of his own prodigious powers of manipulation in the course of breezily informal dealings with other statesmen on a purely per-

sonal basis. All this sometimes exasperated his allies, but when
these last bethought them of who most of his ill-wishers were in
the United States and in the world outside, and what *their* motives
were, their own respect, affection, and loyalty tended to return. No
man made more public enemies, yet no man had a right to take
greater pride in the quality and the motives of some of those
enemies. He could justly call himself the friend of the people, and
although his opponents accused him of being a demagogue, this
charge seems to me unjust. He did not sacrifice fundamental
political principles to a desire to retain power; he did not whip up
evil passions merely in order to avenge himself upon those whom
he disliked or wished to crush, or because it was an atmosphere in
which he found it convenient to operate. He saw to it that his
administration was in the van of public opinion and drew it on
instead of being dragged by it. He made the majority of his fellow
citizens prouder to be Americans than they had been before. He
raised their status in their own eyes, and in those of the rest of the
world. It was an extraordinary transformation of an individual.
Perhaps it was largely brought about by the collapse of his health
in the early twenties, and his marvelous triumph over his disabili-
ties. For he began life as a well-born, polite, agreeable, debonair,
not particularly gifted young man, something of a prig, liked but
not greatly admired by his contemporaries at Groton and at
Harvard, a competent Assistant Secretary of the Navy in the First
World War; in short, he seemed embarked on the routine career of
an American patrician with moderate political ambitions. His
illness and the support and encouragement and political qualities
of his wife—whose greatness of character and goodness of heart
history will duly record—seemed to transfigure his public personality into the strong and beneficent champion who became the
father of his people, in an altogether unique fashion.

He was more than this: it is not too much to say that he altered
the fundamental concept of government and its obligations to the
governed. In this respect Lloyd George was no more than a fore-
runner. The welfare state, so much denounced, has obviously come
to stay: the direct moral responsibility for minimum standards of
living and social services which it took for granted, are today

accepted almost without a murmur by the most conservative politicians in the Western democracies. The Republican party in 1952 made no effort to upset the basic principles—which seemed utopian in the twenties—of Mr. Roosevelt's social legislation.

But Mr. Roosevelt's greatest service to mankind (after ensuring victory against the enemies of freedom) consists in the fact that he showed that it is possible to be politically effective and yet benevolent and civilized: that the fierce left- and right-wing propaganda of the thirties, according to which the conquest and retention of political power is not compatible with human qualities, but necessarily demands from those who pursue it seriously the sacrifice of their lives upon the altar of some ruthless ideology, or the systematic practice of despotism—this propaganda, which filled the art and talk of the day, was simply untrue. Mr. Roosevelt's example strengthened democracy everywhere—that is to say, the view that the promotion of social justice and individual liberty does not necessarily mean the end of all efficient government; that power and order are not identical with a straitjacket of doctrine, whether economic or political; that it is possible to reconcile individual liberty and a loose texture of society with the indispensable minimum of organization and authority. And in this belief lies what Mr. Roosevelt's greatest predecessor once described as the last best hope on earth.

✪

A Little Left of Center

I knew Roosevelt long enough and under enough circumstances to be quite sure that he was no political or economic radical. I take it that the essence of economic radicalism is to believe that the best system is the one in which private ownership of the means of production is abolished in favor of public ownership. But Roosevelt took the status quo in our economic system as much for granted as his family. They were part of his life, and so was our system; he was content with it. He felt that it ought to be humane, fair, and honest, and that adjustments ought to be made so that the people would not suffer from poverty and neglect, and so that all would share.

He thought business could be a fine art and could be conducted on moral principles. He thought the test ought to be whether or not business is conducted partly for the welfare of the community. He could not accept the idea that the sole purpose of business was to make more and more money. He thought business should make and distribute goods with enough profit to give the owners a comfortable living and enable them to save something to invest in other productive enterprises. Yes, he felt that stockholders had a place and right and that a business ought to be conducted so that they would earn modest interest, while the workers got good wages and the community profited by low prices and steady work.

But he couldn't see why a man making enough money should want to go on scheming and plotting, sacrificing and living under nervous tension, just to make more money. That, of course, made him unable to sympathize with the ambitions and drive of much of the American business fraternity. But he liked and got along well with those businessmen who shared, as many did, the point of view that business is conducted partly for the welfare of the country as well as to make money. They liked and trusted him and understood his objectives. Gerard Swope of the General Electric Company, Thomas J. Watson of the International Business Machines Company, Ernest Draper of the Hills Brothers Company, Donald and Hugh Comer, Southern textile manufacturers, who had a humane if not a trade union conception of the rights of their workers and of the employers' duty in relation to them, were all comprehensible to the President. He liked Walter Chrysler, although I am not sure that Chrysler fully embraced the idea that enough is enough, particularly if his rivals were making more. But he did have some of the attitude that there was nothing remarkable in itself about making money.

It is true that Roosevelt never met a payroll, and many businessmen took it into their heads that he could not possibly comprehend business unless he had had that experience. This, of course, is part of the limitation of the business fraternity itself.

Roosevelt was entirely willing to try experiments. He had no theoretical or ideological objections to public ownership when that was necessary, but it was his belief that it would greatly complicate the administrative system if we had too much. He recognized, however, that certain enterprises could best be carried on under public control. He recognized that we probably would never have enough cheap electric power to supply the needs of the people if the government did not undertake vast programs in the Tennessee and Missouri valleys, and he believed that plenty of power at low rates was necessary for the development of a high standard of living and for business progress. Just as the need for production in wartime is so great that the government must take a hand in it, so he was able to accept the idea that in peacetime too the government must sometimes carry on enterprises because of the enormous amount of capital expenditure required or the preponderance of the experimental element. He was willing to concede that there were some fields in which such government participation might be required permanently. But he always resisted the frequent suggestion of the government's taking over railroads, mines, etc., on the ground that it was unnecessary and would be a clumsy way to get the service needed.

A superficial young reporter once said to Roosevelt in my presence, "Mr. President, are you a Communist?"

"No."

"Are you a capitalist?"

"No."

"Are you a Socialist?"

"No," he said, with a look of surprise as if he were wondering what he was being cross-examined about.

The young man said, "Well, what is your philosophy then?"

"Philosophy?" asked the President, puzzled. "Philosophy? I am a Christian and a Democrat—that's all."

Those two words expressed, I think, just about what he was. They expressed the extent of his political and economic radicalism. He was willing to do experimentally whatever was necessary to promote the Golden Rule and other ideals he considered to be Christian, and whatever could be done under the Constitution of the United States and under the principles which have guided the Democratic party.

The young reporter, or his editor, did not think the answer had any news value, and nothing was printed about it. I suppose if the President had answered that he thought there was something remarkable in Communism or capitalism, it would have been a headline story.

I am certain that he had no dream of great changes in the economic or political patterns of our life. I never heard him express any preference for any form of government other than the representative republic and state-federal system which have become the pattern of political organization in the United States under the Constitution. At the beginning of his administration, and also, I think, at the end, he would have said that the states and their administrative systems should be strengthened and maintained. Nevertheless, federal legislation and administration must occur in some fields. If there could be greater cooperation among the states, that would be fine. But they should permit federal intervention on behalf of certain things that could not be done by them alone.

He believed in leadership from the office of the President, a leadership based upon the immense sources of information and analysis which the executive department had and which were available to the President. He fully recognized, however, the importance of Congress and the desirability of maintaining the strength of our Congressional system. For that reason he wished at times that the people of the country would be more careful about whom they sent to Congress, to be sure that the Congressman elected would not only represent his constituents but take part, intelligently and constructively, in making laws for all the people.

When he came to Washington, he had no idea whatever of reforming, changing, or modifying the Supreme Court. He believed strongly that Congress and its lawmaking powers should be seriously regarded by the Court, and that all the courts ought to exercise extreme care not to interfere with the development of law and procedures as times changed. As witness his casual reference that EPIC, even if it won in California, would "make no difference in Dutchess County, New York"—or other states or counties. He believed that Congress, suitably advised by its own legal committees, should be permitted to decide what was best for the country, and that the will of the people as expressed by an act of Congress should not be frustrated by overmeticulous decisions on abstract constitutional lines.

Roosevelt was not very familiar with economic theory. He thought of wealth in terms of the basic wealth in agriculture, transportation, and services which were the familiar pattern of his youth. He recognized or took for granted the changes that had come about in our economy in his own lifetime: the shift in emphasis from agriculture to industry and distribution, the importance of the financial elements. Honorable methods in all business matters seemed to him imperative and to be insisted upon, by changes in the law if necessary. And under "honorable" he instinctively included wages and working conditions of the best, together with friendly, fair industrial relations. But, he had, I am sure, no thought or desire to impose any over-all economic or political change on the United States. Some of the high-strung people who advised him from time to time did, I think, have ideas of this sort, but he always laughed them off and used their brilliant analyses for some project that would do some immediate good to people in distress.

It was his way to be concerned about the concrete situations. One recalls his ideas for salvaging and preserving the fertility of the soil where this was needed, his plans to develop and preserve the forests for their value not only as timber but as aids to the soil and the water supply. He had ideas for developing water power all over the country by great dams and irrigation systems and for distributing electric power and light to remote areas at low prices. He had plans for a transcontinental through highway with a network of feeders to serve farmers and city folk. He had plans for a chain of small hospitals all over the country with medical services available as the people needed them.

The objective of all these plans was to make human life on this planet in this generation more decent. "Decent" was the word he often used to express what he meant by a proper, adequate, and intelligent way of living.

If the application of these and similar ideas constitute[s] revolution, then the phrase "Roosevelt revolution," used half in jest, may be correct. If such it was, it was a social revolution—a revolution in living—not an economic or a political revolution.

Radicals were always getting angry at Roosevelt for not being interested in over-all economic and political changes. For him, the economic and political measures were not the end but the means. He was not even a vigorous antimonopolist. Big enterprises, if morally and socially responsible, seemed entirely all right. Efficiency interested him only as it produced more comforts for more people and a better standard of living. Bigness did not frighten him as it did many people. He would insist on moral and social responsibility for all the institutions of human life; for the school, for the family, for business and industry, for labor, for professional services, for money management, for government—yes, even for the Church. He would insist in his way of thinking that all of these institutions should accept and practice a moral responsibility for making the life of the individuals who make up the life of the common people "more decent," and in the common people he included the rich and the poor alike. I remember that he wanted to find a way for well-to-do boys, as well as relief boys, to go to C.C.C. camps (to get the advantages of the training and democratic living).

What he cared about was improvement in people's lives. If economic changes were necessary, he would make them, but only to do a specific task. When he said of himself that he was "a little to the left of center" he described accurately his thinking and feeling in political and economic matters.

JAMES MAC GREGOR BURNS

✪

Roosevelt: The Lion and the Fox

DEMOCRACY'S ARISTOCRAT

Those who knew Roosevelt best could agree fully on only one
point—that he was a man infinitely complex and almost incompre-
hensible. "I cannot come to grips with him!" Ickes cried more than
once, and the words were echoed by a host of Congressmen,
politicos, diplomats, and bureaucrats who dealt with the canny
politician in the White House. His character was not only complex,
Robert Sherwood observed, it was contradictory to a bewildering
degree.

The contradictions continually bemused or galled Roosevelt's
lieutenants. He was almost unvaryingly kind and gracious, yet a
thin streak of cruelty ran through some of his behavior. He
remained unruffled and at ease under the most intense pressures;
yet when pricked in certain ways he struck out at his enemies in
sharp, querulous words. He found ways to evade bores and know-
it-alls, yet he patiently listened to Ickes's complaints and demands
hour after hour, week after week, year after year. He juggled huge
figures with an almost casual air, yet he could work long minutes
over a knot to save the string and over a telegram to cut it down to
ten words. He liked new ideas, people, and projects, but he wanted

Reprinted from *Roosevelt: The Lion and the Fox*, pp. 472–477, © 1956,
by James MacGregor Burns. Reprinted by permission of Harcourt, Brace &
World, Inc.

an element of fixity in his surroundings. He shifted nimbly from one set of policies to another—from economy to spending, from central planning to trust busting, from intervention abroad to neutrality, from party action to national action.

In many little ways inconsistency ruled: in the way he thanked some subordinates for their efforts and said nothing to others, intervened in some administrative matters and ignored others, had four men doing a single job in some instances (as Flynn once complained) and one man doing four jobs in others, was unaccountably frivolous about some matters and grave about others.

And there was the most baffling quality of all—his sheer, superb courage in facing some challenges, and his caution and indirection in facing others. He acted instantly, electrically, on certain decisions, and unaccountably postponed others for months. It was not strange that he should follow Machiavelli's advice that a leader must be as brave as the lion and as shrewd as the fox, for this had long been the first lesson for politicians. But his metamorphoses from lion to fox and back to lion again mystified even his intimates.

Roosevelt's complexities stemmed in part from the demands of political life. Gladstone once remarked that he had known and studied politicians for sixty years and they still remained to him a mysterious breed. Democratic politics is a highly competitive profession, and the successful politician must know how to conceal his hand and present different faces to different groups. Too, Roosevelt took a particular delight in mystifying people by keeping something up his sleeve. But the source of his complexity lay deeper than this.

Roosevelt was a complex man mainly because he was a deeply divided man. More than almost any other political leader of his time, he experienced a lingering between two worlds.

He had been born and raised in a class and in a tradition that formed the closest American approximation to an aristocracy. At home, at Groton, at Harvard, at the right houses of Boston and New York, he had absorbed a core of beliefs and a sense of security and assurance he would never lose. His background always brought the needle of his compass, no matter how it might waver for a time, back to true north. The major premises on which this society operated might be inarticulate, or at least fuzzy, but they had meaning. These premises were: that men can live together only on the basis of certain simple, traditional ethical rules; that men are essentially good and those who are not can be improved by example and precept; that despite ups and downs the world is getting better; that the wellborn must never compromise with evil; that the gentleman must enter government to help the less fortunate, that he must enter politics to purify it. And the turn-of-the-century world seemed to validate these ideas: it was stable, secure, peaceful, expansive.

Roosevelt was projected out of this world into bizarre and unanticipated phases of the twentieth century—a decade of muckraking, a decade of Wilsonian reform at home and Wilsonian idealism abroad; a decade of postwar cynicism and reaction; then the climactic years of Depression, the New Deal, abroad the rise of brutish men to power, and the coming of a new war.

Some nineteenth-century men could not effectively make the shift to the new century; insecure and frightened, they clung not only to the old moralities, as did Roosevelt, but also to the old methods, the old ways of business, the old distrust for government; they huddled within their class barriers. Roosevelt, however, made the jump with ease. He did so for several reasons: because he had not met absolute success socially at Groton or Harvard—for example, in his failure to make the best club in Cambridge—and thus was not absolutely committed to the old ways and institutions; because of the influence of Eleanor and Theodore Roosevelt; because he was drawn into the variegated political life of New York State; because he was vital and curious and ambitious.

Still other men of his generation, rejecting the past completely, found some kind of fixed mooring somewhere in this strange new world—but, again, not Roosevelt. He made no final commitment to any part of that world—not to Wilsonian idealism, nor to business money-making, nor to radicalism, nor to internationalism. Partly because of quick adaptability, partly because of the diverse make-up of his intimates, partly because he had little need for personal introspection, partly because of his tremendous self-assurance, he was able to shift back and forth among segments of this world and to make himself at home in all of them.

Success fed on success: as Roosevelt found that he could carry off brilliantly a variety of roles—as party leader, as man of affairs, as bureaucrat, as Hyde Park squire, as Governor, as campaigner, as a heroic battler against polio—he played the roles more and more to the hilt. This was one reason why he presided so joyously in the White House, for today the great President must be a man of many roles. Roosevelt was a superb actor in the literal sense—in the way his face, his gestures, the tilt of his head communicated feeling, in the perfect modulation of voice and the timing with which he read his speeches, in his sense of the dramatic. He was a superb actor in the far more significant sense that he was responding in each of his roles not merely to an assigned script but to something within himself.

The result was a man of no fixed convictions about methods and policies, flexible as a broker because he had to mediate among conflicting worlds and experiences. To some, like Hoover, he seemed a "chameleon on plaid" because of this enormous flexibility. Indeed, even to some of his friends he seemed almost in a state of anomie, lacking any guideposts at all, because he rejected so many doctrines and dogmas. Quite naturally, because the mask often was almost impenetrable, they could not see the inner compass of certainty and rightness.

Caught between two worlds, Roosevelt compartmentalized his life. The results sometimes were ludicrous, as when he tried to force opposites to work together and could not understand why they failed. The results were at times unfortunate, for Roosevelt's pseudointegration of his roles weakened his capacity to supply strong leadership and to make long-term strategic decisions or commitments when these were needed. It allowed the warring ideas and forces in American society not only to beat against him from outside but, because he *incorporated* as well as reflected these forces, to divide him from within.

Yet Roosevelt's flexibility and opportunism had tremendous advantages too. In a time of whirling social change he could move fast to head off crisis at home and abroad. In a time when experimentation was vital, he could try one method, quickly drop it, and turn to another. In a time when Americans had to be educated in the meaning of events, he could act as an interpreter all the more effectively because he spoke so many languages of social experience. Leading a people of sublime diversity, presiding over a nation of nations, he could say with Walt Whitman:

> Do I contradict myself?
> Very well, then, I contradict myself,
> (I am large, I contain multitudes.)

Lincoln Steffens once remarked that Theodore Roosevelt thought with his hips. Franklin Roosevelt's thinking was perhaps no more cerebral, but he thought with all five senses, perhaps with a sixth too. He had a radar set that could point in all directions, acute, sensitive, recording everything indiscriminately, and restoring the image in the responsive instrument that was Roosevelt's mind.

Was there then no hard center, no core personality, no final commitment in this man? Watching his quicksilver mind run from idea to idea, visitors could hardly believe that stone or steel lay under the bright, smooth flow of talk. But something did. The more that mask and costume are stripped away from Roosevelt, the more the turn-of-century man of Hyde Park, Groton, and Harvard stands out.

Roosevelt, for all his deviousness, was basically a moral man in the sense that he felt so intensely the need to do right that he had to *think* he did right. He believed in doing good, in showing other people how to do good, and he assumed that ultimately people would do good. By "good" he meant the ten commandments and the Golden Rule, as interpreted by Endicott Peabody. He meant the "simple rules of human conduct to which we always go back," as he said in 1932. He meant "old-fashioned standards of rectitude," as he said in signing the truth-in-securities bill in 1933. Significantly, Roosevelt always looked back into the past for his moralities; he did not try to fashion them anew.

These rules were not very precise, and Roosevelt did not want them to be precise. It was enough that they were there. Once when Eleanor Roosevelt raised with him the question of their children's religious upbringing, he said simply that they should go to church and learn what he had learned. "But are you sure that you believe in everything you learned?" his wife persisted. "I really never thought about it," he said with a quizzical look. "I think it is just as well not to think about things like that. . . ." But he expected others to understand his simple rules of conduct, and to understand his own allegiance to them. When Richard Whitney's financial irresponsibilities were disclosed, Roosevelt's wealthy friends wrote to compliment him on not using the unhappy incident as part of a political attack on Wall Street. The President was amazed at the letters. "I wonder what sort of man they think I am," he said.

Vague though it was, this set of moral rules embraced one idea in particular that was of cardinal importance to Roosevelt and to his country. This was the idea of man's responsibility for the well-being of his fellow man. It was simply an extension of Sara Roosevelt's notions of noblesse oblige, but it found enormous meaning in the new conditions of the twentieth century. For it underlay Roosevelt's most important single idea—the idea that government had a positive responsibility for the general welfare. Not that government itself must do everything, but that everything practicable must be done. Whether government does it, or private enterprise, is an operating decision dependent on many factors— but government must insure that something *is* done.

Such was the essence of Roosevelt's morality; such was the core of beliefs far below the surface.

Some politicians preach morality because it is safe to do so, because they prove thereby that they are on the right side between Good and Evil, because they reach the largest common denominator among their audience, not because they take their own preachments too seriously. Not so Roosevelt. Probably no American politician has given so many speeches that were essentially sermons rather than statements of policy. Like a preacher, he wanted and expected his sermons to serve as practical moral guides to his people. Roosevelt was so theatrical that his moral preachments were often dismissed with a smile. Actually he was deadly serious.

Only a man deadly serious and supremely confident could have spent the time Roosevelt did trying to educate and elevate not only his own people but foreign leaders who seemed to others to be beyond redemption. There was something pathetic and yet almost sublime in the way that Roosevelt sent message after message to Hitler and other dictators. Partly, of course, it was for the record; but even more it was an expression of Roosevelt's faith in the ultimate goodness and reasonableness of all men. His eternal desire to talk directly with his enemies, whether Congressmen or dictators, reflected his confidence in his own persuasiveness and, even more, in the essential ethical rightness of his own position.

To Theodore Roosevelt the Presidency was a "bully pulpit." To Franklin Roosevelt it was the same—"pre-eminently a place of moral leadership. . . ."

How explain, then, the "other side" of Roosevelt—his shiftiness, his compromises, his manipulations? Why did he so often act like a fox?

Roosevelt was not an absolute moralist about means because, whatever his hopes or illusions about man's possible redemption and *ultimate* goodness and reasonableness, he had few illusions about man's nature. He knew that some men were selfish, irrational, vengeful, and mean. The practical statesman or man of affairs encounters ambitions and passions in his daily experience that put man in a strong, harsh light. Roosevelt got his education at the hands of tough labor leaders like Lewis, city bosses like Murphy and Hague, agrarian demagogues like Long, and—on the level of pure evil—Hitler and his camp followers. He learned the uses of power.

Roosevelt overcame these men because he liked and wanted power and, even more, because he wanted to defend the position of strength from which he could lead *and teach* the people. To seize and hold power, to defend that position, he got down into the dusty arena and grappled with rival leaders on their own terms. So sure was he of the rightness of his aims that he was willing to use Machiavellian means; and his moral certainties made him all the more effective in the struggle. To the idealists who cautioned him he responded again and again that gaining power—winning elections—was the first, indispensable task. He would use the tricks of the fox to serve the purposes of the lion.

During the war years Roosevelt became interested in Kierkegaard, and this was not surprising. The Danish theologian, with his emphasis on man's natural sinfulness, helped explain to him, Roosevelt said, why the Nazis "are human, yet they behave like demons." From Peabody's homilies to Kierkegaard's realities, from the world of Hyde Park to the world of Hitler, the way was long and tortuous; the fact that Roosevelt could traverse that road so surely, with so little impairment to his loftiest ideals, and with such courage and good humor, was the final and true test of the man.

Holmes had been right—a second-rate intellect but a first-rate temperament. To examine closely single aspects of Roosevelt's character—as thinker, as organizer, as manipulator, as strategist—is to see failings and deficiencies closely interwoven with the huge capacities. But to stand back and look at the man as a whole, against the backdrop of his people and his times, is to see the lineaments of greatness—courage, joyousness, responsiveness, vitality, faith, and above all, concern for his fellow man. A democrat in manner and conviction, he was yet a member of that small aristocracy once described by E. M. Forster—sensitive but not weak, considerate but not fussy, plucky in his power to endure, capable of laughing and of taking a joke. He was the true happy warrior.

WILLIAM E. LEUCHTENBURG

✪

The Roosevelt Reconstruction

In eight years, Roosevelt and the New Dealers had almost revolutionized the agenda of American politics. "Mr. Roosevelt may have given the wrong answers to many of his problems," concluded the editors of *The Economist*. "But he is at least the first President of modern America who has asked the right questions." In 1932, men of acumen were absorbed to an astonishing degree with such questions as prohibition, war debts, and law enforcement. By 1936, they were debating social security, the Wagner Act, valley authorities, and public housing. The thirties witnessed a rebirth of issues politics, and parties split more sharply on ideological lines than they had in many years past. "I incline to think that for years up to the present juncture thinking Democrats and thinking Republicans had been divided by an imaginary line," reflected a Massachusetts Congressman in 1934. "Now for the first time since the period before the Civil War we find vital principles at stake." Much of this change resulted simply from the Depression trauma, but much too came from the force of Roosevelt's personality and his use of his office as both pulpit and lectern. "Of course you have fallen into some errors—that is human," former Supreme Court Justice John Clarke wrote the President, "but you

Reprinted from *Franklin D. Roosevelt and the New Deal, 1932–1940*, pp. 326–334, 335–336, 344–348, by William E. Leuchtenburg. Copyright © 1963 by William E. Leuchtenburg. Reprinted by permission of Harper & Row, Publishers.

have put a new face upon the social and political life of our country."

Franklin Roosevelt re-created the modern Presidency. He took an office which had lost much of its prestige and power in the previous twelve years and gave it an importance which went well beyond what even Theodore Roosevelt and Woodrow Wilson had done. Clinton Rossiter has observed: "Only Washington, who made the office, and Jackson, who remade it, did more than [Roosevelt] to raise it to its present condition of strength, dignity, and independence." Under Roosevelt, the White House became the focus of all government—the fountainhead of ideas, the initiator of action, the representative of the national interest.

Roosevelt greatly expanded the President's legislative functions. In the nineteenth century, Congress had been jealous of its prerogatives as the lawmaking body, and resented any encroachment on its domain by the chief executive. Woodrow Wilson and Theodore Roosevelt had broken new ground in sending actual drafts of bills to Congress and in using devices like the caucus to win enactment of measures they favored. Franklin Roosevelt made such constant use of these tools that he came to assume a legislative role not unlike that of a prime minister. He sent special messages to Congress, accompanied them with drafts of legislation prepared by his assistants, wrote letters to committee chairmen or members of Congress to urge passage of the proposals, and authorized men like Corcoran to lobby as Presidential spokesmen on the Hill. By the end of Roosevelt's tenure in the White House, Congress looked automatically to the executive for guidance; it expected the administration to have a "program" to present for consideration.

Roosevelt's most important formal contribution was his creation of the Executive Office of the President on September 8, 1939. Executive Order 8248, a "nearly unnoticed but none the less epoch-making event in the history of American institutions," set up an Executive Office staffed with six administrative assistants with a "passion for anonymity." In 1939, the President not only placed obvious agencies like the White House Office in the Executive Office but made the crucial decision to shift the Bureau of the

Budget from the Treasury and put it under his wing. In later years, such pivotal agencies as the Council of Economic Advisers, the National Security Council, and the Central Intelligence Agency would be moved into the Executive Office of the President. Roosevelt's decision, Rossiter has concluded, "converts the Presidency into an instrument of twentieth-century government; it gives the incumbent a sporting chance to stand the strain and fulfill his constitutional mandate as a one-man branch of our three-part government; it deflates even the most forceful arguments, which are still raised occasionally, for a plural executive; it assures us that the Presidency will survive the advent of the positive state. Executive Order 8248 may yet be judged to have saved the Presidency from paralysis and the Constitution from radical amendment."

Roosevelt's friends have been too quick to concede that he was a poor administrator. To be sure, he found it difficult to discharge incompetent aides, he procrastinated about decisions, and he ignored all the canons of sound administration by giving men overlapping assignments and creating a myriad of agencies which had no clear relation to the regular departments of government. But if the test of good administration is not an impeccable organizational chart but creativity, then Roosevelt must be set down not merely as a good administrator but as a resourceful innovator. The new agencies he set up gave a spirit of excitement to Washington that the routinized old-line departments could never have achieved. The President's refusal to proceed through channels, however vexing at times to his subordinates, resulted in a competition not only among men but among ideas, and encouraged men to feel that their own beliefs might win the day. "You would be surprised, Colonel, the remarkable ideas that have been turned loose just because men have felt that they can get a hearing," one Senator confided. The President's "procrastination" was his own way both of arriving at a sense of national consensus and of reaching a decision by observing a trial by combat among rival theories. Periods of indecision—as in the spring of 1935 or the beginning of 1938—were inevitably followed by a fresh outburst of new proposals.

Most of all, Roosevelt was a successful administrator because he attracted to Washington thousands of devoted and highly skilled men. Men who had been fighting for years for lost causes were given a chance: John Collier, whom the President courageously named Indian Commissioner; Arthur Powell Davis, who had been ousted as chief engineer of the Department of the Interior at the demand of power interests; old conservationists like Harry Slattery, who had fought the naval oil interests in the Harding era. When Harold Ickes took office as Secretary of the Interior, he looked up Louis Glavis—he did not even know whether the "martyr" of the Ballinger-Pinchot affair was still alive—and appointed him to his staff.

The New Dealers displayed striking ingenuity in meeting problems of governing. They coaxed salmon to climb ladders at Bonneville; they sponsored a Young Choreographers Laboratory in the W.P.A.'s Dance Theater; they gave the pioneer documentary film maker Pare Lorentz the opportunity to create his classic films *The Plow That Broke the Plains* and *The River*. At the Composers Forum-Laboratory of the Federal Music Project, William Schuman received his first serious hearing. In Arizona, Father Berard Haile of St. Michael's Mission taught written Navajo to the Indians. Roosevelt, in the face of derision from professional foresters and prairie states' Governors, persisted in a bold scheme to plant a mammoth "shelterbelt" of parallel rows of trees from the Dakotas to the Panhandle. In all, more than two hundred million trees were planted—cottonwood and willow, hackberry and cedar, Russian olive and Osage orange; within six years, the President's visionary windbreak had won over his former critics. The spirit behind such innovations generated a new excitement about the potentialities of government. "Once again," Roosevelt told a group of young Democrats in April, 1936, "the very air of America is exhilarating."

Roosevelt dominated the front pages of the newspapers as no other President before or since has done. "Frank Roosevelt and the N.R.A. have taken the place of love nests," commented Joe Patterson, publisher of the tabloid New York *Daily News*. At his very first press conference, Roosevelt abolished the written question and told reporters they could interrogate him without warning. Skeptics predicted the free and easy exchange would soon be abandoned, but twice a week, year in and year out, he threw open the White House doors to as many as two hundred reporters, most of them representing hostile publishers, who would crowd right up to the President's desk to fire their questions. The President joshed them, traded wisecracks with them, called them by their first names; he charmed them by his good-humored ease and impressed them with his knowledge of detail. To a degree, Roosevelt's press conference introduced, as some observers claimed, a new institution like Britain's parliamentary questioning; more to the point, it was a device the President manipulated, disarmingly and adroitly, to win support for his program. It served too as a classroom to instruct the country in the new economics and the new politics.

Roosevelt was the first President to master the technique of reaching people directly over the radio. In his fireside chats, he talked like a father discussing public affairs with his family in the living room. As he spoke, he seemed unconscious of the fact that he was addressing millions. "His head would nod and his hands would move in simple, natural, comfortable gestures," Frances Perkins recalled. "His face would smile and light up as though he were actually sitting on the front porch or in the parlor with them." Eleanor Roosevelt later observed that after the President's death people would stop her on the street to say "they missed the way the President used to talk to them. They'd say 'He used to talk to me about my government.' There was a real dialogue between Franklin and the people," she reflected. "That dialogue seems to have disappeared from the government since he died."

For the first time for many Americans, the federal government became an institution that was directly experienced. More than state and local governments, it came to be *the* government, an agency directly concerned with their welfare. It was the source of their relief payments; it taxed them directly for old-age pensions; it even gave their children hot lunches in school. As the role of the state changed from that of neutral arbiter to a "powerful promoter of society's welfare," people felt an interest in affairs in Washington they had never had before.

Franklin Roosevelt personified the state as protector. It became commonplace to say that people felt toward the President the kind of trust they would normally express for a warm and understanding father who comforted them in their grief or safeguarded them from harm. An insurance man reported: "My mother looks upon the President as someone so immediately concerned with her problems and difficulties that she would not be greatly surprised were he to come to her house some evening and stay to dinner." From his first hours in office, Roosevelt gave people the feeling that they could confide in him directly. As late as the Presidency of Herbert Hoover, one man, Ira Smith, had sufficed to take care of all the mail the White House received. Under Roosevelt, Smith had to acquire a staff of fifty people to handle the thousands of letters written to the President each week. Roosevelt gave people a sense of membership in the national community. Justice Douglas has written: "He was in a very special sense the people's President, because he made them feel that with him in the White House they shared the Presidency. The sense of sharing the Presidency gave even the most humble citizen a lively sense of belonging."

When Roosevelt took office, the country, to a very large degree, responded to the will of a single element: the white, Anglo-Saxon, Protestant property-holding class. Under the New Deal, new groups took their place in the sun. It was not merely that they received benefits they had not had before but that they were "recognized" as having a place in the commonwealth. At the beginning of the Roosevelt era, charity organizations ignored labor when seeking "community" representation; at the end of the period, no fund-raising committee was complete without a union representative. While Theodore Roosevelt had founded a lily-white Progressive party in the South and Woodrow Wilson had introduced segregation into the federal government, Franklin Roosevelt had quietly brought the Negro into the New Deal coalition. When the distinguished Negro contralto Marian Anderson was denied a concert hall in Washington, Secretary Ickes arranged for her to perform from the steps of the Lincoln Memorial. Equal representaton for religious groups became so well accepted that, as one priest wryly complained, one never saw a picture of a priest in a newspaper unless he was flanked on either side by a minister and a rabbi.

The devotion Roosevelt aroused owed much to the fact that the New Deal assumed the responsibility for guaranteeing every American a minimum standard of subsistence. Its relief programs represented an advance over the barbaric pre-depression practices that constituted a difference not in degree but in kind. One analyst wrote: "During the ten years between 1929 and 1939 more progress was made in public welfare and relief than in the three hundred years after this country was first settled." The Roosevelt administration gave such assistance not as a matter of charity but of right. This system of social rights was written into the Social Security Act. Other New Deal legislation abolished child labor in interstate commerce and, by putting a floor under wages and a ceiling on hours, all but wiped out the sweatshop.

Roosevelt and his aides fashioned a government which consciously sought to make the industrial system more humane and to protect workers and their families from exploitation. In his acceptance speech in June, 1936, the President stated: "Governments can err, Presidents do make mistakes, but the immortal Dante tells us that divine justice weighs the sins of the cold-blooded and the sins of the warmhearted in different scales.

"Better the occasional faults of a Government that lives in a spirit of charity than the constant omission of a Government frozen in the ice of its own indifference." Nearly everyone in the Roosevelt government was caught up to some degree by a sense of participation in something larger than themselves. A few days after he took office, one of the more conservative New Deal administrators wrote in his diary: "This should be a Gov't of humanity."

The federal government expanded enormously in the Roosevelt years. The crisis of the Depression dissipated the distrust of the state inherited from the eighteenth century and reinforced in diverse ways by the Jeffersonians and the Spencerians. Roosevelt himself believed that liberty in America was imperiled more by the agglomerations of private business than by the state. The New Dealers were convinced that the Depression was the result not simply of an economic breakdown but of a political collapse;

hence, they sought new political instrumentalities. The reformers of the 1930's accepted almost unquestioningly the use of coercion by the state to achieve reforms. Even Republicans who protested that Roosevelt's policies were snuffing out liberty voted overwhelmingly in favor of coercive measures.

This elephantine growth of the federal government owed much to the fact that local and state governments had been tried in the crisis and found wanting. When one magazine wired state Governors to ask their views, only one of the thirty-seven who replied announced that he was willing to have the states resume responsibility for relief. Every time there was a rumored cutback of federal spending for relief, Washington was besieged by delegations of mayors protesting that city governments did not have the resources to meet the needs of the unemployed. . . . Under the New Deal, the federal government greatly extended its power over the economy. By the end of the Roosevelt years, few questioned the right of the government to pay the farmer millions in subsidies not to grow crops, to enter plants to conduct union elections, to regulate business enterprises from utility companies to airlines, or even to compete directly with business by generating and distributing hydroelectric power. All of these powers had been ratified by the Supreme Court, which had even held that a man growing grain solely for his own use was affecting interstate commerce and hence subject to federal penalties. The President, too, was well on his way to becoming "the chief economic engineer," although this was not finally established until the Full Employment Act of 1946. In 1931, Hoover had hooted that some people thought "that by some legerdemain we can legislate ourselves out of a world-wide depression." In the Roosevelt era, the conviction that government both should and could act to forestall future breakdowns gained general acceptance. The New Deal left a large legacy of antidepression controls—securities regulation, banking reforms, unemployment compensation—even if it could not guarantee that a subsequent administration would use them.

In the 1930's, the financial center of the nation shifted from Wall Street to Washington. In May, 1934, a writer reported: "Financial news no longer originates in Wall Street." That same month, *Fortune* commented on a revolution in the credit system which was "one of the major historical events of the generation." "Mr. Roosevelt," it noted, "seized the Federal Reserve without firing a shot." The federal government had not only broken down the old separation of bank and state in the Reserve system but had gone into the credit business itself in a wholesale fashion under the aegis of the R.F.C., the Farm Credit Administration, and the housing agencies. Legislation in 1933 and 1934 had established federal regulation of Wall Street for the first time. No longer could the New York Stock Exchange operate as a private club free of national supervision. In 1935, Congress leveled the mammoth holding-company pyramids and centralized yet more authority over the banking system in the federal government. After a tour of the United States in 1935, Sir Josiah Stamp wrote: "Just as in 1929 the whole country was 'Wall Street-conscious' now it is 'Washington-conscious.' "

Despite this encroachment of government on traditional business prerogatives, the New Deal could advance impressive claims to being regarded as a "savior of capitalism." Roosevelt's sense of the land, of family, and of the community marked him as a man with deeply ingrained conservative traits. In the New Deal years, the government sought deliberately, in Roosevelt's words, "to energize private enterprise." The R.F.C. financed business, housing agencies underwrote home financing, and public works spending aimed to revive the construction industry. Moreover, some of the New Deal reforms were Janus-faced. The N.Y.A., in aiding jobless youth, also served as a safety valve to keep young people out of the labor market. A New Deal Congressman, in pushing for public power projects, argued that the country should take advantage of the sea of "cheap labor" on the relief rolls. Even the Wagner Act and the movement for industrial unionism were motivated in part by the desire to contain "unbalanced and radical" labor groups. Yet such considerations should not obscure the more important point: that the New Deal, however conservative it was in some respects and however much it owed to the past, marked a radically new departure. As Carl Degler writes: "The conclusion seems inescapable that, traditional as the words may have been in which the New Deal expressed itself, in actuality it was a revolutionary response to a revolutionary situation." . . .

Commentators on the New Deal have frequently characterized it by that much-abused term "pragmatic." If one means by this that the New Dealers carefully tested the consequences of ideas, the term is clearly a misnomer. If one means that Roosevelt was exceptionally anti-ideological in his approach to politics, one may question whether he was, in fact, any more "pragmatic" in this sense than Van Buren or Polk or even "reform" Presidents like Jackson and Theodore Roosevelt. The "pragmatism" of the New Deal seemed remarkable only in a decade tortured by ideology, only in contrast to the rigidity of Hoover and of the Left.

The New Deal was pragmatic mainly in its skepticism about utopias and final solutions, its openness to experimentation, and its suspicion of the dogmas of the Establishment. Since the advice of economists had so often been wrong, the New Dealers distrusted the claims of orthodox theory—"All this is perfectly terrible because it is all pure theory, when you come down to it," the President said on one occasion—and they felt free to try new approaches. Roosevelt refused to be awed by the warnings of economists and financial experts that government interference with the "laws" of the economy was blasphemous. "We must lay hold of the fact that economic laws are not made by nature," the President stated. "They are made by human beings." The New Dealers denied that depressions were inevitable events that had to be borne stoically, most of the stoicism to be displayed by the most impoverished, and they were willing to explore novel ways to make the social order more stable and more humane. "I am for experimenting . . . in various parts of the country, trying out schemes which are supported by reasonable people and see if they work," Hopkins told a conference of social workers. "If they do not work, the world will not come to an end."

Hardheaded, "anti-utopian," the New Dealers nonetheless had their Heavenly City: the greenbelt town, clean, green, and white, with children playing in light, airy, spacious schools; the government project at Longview, Washington, with small houses, each of

different design, colored roofs, and gardens of flowers and vege-
tables; the Mormon villages of Utah that M. L. Wilson kept in his
mind's eye—immaculate farmsteads on broad, rectangular streets;
most of all, the Tennessee Valley, with its model town of Norris,
the tall transmission towers, the white dams, the glistening wire
strands, the valley where "a vision of villages and clean small
factories has been growing into the minds of thoughtful men."
Scandinavia was their model abroad, not only because it sum-
moned up images of the countryside of Denmark, the beauties of
Stockholm, not only for its experience with labor relations and
social insurance and currency reform, but because it represented
the "middle way" of happy accommodation of public and private
institutions the New Deal sought to achieve. "Why," inquired
Brandeis, "should anyone want to go to Russia when one can go to
Denmark?"

Yet the New Deal added up to more than all of this—more than
an experimental approach, more than the sum of its legislative
achievements, more than an antiseptic utopia. It is true that there
was a certain erosion of values in the thirties, as well as a narrow-
ing of horizons, but the New Dealers inwardly recognized that
what they were doing had a deeply moral significance however
much they eschewed ethical pretensions. Heirs of the Enlighten-
ment, they felt themselves part of a broadly humanistic movement
to make man's life on earth more tolerable, a movement that might
someday even achieve a cooperative commonwealth. Social insurance, Frances Perkins declared, was "a fundamental part of
another great forward step in that liberation of humanity which
began with the Renaissance."

Franklin Roosevelt did not always have this sense as keenly as
some of the men around him, but his greatness as a President lies
in the remarkable degree to which he shared the vision. "The new
deal business to me is very much bigger than anyone yet has
expressed it," observed Senator Elbert Thomas. Roosevelt "seems
to really have caught the spirit of what one of the Hebrew prophets
called the desire of the nations. If he were in India today they
would probably decide that he had become Mahatma—that is, one
in tune with the infinite." Both foes and friends made much of

Roosevelt's skill as a political manipulator, and there is no doubt that up to a point he delighted in schemes and stratagems. As Donald Richberg later observed: "There would be times when he seemed to be a Chevalier Bayard, *sans peur et sans reproche,* and times in which he would seem to be the apotheosis of a prince who had absorbed and practiced all the teachings of Machiavelli." Yet essentially he was a moralist who wanted to achieve certain humane reforms and instruct the nation in the principles of government. On one occasion, he remarked: "I want to be a *preaching President*—like my cousin." His courtiers gleefully recounted his adroitness in trading and dealing for votes, his effectiveness on the stump, his wicked skill in cutting corners to win a point. But Roosevelt's importance lay not in his talents as a campaigner or a manipulator. It lay rather in his ability to arouse the country and, more specifically, the men who served under him, by his breezy encouragement of experimentation, by his hopefulness, and—a word that would have embarrassed some of his lieutenants—by his idealism.

The New Deal left many problems unsolved and even created some perplexing new ones. It never demonstrated that it could achieve prosperity in peacetime. As late as 1941, the unemployed still numbered six million, and not until the war year of 1943 did the army of the jobless finally disappear. It enhanced the power of interest groups who claimed to speak for millions, but sometimes represented only a small minority. It did not evolve a way to protect people who had no such spokesmen, nor an acceptable method for disciplining the interest groups. In 1946, President Truman would resort to a threat to draft railway workers into the army to avert a strike. The New Deal achieved a more just society by recognizing groups which had been largely unrepresented— staple farmers, industrial workers, particular ethnic groups, and the new intellectual-administrative class. Yet this was still a halfway revolution; it swelled the ranks of the bourgeoisie but left many Americans—sharecroppers, slum dwellers, most Negroes— outside of the new equilibrium.

Some of these omissions were to be promptly remedied. Subsequent Congresses extended social security, authorized slum clearance projects, and raised minimum-wage standards to keep step with the rising price level. Other shortcomings are understandable. The havoc that had been done before Roosevelt took office was so great that even the unprecedented measures of the New Deal did not suffice to repair the damage. Moreover, much was still to be learned, and it was in the Roosevelt years that the country was schooled in how to avert another major depression. Although it was war which freed the government from the taboos of a balanced budget and revealed the potentialities of spending, it is conceivable that New Deal measures would have led the country into a new cycle of prosperity even if there had been no war. Marked gains had been made before the war spending had any appreciable effect. When recovery did come, it was much more soundly based because of the adoption of the New Deal program.

Roosevelt and the New Dealers understood, perhaps better than their critics, that they had come only part of the way. Henry Wallace remarked: "We are children of the transition—we have left Egypt but we have not yet arrived at the Promised Land." Only five years separated Roosevelt's inauguration in 1933 and the adoption of the last of the New Deal measures, the Fair Labor Standards Act, in 1938. The New Dealers perceived that they had done more in those years than had been done in any comparable period in American history, but they also saw that there was much still to be done, much, too, that continued to baffle them. "I believe in the things that have been done," Mrs. Roosevelt told the American Youth Congress in February, 1939. "They helped but they did not solve the fundamental problems. . . . I never believed the Federal government could solve the whole problem. It bought us time to think." She closed not with a solution but with a challenge: "Is it going to be worth while?"

"This generation of Americans is living in a tremendous moment of history," President Roosevelt stated in his final national address of the 1940 campaign.

"The surge of events abroad has made some few doubters among us ask: Is this the end of a story that has been told? Is the book of democracy now to be closed and placed away upon the dusty shelves of time?

"My answer is this: All we have known of the glories of democracy—its freedom, its efficiency as a mode of living, its ability to meet the aspirations of the common man—all these are merely an introduction to the greater story of a more glorious future.

"We Americans of today—all of us—we are characters in the living book of democracy.

"But we are also its author. It falls upon us now to say whether the chapters that are to come will tell a story of retreat or a story of continued advance."

Bibliography

The definitive biography of Franklin D. Roosevelt is being written by Frank Freidel. He has turned out three volumes, *The Apprenticeship* (1952), *The Ordeal* (1954), and *The Triumph* (1956); they carry Roosevelt through the 1932 election. The major multivolume study of the New Deal is Arthur M. Schlesinger, Jr.'s "The Age of Roosevelt." He, too, has written three volumes: *The Crisis of the Old Order, 1919–1933* (1957), *The Coming of the New Deal* (1959), and *The Politics of Upheaval* (1960); they embrace the history of the Roosevelt era, save for foreign affairs, through the 1936 election. A one-volume history of the New Deal is William E. Leuchtenburg, *Franklin D. Roosevelt and the New Deal, 1932–1940* (1963). Basil Rauch's *The History of the New Deal* (1944) broke new ground.

There are several excellent one-volume studies of F.D.R., of which the best are James MacGregor Burns, *Roosevelt: The Lion and the Fox* (1956), and Rexford G. Tugwell, *The Democratic Roosevelt* (1957). The most discerning of the early biographies are Ernest K. Lindley, *Franklin D. Roosevelt* (1931), and Gerald Johnson, *Roosevelt: Dictator or Democrat?* (1941). John Gunther's *Roosevelt in Retrospect* (1950) is rich in detail but must be used with caution. William S. White's *Majesty and Mischief: A Mixed Tribute to F.D.R.* (1961) is more critical. Especially hostile are two conservative accounts, Edgar E. Robinson, *The Roosevelt Leadership, 1933–1945* (1955), and John T. Flynn, *Country Squire in the White House* (1940).

Roosevelt is illuminated in a number of memoirs. Frances Perkins,

The Roosevelt I Knew (1946), is a classic. Robert E. Sherwood, *Roosevelt and Hopkins* (1948), is also rewarding. Eleanor Roosevelt is revealing in *This Is My Story* (1937) and *This I Remember* (1949), and one of F.D.R.'s sons reminisces in James Roosevelt and Sidney Shalett, *Affectionately, F.D.R.* (1959). Among the more important recollections by Roosevelt's aides are Grace Tully, *F.D.R., My Boss* (1949), Samuel I. Rosenman, *Working with Roosevelt* (1952), James A. Farley, *Behind the Ballots* (1938) and *Jim Farley's Story* (1948), William Hassett, *Off the Record with F.D.R., 1942–1945* (1958), and Raymond Moley, *After Seven Years* (1939). Moley has gone over much the same ground in *The First New Deal* (1966). There is a wealth of material in John M. Blum, *From the Morgenthau Diaries* (2 vols., 1959, 1965) and *The Secret Diaries of Harold L. Ickes* (3 vols., 1953–1954).

Scholars have already turned their hand to monographs on different phases of Roosevelt's life. Alfred Rollins, Jr., *Roosevelt and Howe* (1962), is first-rate. Helpful for F.D.R.'s pre-Presidential years are Daniel Fusfeld, *The Economic Thought of Franklin D. Roosevelt and the Origins of the New Deal* (1956), and Bernard Bellush, *Franklin D. Roosevelt as Governor of New York* (1955). Roosevelt's political activities are reviewed in Harold Gosnell, *Champion Campaigner: Franklin D. Roosevelt* (1952). A useful guide to this literature is Richard L. Watson, Jr., "Franklin D. Roosevelt in Historical Writing, 1950–1957," *South Atlantic Quarterly* (1958), pp. 104–126.

Less attention has been paid to Roosevelt's conception of foreign policy, except in general studies of foreign affairs in this period. One exception to this generalization is Willard Range, *Franklin D. Roosevelt's World Order* (1959). Roosevelt's foreign policy has been attacked in such works as Charles A. Beard, *American Foreign Policy in the Making, 1932–1940* (1946) and *President Roosevelt and the Coming of the War, 1941* (1948), and in Charles C. Tansill, *Back Door to War* (1952). These criticisms have been answered in Basil Rauch, *Roosevelt: From Munich to Pearl Harbor* (1950), and in Arthur M. Schlesinger, Jr., "Roosevelt and His Detractors," *Harper's Magazine,* CC (June 1950), 62–68. Among the judicious accounts of foreign policy in this period are Robert A. Divine, *The Illusion of Neutrality* (1961), and the semiofficial William L. Langer and S. Everett Gleason, *The World Crisis and American Foreign Policy* (2 vols., 1952–1953).

Roosevelt's own words are collected in Samuel Rosenman, ed.,

The Public Papers and Addresses of Franklin D. Roosevelt (13 vols., 1938–1950), Elliott Roosevelt, *F.D.R.: His Personal Letters, 1928–1945* (2 vols., 1950), Carroll Kilpatrick, ed., *Roosevelt and Daniels* (1952), and Edgar B. Nixon, ed., *Franklin D. Roosevelt and Conservation, 1911–1945* (2 vols., 1957). F.D.R.'s ideas are analyzed in Thomas Greer, *What Roosevelt Thought* (1958).

WILLIAM E. LEUCHTENBURG was born in New York in 1922, attended Cornell University, and received his advanced degrees in history from Columbia University. He has taught at Smith and Harvard and since 1952 has been a member of the history department at Columbia. Professor Leuchtenburg has lectured in American Studies at Salzburg, Austria, and has been a fellow at the Center for Advanced Studies in the Behavioral Sciences in Stanford, California. His book, *Franklin D. Roosevelt and the New Deal,* won a Bancroft Award in 1964. His other published works are *The Perils of Prosperity, 1914–32, Flood Control Politics, New Deal and Global War,* and *The Great Age of Change.*

✪

AÏDA DiPACE DONALD, General Editor of the American Profiles series, holds degrees from Barnard and Columbia, where she taught American history, and a doctorate from the University of Rochester. Mrs. Donald has been awarded A.A.U.W. and Fulbright fellowships and has edited *John F. Kennedy and the New Frontier.* She is also co-editor of the *Charles Francis Adams Diary.*

AMERICAN CENTURY SERIES